Deliberative Peace Referendums

OXFORD COMPARATIVE CONSTITUTIONALISM

Comparative constitutional law has a long and distinguished history in intellectual thought and in the construction of public law. As political actors and the people who create or modify their constitutional orders, they often wish to learn from the experience and learning of others. This cross-fertilization and mutual interaction has only accelerated with the onset of globalization, which has transformed the world into an interconnected web that facilitates dialogue and linkages across international and regional structures. Oxford Comparative Constitutionalism seeks to publish scholarship of the highest quality in constitutional law that deepens our knowledge of local, national, regional, and global phenomena through the lens of comparative public law.

Deliberative Peace Referendums

RON LEVY

Associate Professor at the ANU College of Law,
The Australian National University

IAN O'FLYNN

Senior Lecturer in Political Theory at
Newcastle University, UK

and

HOI L KONG

The Rt. Hon. Beverley McLachlin, P.C.,
UBC Professor in Constitutional Law, and Scholar at
the Peter Wall Institute for Advanced Studies,
The University of British Columbia

OXFORD
UNIVERSITY PRESS

OXFORD
UNIVERSITY PRESS

Great Clarendon Street, Oxford, OX2 6DP,
United Kingdom

Oxford University Press is a department of the University of Oxford.
It furthers the University's objective of excellence in research, scholarship,
and education by publishing worldwide. Oxford is a registered trade mark of
Oxford University Press in the UK and in certain other countries

First Edition published in 2021

Impression: 1

Published in the United States of America by Oxford University Press
198 Madison Avenue, New York, NY 10016, United States of America

British Library Cataloguing in Publication Data

Data available

Library of Congress Control Number: 2020948247

ISBN 978–0–19–886703–6

DOI: 10.1093/oso/9780198867036.001.0001

Printed and bound in the UK by
TJ Books Limited

Acknowledgements

There are many people whom we wish to thank deeply for their support. At the earliest stages, the ideas within these pages developed in part through conversations with colleagues at our home institutions, the Australian National University, Newcastle University, and the University of British Columbia (as well as, previously, McGill University). We also had the benefit of engaged colleagues and seminar audiences at the Centre for Deliberative Democracy and Global Governance (University of Canberra), the Center for Deliberative Democracy (Stanford), the Centre for Human Rights and Legal Pluralism (McGill University), the Political Theory Workshop (University of British Columbia), Griffith University, Hebrew University, and the Universities of Edinburgh, Indiana (Bloomington), Leuven, Melbourne, Montreal, New Caledonia, Oxford, Ottawa, Turku, Victoria, and Western Australia. We are indebted to many who kindly hosted us, and to many more who gave their insights at these places and elsewhere. Among them were Elisa Arcioni, André Bächtiger, Bruce Baum, Didier Caluwaerts, Satish Chand, Manlio Cinalli, Nicole Curato, Ros Dixon, Yoav Dotan, John Dryzek, Anna Dziedzic, Pavlos Eleftheriadis, Stephen Elstub, Graham Gee, Alon Harel, Bal Kama, Jeffrey Kennedy, Alana Klein, Vanessa MacDonnell, Vrinda Narain, Simon Neimeyer, Peter Oliver, Mike Pal, Will Partlett, Sagi Peari, Nandini Ramanujam, Anthony Regan, David Russell, Maija Setälä, Stephen Scott, Amelia Simpson, Jürg Steiner, Scott Stephenson, Nadera Shalhoub-Kevorkian, James Tanis, Leah Trueblood, Anne Twomey, Ronald Van Crombrugge, Shauna Van Praagh, Albert Weale, Jeremy Webber, Daniel Weinstock, Lulu Weis, David Williams, Susan Williams, and many others. We are extremely grateful to Peter Jones from whom we learned a great deal about Rawls's idea of public reason. We would also like to express our thanks to James Fishkin, Robert Luskin, and Gaurav Sood for helping us to better understand the nature and prospects for mini-publics. And we thank Chuck Sabel for helping us to see how deliberative democracy's norms can be translated into institutional design principles. Finally, we thank Donald Horowitz for inspiring us to think harder about how a more conciliatory politics might be possible, even in conflict societies.

Mike Pal, Donald Bello Hutt, Justin McCaul, Joshua Neoh, Kate Ogg, and Graeme Orr generously offered comments on the developing drafts, even as—in the final months—the Covid-19 crisis arose and they, like everyone, were doubtless affected. Special thanks as well to this series' wonderful and encouraging editors, Richard Albert and Robert Schuetze, for their support throughout, and to the book's very incisive anonymous reviewers. At Oxford University Press, Imogen Hill and earlier Jamie Berezin, assisted by Eleanor Hanger, very ably shepherded the project. We also wish to thank Suchitra Suresh and Elissa Connor for their very careful editorial work. External funding at various stages came from the Australian Research Council and the Social Sciences and Humanities Research Council of Canada and was received with gratitude. We are also grateful for funding from the Allard School of Law (UBC), which allowed us to host a meeting of the research programme on Deliberative Governance and the Law; the three of us presented portions of this work in Vancouver to an audience that included law school and political theory colleagues, including, notably, Mark Warren. We were also fortunate to be able to employ a team of brilliant research assistants in the preparation of this work on peacemaking: Oluwaseun Ajaja, Ryan Brown, Georgina Flaherty, Jared Hee, Alexander Parkinson, Nicholas Rosati, and Sam Rutherford. Lastly, but most of all, we wish to thank our partners, Kate Ogg, Laura O'Flynn, and Ramona Rothschild. This book is dedicated to Malka Levy, Eli Levy, Catherine O'Flynn, and Mabel Wong, peacemakers.

Contents

PART I

INTRODUCTION

1

Introduction

I. Peace Referendums and Deliberation in Conflict Societies

Referendums are now common in 'conflict societies'—societies where a widespread and concerted campaign of violence between groups recently occurred, is occurring, or is liable to occur.[1] More particularly, 'peace referendums', which aim to manage conflict, have occurred in Colombia, Croatia, Cyprus, the Democratic Republic of the Congo, Eritrea, France/Algeria, Guatemala, Iraq, Kenya, Kyrgyzstan, Montenegro, New Caledonia, Northern Ireland, Papua New Guinea, Somalia, South Africa, South Sudan, Tanzania, Timor-Leste, and elsewhere. More peace referendums are planned, and many more are likely.[2]

In the ideal case, a peace referendum can secure consent for a new formal peace settlement among warring groups and provide the settlement with a popular mandate.[3] The referendum can lend the pursuit of settlement broader appeal, potentially generating common sentiments across groups not usually accustomed to agreeing. In principle, it can also bypass differences of interest, ideology, or worldview. And it may even circumvent the vocal 'spoilers' of peacemaking—typically 'elites'[4] who, for reasons of their own, seek to derail the process—by turning directly to the people.[5] Ordinary citizens may feel less

[1] We use 'referendum' broadly: it is any voting process by which a substantial portion of a population can endorse or rank propositions put to them on a ballot (including via non-binding processes, which some jurisdictions call 'plebiscites').

[2] For a global overview of ethno-national referendums, see Matt Qvortrup, 'The History of Ethno-National Referendums 1791–2011' (2012) 18(1) Nationalism and Ethnic Politics 129; see also Matt Qvortrup, *Referendums and Ethnic Conflict* (University of Pennsylvania Press 2014). For a global overview of sovereignty referendums, see Fernando Mendez and Micha Germann, 'Contested Sovereignty: Mapping Referendums on Sovereignty over Time and Space' (2018) 48(1) British Journal of Political Science 141.

[3] Joanne McEvoy, 'Letting "the People(s)" Decide: Peace Referendums and Power-Sharing Settlements' (2018) 25(5) Democratization 864, 867.

[4] Except where we specify particular usages, 'elites' will mean governmental leaders (elected or appointed), prominent media and business personalities and leaders, and other social and cultural leaders (eg, those who speak, influentially, on behalf of religious, ethnic, tribal, or other identity groups).

[5] Stephen Stedman, 'Spoiler Problems in Peace Processes' (1997) 22(2) International Security 5.

Deliberative Peace Referendums. Ron Levy, Ian O'Flynn, Hoi L Kong, Oxford University Press (2021). © Ron Levy, Ian O'Flynn, and Hoi L Kong. DOI: 10.1093/oso/9780198867036.003.0001

committed to sustaining a conflict, and more eager to reach an agreement.[6] If well designed, a peace referendum can therefore improve the prospects of achieving a settlement. The referendum's perceived legitimacy may even help to ensure against breaches, once the settlement is reached.

Of course, many peace referendums fall well short of such high aspirations. While referendums have entered common use in conflict settings and have been involved in peace settlements—in Algeria, Northern Ireland, South Africa, and Timor-Leste, for example—their utility has been (to say the least) inconsistent. A referendum might lend a settlement little more than a fig leaf of legitimacy. There may be no neutral authority available to administer the vote. Ballot questions can mislead, and those in control can exclude or intimidate classes of voters. Even a referendum that contributes towards long-term peacemaking can in the interim increase divisions and violence, as for instance in 1999 in Timor-Leste and after 1962 in Algeria.[7] Worse yet, a purported peace referendum might only entrench an unstable balance of power between conflicting groups, or provide new outlets for divisive social discourse. Although a referendum amplifies the voices of the many, it does not necessarily quiet those of the demagogic few. Some referendums do more to exacerbate than to resolve intercommunal friction.

In this book we consider when—despite their risks—peace referendums might have useful roles to play in securing settlements and managing conflicts. The *substance* of the peacemaking proposal is obviously crucial. In conflict societies, this often focuses on the question of how power should be shared.[8] Depending on the context, it may also focus on matters such as equality legislation, policing, demilitarization, the reintegration into society of former

[6] See, eg, ARK, 'Northern Ireland Life and Times Survey, 2017', Northern Ireland LIFE & TIMES (Survey, June 2018); Palestinian Center for Policy and Survey Research and Tami Steinmetz Center for Peace Research, Tel Aviv University, 'The Palestinian-Israeli Pulse: A Joint Poll' (June–July 2017).

[7] Neophytos Loizides, 'Negotiated Settlements and Peace Referendums' (2014) 53(2) European Journal of Political Research 234, 235; Jonathan NC Hill, 'Remembering the War of Liberation: Legitimacy and Conflict in Contemporary Algeria' (2012) 23(1) Small Wars & Insurgencies 4, 10.

[8] On options for sharing power such as consociationalism or centripetalism, see, eg, Donald Horowitz, 'Electoral Systems: A Primer for Decision Makers' (2003) 14(4) Journal of Democracy 115; Caroline Hartzell and Matthew Hoddie, 'The Art of the Possible: Power Sharing and Post-Civil War Democracy' (2015) 67(1) World Politics 37; Arend Lijphart, 'Constitutional Design for Divided Societies' (2004) 15(2) Journal of Democracy 96; Pippa Norris, *Driving Democracy: Do Power-Sharing Institutions Work?* (CUP 2008); Brendan O'Leary, 'Debating Consociational Politics: Normative and Explanatory Arguments' in Sidney JR Noel (ed), *From Power Sharing to Democracy: Post-Conflict Institutions in Ethnically Divided Societies* (McGill-Queen's University Press 2005) 3–43; Benjamin Reilly, *Democracy in Divided Societies: Electoral Engineering for Conflict Management* (CUP 2001); Philip G Roeder and Donald S Rothchild, *Sustainable Peace: Power and Democracy after Civil Wars* (Cornell University Press 2005); Scott Gates and others, 'Inclusion, Dispersion, and Constraint: Powersharing in the World's States, 1975–2010' (2017) 47(1) British Journal of Political Science 165.

combatants and the right of return of refugees.[9] However, the primary focus of this book is on the *process* of the peace referendum itself. What are the rationales for using referendums as tools for conflict settlement? What, in turn, are the prospects and limitations of the approach? The referendum is an erratic force, liable as often to aggravate as it is to resolve tensions. Ultimately, we will argue, the referendum's utility for conflict management in large part depends on its design, including how such design incorporates cautionary lessons from past trials.

At the broadest level, by addressing these issues we hope to contribute to the large and complex literature on the management of armed intergroup conflict. Within this literature, however, we focus on a relatively novel strand drawing on deliberative democratic theory.[10] This theory assumes that those who are bound by a decision should have a right to participate in the making of that decision—a standard democratic assumption—but also that the participation should be as deliberative as possible. In deliberative democracy, citizens (or their representatives) 'are expected to justify the laws they would impose on one another by giving reasons for their political claims and responding to others' reasons in return'.[11] They may eventually have to vote or compromise or agree to go to arbitration, once deliberation has run its course. But, in the ideal

[9] On policing see, eg, John McGarry and Brendan O'Leary, *Policing Northern Ireland: Proposals for a New Start* (Blackstaff Press 1999); on dealing with issues arising from the legacy of the past, including those mentioned in the main text, see, eg, Christine Bell, 'Contending with the Past: Transitional Justice and Political Settlement Processes' in Roger Duthie and Paul Seils (eds), *Justice Mosaics: How Context Shapes Transitional Justice in Fractured Societies* (International Center for Transitional Justice 2017) 85–115.

[10] For an overview, see Ian O'Flynn and Didier Caluwaerts, 'Deliberation in Deeply Divided Societies' in André Bächtiger and others (eds), *Oxford Handbook of Deliberative Democracy* (OUP 2018) 742–54. See also Adeno Addis, 'Deliberative Democracy in Severely Fractured Societies' (2009) 16(1) Indiana Journal of Global Legal Studies 59; Didier Caluwaerts and Kris Deschouwer, 'Building Bridges Across Political Divides: Experiments on Deliberative Democracy in Deeply Divided Belgium' (2014) 6(3) European Political Science Review 427; Anna Drake and Allison McCulloch, 'Deliberative Consociationalism in Deeply Divided Societies' (2011) 10(3) Contemporary Political Theory 372; John Dryzek, 'Deliberative Democracy in Divided Societies: Alternatives to Agonism and Analgesia' (2005) 33(2) Political Theory 218; Michael R James, *Deliberative Democracy and the Plural Polity* (University Press of Kansas 2004); Robert Luskin and others, 'Deliberating Across Deep Divides' (2014) 62(1) Political Studies 116; Ian O'Flynn, 'Pulling Together: Shared Intentions, Deliberative Democracy and Deeply Divided Societies' (2017) 47(1) British Journal of Political Science 187; Ian O'Flynn, 'Deliberative Democracy, the Public Interest and the Consociational Model' (2010) 58(3) Political Studies 572; Ian O'Flynn, 'Divided Societies and Deliberative Democracy' (2007) 37(4) British Journal of Political Science 731; Ian O'Flynn, *Deliberative Democracy and Divided Societies* (Edinburgh University Press 2006); Maria C Jaramillo and others, *Deliberation Across Deeply Divided Societies: Transformative Moments* (CUP 2017); Juan Ugarriza and Enzo Nussio, 'There is No Pill for Deliberation: Explaining Discourse Quality in Post-Conflict Communities' (2015) 22(1) Swiss Political Science Review 145; George Vasilev, 'Preaching to the Choir or Converting the Uninitiated? The Integrative Potential of In-group Deliberations' (2013) 16(1) Critical Review of International Social and Political Philosophy 109.

[11] Dennis Thompson, 'Deliberative Democratic Theory and Empirical Political Science' (2008) 11 Annual Review of Political Science 497, 498.

case, the eventual decision turns not on the strength of numbers, the balance of advantage or the threat of coercion, but on what Jürgen Habermas famously terms the 'force of the better argument'.[12]

The central place that deliberative theorists reserve for reason-giving is bound up with commitments to well-informed,[13] reflective,[14] flexible,[15] co-operative,[16] and other-regarding decision-making.[17] Beyond this, deliberative theorists take somewhat different views on what counts as an adequate reason.[18] On one influential approach, the reasons that we give to one another when deliberating about important matters of law and policy should be couched in terms of general 'public' values, and in particular in terms of political values such as freedom, equality, inclusion, and respect that can be widely shared. This limit need not apply to our personal deliberations about such matters or to the internal reasoning about them of churches, ethno-cultural networks, and other such associations. In the personal and associational domains, particular 'non-public' values may properly apply. But once we step into the political domain, those values must be set aside in favour of public values.[19]

This 'public reason' approach is not without its detractors. In particular, 'difference democrats' have criticized it for failing to see that disadvantaged groups (eg, groups with limited access to formal education or certain indigenous minorities) may struggle to express themselves in terms of 'lofty' public values.[20]

[12] Jürgen Habermas, *The Theory of Communicative Action: Reason and the Rationalisation of Society*, vol 1 (Thomas McCarthy tr, Polity 1984) 25.

[13] James Fishkin, *When the People Speak: Deliberative Democracy and Public Consultation* (OUP 2009) 14.

[14] John Dryzek, *Deliberative Democracy and Beyond: Liberals, Critics, Contestations* (OUP 2000) 68.

[15] Amy Gutmann and Dennis Thompson, *Democracy and Disagreement: Why Moral Conflict Cannot Be Avoided and What Should be Done About It* (Belknap Press of Harvard University Press 1996) 57–9, 110–19.

[16] Simone Chambers, 'Deliberative Democratic Theory' (2003) 6(1) Annual Review of Political Science 307, 317.

[17] Jon Elster, 'The Market and the Forum: Three Varieties of Political Theory' in Jon Elster and Aanund Hylland (eds), *Foundations of Social Choice Theory* (CUP 1986) 113, 132; David Miller, 'Deliberative Democracy and Social Choice' (1992) 40(1) Political Studies 54, 61. Alternatively we may say 'not wholly self-regarding' decision-making: see, eg, Jane Mansbridge and others, 'The Place of Self-Interest and the Role of Power in Deliberative Democracy' (2010) 18(1) Journal of Political Philosophy 64.

[18] Thompson, 'Deliberative Democratic Theory' (n 11).

[19] Seminal works on public reason include Joshua Cohen, 'Deliberation and Democratic Legitimacy' in Alan Hamlin and Philip Pettit (eds), *The Good Polity: Normative Analysis of the State* (Blackwell 1989) 17–34; Gutmann and Thompson, *Democracy and Disagreement* (n 15); John Rawls, *Political Liberalism* (Columbia University Press 1996) Lecture 6; and John Rawls, 'The Idea of Public Reason Revisited' (1997) 64(3) University of Chicago Law Review 765. See also Gerald F Gaus, *The Order of Public Reason: A Theory of Freedom and Morality in a Diverse and Bounded World* (CUP 2011); Stephen Macedo, *Liberal Virtues: Citizenship, Virtue, and Community in Liberal Constitutionalism* (OUP 1990); Charles Larmore, *The Morals of Modernity* (CUP 1996); and Jeremy Waldron, 'Theoretical Foundations of Liberalism' in Jeremy Waldron (ed), *Liberal Rights: Collected Papers 1981–1991* (CUP 1993) 35–62.

[20] See, eg, Iris Young, *Inclusion and Democracy* (OUP 2000); see also Jane Mansbridge, 'Everyday Talk in the Deliberative System' in Stephen Macedo (ed), *Deliberative Politics: Essays on Democracy*

In these critics' view, testimony, storytelling, humour, and rhetoric may be just as necessary—perhaps in some circumstances even more so—to further the goal of democratic voice.[21] We will have more to say in response to this line of criticism later in the book, including a discussion of the scope of public reason. Yet, for now, we highlight one important rationale for prioritizing the public reason approach in conflict societies: since non-public values are not shared by all, reasons couched in non-public terms may exacerbate conflict rather than reduce it. By contrast, reasons cast in terms of public values proceed from common ground. As such, they remind people not of what divides them, but of what they share—in our view a *sine qua non* of any peace process. Crucially, the public reason approach can therefore facilitate agreement, people's differing religious, moral, or philosophical worldviews notwithstanding.[22] The idea that agreements should be based on public reasons need not be extended to every area of political life or to every question that may arise, but—as we argue in this book—the idea is vital to the success of the constitutional settlements that peace referendums usually aim to produce.

Given its concern for channelling disagreement into reasoned forms of decision-making, it is clear why deliberative democratic theory has forcefully entered the field of conflict research. By reworking institutions of decision-making we might incrementally improve the quality of deliberation, which in turn might improve prospects for achieving a peace settlement. As yet, however, few deliberative democracy scholars have advanced arguments for referendums in conflict societies. Indeed, deliberative democrats have been at best ambivalent about referendums.[23] And standard assumptions about good referendum design—including guidelines developed by official bodies—still largely omit deliberation as an objective.[24]

and Disagreement (OUP 1999); Lynn Sanders, 'Against Deliberation' (1997) 25(3) Political Theory 347; Melissa Williams, 'The Uneasy Alliance of Group Representation and Deliberative Democracy' in Will Kymlicka and Wayne Norman (eds), *Citizenship in Diverse Societies* (OUP 2000) 124.

[21] Young (n 20) 56.

[22] John Rawls, *A Theory of Justice* (Harvard University Press 1971) 340; Rawls, *Political Liberalism* (n 19) 134–49. See, further, Chapter 2.

[23] See, eg, James Fishkin, *Democracy and Deliberation: New Directions for Democratic Reform* (Yale University Press 1993) 54–64 (but Fishkin does allow that referendums can serve political equality or inclusion, an important value in his democratic scheme); Claus Offe, 'Referendum vs. Institutionalized Deliberation: What Democratic Theorists Can Learn from the 2016 Brexit Decision' (2017) 146(3) Daedalus 14. On the more positive side of the ledger, see Stephen Tierney, *Constitutional Referendums: The Theory and Practice of Republican Deliberation* (OUP 2012).

[24] See, eg, the Council of Europe (Venice Commission), *Code of Good Practice on Referendums: an official compendium of best practices adopted in 2007* (19 March 2007) Study No 371, 2006 CDL-AD (2007) 008 Or. Fr. The document's few, implicit pro-deliberative provisions include those promoting balance in the funding and official advocacy of contending positions.

To be sure, authors have increasingly considered how to construct 'deliberative referendums'—referendums institutionally geared towards enhancing deliberation, both in the lead up to voting and in the act of voting itself.[25] These authors focus on features such as mini-publics, instruction of voters on the proposals presented in the ballot and specialized ballot designs. However, this body of work, too, is incomplete: only a very few contributions have strayed beyond polities with relatively modest social divisions.[26] On one level, this is unsurprising: while designing deliberative referendums is a challenge even in the most peaceable societies, designing them for conflict societies is harder still.

Nevertheless, discounting deliberative institutional schemes because deliberation appears too difficult, and a society too conflictual, overlooks the possibility that some violent conflict can be traced to scarce opportunities to deliberate in the first place.[27] When, if ever, can referendums provide such opportunities? As there have been few genuine experiences with deliberative referendums in conflict societies thus far, there is only a limited empirical record and any answers must be tentative. In this book, using a distinctive combination of deliberative democratic and constitutional theory, we develop what we call a 'Deliberative Peace Referendum', or 'DPR'. A DPR is a purpose-designed deliberative referendum held under conditions of conflict.

A principal feature of our model of DPR is the requirement that voters choose settlement options framed as generalizable principles and values—hence the model's coherence with the public reason approach outlined above. This innovation compels participants to make choices that are not based (or at least not purely based) on self-interest.[28] As we shall see, other institutional features of the DPR can also support deliberation in the course of the referendum campaign and the vote itself.

[25] See, eg, Ron Levy, '"Deliberative Voting": Realising Constitutional Referendum Democracy' (2013) Public Law 555; Stephen Tierney, 'Using Electoral Law to Construct a Deliberative Referendum: Moving Beyond the Democratic Paradox' (2013) 12(4) Election Law Journal 508; John Gastil and Robert Richards, 'Making Direct Democracy Deliberative Through Random Assemblies' (2013) 41(2) Politics & Society 253; Ethan J Leib, 'Can Direct Democracy be Made Deliberative?' (2006) 54 Buffalo Law Review 903, 911; Alice el-Wakil, 'The Deliberative Potential of Facultative Referendums: Procedure and Substance in Direct Democracy' (2017) 4(1) Democratic Theory 59; Lawrence LeDuc, 'Referendums and Deliberative Democracy' (2015) 38 Electoral Studies 139; Hélène Landemore, 'Referendums are Never Merely Referendums: On the Need to Make Popular Vote Processes More Deliberative' (2018) 24(3) Swiss Political Science Review 320.

[26] Exceptions include sections in Tierney, *Constitutional Referendums* (n 23) 241–59; and Ron Levy, '"Shotgun Referendums": Popular Deliberation and Constitutional Settlement in Conflict Societies' (2018) 41(3) Melbourne University Law Review 1237.

[27] Jürg Steiner and Maria C Jaramillo, 'How to Arrive at Peace in Deeply Divided Societies? Using Deliberation to Refine Consociational Theory' (2019) 15(3) Journal of Public Deliberation 9.

[28] Mansbridge and others, 'The Place of Self Interest' (n 17) 77–78; Miller (n 17) 55; Dryzek, *Deliberative Democracy and Beyond* (n 14) 68–69. See also Chapter 2.

The DPR has two broad objectives. We call the first of these *settlement achievement*. The DPR is initially intended to enhance the public-value deliberation of voters just long enough to enact a peace settlement. Promoting such deliberation may enable a limited sort of agreement, at a 'ripe' if fleeting moment in time,[29] among the conflicting parties. The first aim of the DPR, therefore, is not to eliminate social division at a broad level—an aspiration that we will describe as quixotic—but to encourage members of each group in conflict to alight on just those few places of agreement that may exist between them. In the first instance, at least for many conflicts, only this minimal agreement may be realistic.

Yet crucially, only this bare level of agreement may be necessary. If the DPR exposes or prompts popular agreement, then the objective shifts to ensuring that this agreement crystallizes as a lasting settlement. This is the objective of *settlement endurance*. The constitutional nature of our subject informs our reasoning here. An effective settlement usually involves changes to norms that are constitutional (or similar), as it requires fundamental alterations to political powers or territorial arrangements. Conceptualizing settlement as 'constitutional settlement' has key implications for how settlement should be understood and approached. A constitutional norm is definitionally a norm that endures (among its other features). Whether settlement norms are perceived as having constitutional status and legitimacy thus substantially affects whether and why such norms persist.

We will look at empirical evidence about whether peace referendums may affect the perception of constitutional legitimacy. And we will find, broadly, that they can. But peace referendums can vary widely, and thus we must be careful not overlook the referendum's institutional design dimensions—and especially the roles of deliberation. Indeed, we will show why the endurance of a constitutional settlement may especially depend on the degree to which a peace referendum incorporates DPR design principles to support the deliberation of voters.

In sum, rather than seek in the first instance to design deliberation to mend deep social divisions, some referendums can—far more manageably—contribute towards deliberation of limited scope and duration, but with potentially enduring consequences. This possibility helps to address a wide gap in deliberative conflict studies. Although experiments on deliberation across deeply divided settings 'are, on balance, encouraging', it remains the case that

[29] On 'ripe' moments in peace processes, see Ira W Zartman, 'The Timing of Peace Initiatives: Hurting Stalemates and Ripe Moments' (2001) 1(1) The Global Review of Ethnopolitics 8.

'very little work has hitherto been done to study the long-term effects of deliberative experiences on intergroup relations'.[30] Is deliberative democracy in conflict settings limited to prompting a mere transient meeting of minds? Or, after scaffolding a tenuous agreement, can the referendum help to concretize the agreement as a lasting constitutional settlement by drawing on the perceived legitimacy of the process?

In this book we seek to place the aspirations and the boundaries of peace referendums, and especially DPRs, into a useful theoretical frame. Against this frame we will specify institutional means meant to chip away at (to diminish, rather than solve outright) the problems of deliberation in conflict settings. Even a marginal improvement in deliberative quality may help to reconstruct the referendum from a potentially destabilizing factor to a more effective peacebuilding tool. The pathologies of standard referendums must be explicitly addressed if any referendum is to avoid repeating problems that have derailed settlement so often in the past. In short, our purpose in writing this book is to rescue the referendum from its under-theorization and habitually poor design in conflict settings, and to rehabilitate it as a tool of conflict management.

II. Conflict Societies' Challenges to Deliberation

Designing a referendum to be more deliberative is a challenge under any circumstances. It may be hardest of all amid armed intercommunal conflict. Conflict societies have relatively pronounced deliberative pathologies. At least six interlaced characteristics of these societies tend to diminish the quality of elite or popular deliberation, or indeed of both. Some of these characteristics are not unique to conflict societies, but in such societies they may be more extreme.

(i) Low information and misinformation: Conflict societies are usually marked by relatively low levels of information and relatively high levels of misinformation or disinformation.[31] For instance, conflict frequently coincides with low general rates of education. This information deficit leaves ordinary people, especially, vulnerable to elite propaganda and oversimplification. In

[30] O'Flynn and Caluwaerts, 'Deliberation in Deeply Divided Societies' (n 10).

[31] Influenced by rational choice theory, a prominent strand within the conflict literature treats the occurrence of conflict as itself the result of information failures and concomitant problems of trust or commitment. For an overview, see Barbara Walter, 'Bargaining Failures and Civil War' (2009) 12 Annual Review of Political Science 243. See also David Lake and Donald Rothchild, 'Containing Fear: The Origins and Management of Ethnic Conflict' (1996) 21(2) International Security 41; Barry Posen, 'The Security Dilemma and Ethnic Conflict' (1993) 35(1) Survival 27.

the extreme, disinformation can involve some combatant groups' control of media outlets in order to silence critics and valorize 'desirable' voices.[32]

(ii) Enclave deliberation: To an appreciable extent, the problems of low information and misinformation stem from enclave deliberation, that is, deliberation conducted exclusively among people on the same side of a conflict, usually from the same group or community. In conflict societies, concerns about security will typically drive people to live within their own communities, to marry within their own traditions, to send their children to segregated schools, and so forth. As a result, they may go their entire lives without ever engaging in a serious conversation with someone from another side. From within these enclaves, stereotyping assumptions and prejudicial social comparisons—based on distinctions both real and imagined, and both large and trivial—often flourish.[33]

Ordinary people are frequently prevented from knowing or understanding the salience of others' histories and values, and hence from developing any sense of empathy for them.[34] According to Brendan O'Leary, one reason why 'it is not possible to create "ideal speech situations"' in conflict societies is that 'deliberation takes place in languages, dialects, accents, and ethnically toned voices'.[35] For instance, in Lebanon the existence of separate linguistic, educational, religious, and media institutions and norms meant that 'powerful internal social barriers impeded contact between the communities'.[36]

To be sure, we know little as yet about how cultural differences affect the scope for intergroup deliberation.[37] (One could take an interpretative or hermeneutic approach to understanding the specific meanings different groups attach to specific words. That would obviously be important. However, the worry is that hermeneutics does not tell anything specific about how best to build from common ground.[38]) What we do know is that conflict can intensify

[32] At the time of writing, India's restive Jammu and Kashmir region has had its internet shut down for over a year: Fahad Shah and Adam Withnall, 'Kashmir at Breaking Point One Year After Losing Statehood', *Independent* (news article, 5 August 2020).

[33] Michael Billig and Henri Tajfel, 'Social Categorization and Similarity in Intergroup Behaviour' (1973) 3(1) European Journal of Social Psychology 27.

[34] On the role of empathy in deliberative democracy, see Michael Morrell, *Empathy and Democracy: Feeling, Thinking, and Deliberation* (Penn State University Press 2010).

[35] O'Leary, 'Debating Consociational Politics' (n 8).

[36] John Coakley, 'Ethnic Conflict Resolution: Routes Towards Settlement' (2009) 15(3–4) Nationalism and Ethnic Politics 462, 467.

[37] See, eg, Jensen Sass and John Dryzek, 'Deliberative Cultures' (2014) 42(1) Political Theory 3; cf Manlio Cinalli and Ian O'Flynn, 'Pluralism and Deliberative Democracy' in Peter McLaverty and Stephen Elstub (eds), *Deliberative Democracy: Issues and Cases* (Edinburgh University Press 2014) 82–97.

[38] Hans-Georg Gadamer, *Truth and Method* (2nd edn, Continuum 1997) 302. For an hermeneutic approach to the case of Northern Ireland, see Norman Porter, *The Elusive Quest: Reconciliation in Northern Ireland* (Blackstaff Press 2003).

information deficiencies. Groups will know that they may benefit from sharing information about their intentions, since sharing information reduces the scope for strategic misunderstanding. But, since conflicting groups are wary of one another, and are also perhaps anxious to get the best deal possible for themselves in any future settlement, the incentive to withhold information in the hope of strengthening their bargaining hand is often what prevails.[39] In turn, this reduces the scope for genuine deliberation.

(iii) Polarization and intragroup outbidding: According to Sunstein, enclave deliberation increases the chances that the group's deliberations will conform to 'the law of group polarisation'.[40] That law refers to a statistical regularity that allows us to predict that when like-minded people meet to discuss an issue of importance to them, they will move to a more extreme point in the direction indicated by the median point of their prior views and opinions. Of course, the mere fact of moving in a more extreme direction is neither good nor bad in itself. But if people only engage in political discussions with members of their own group or faction, the chances are that they will become more entrenched in their views and hence less responsive to the views of others.

More specifically, enclave deliberation encourages the conceptualization of values and policy in rivalrous terms. In conflict, sub-cultural narratives of oppression may particularly reinforce this effect.[41] Dryzek observes how agonistic approaches to intergroup negotiation—which eschew deliberation and instead see groups strenuously promote clashing positions—can 'freez[e] cleavages' into place and reinforce a 'vicious symbolic politics . . . tied to myths of victimhood and destiny'.[42] Under such conditions '[d]ebate leads only to the group position becoming more extreme, as individuals only get their prejudices confirmed in talk with like-minded others'.[43] These patterns are contrary to deliberative democratic ideals, such as reasoning that is flexible, open-minded, cooperative and other-regarding. Hence it may be easier to deliberate towards common ground in stable democracies where, by definition, political cleavages are relatively shallow. Of course, no society is wholly unitary; all have

[39] Cf James Fearon and David Laitin, 'Explaining Interethnic Cooperation' (1996) 90(4) American Political Science Review 715.

[40] See Cass Sunstein, *Going to Extremes: How Like Minds Unite and Divide* (OUP 2009); cf André Bächtiger and others, 'What Drives the Polarization and Moderation of Opinions? Evidence from a Finnish Citizen Deliberation Experiment on Immigration' (2017) 56(1) European Journal of Political Research 23; Vasilev (n 10).

[41] Ralph R Premdas, 'The Guyana Ethnic Quagmire: Problems and Solutions for Reconciliation' (2004) 10(2) Nationalism and Ethnic Politics 251, 254–55.

[42] Dryzek, 'Deliberative Democracy in Divided Societies' (n 10) 223.

[43] ibid.

distinctions of identity and ideology. The question therefore is why not every such mixed society suffers from extreme political division.[44]

In conflict societies, the main contending groups will each tend to contain several sub-groups or factions, and those factions will often compete with one another for control or influence. To that end, each faction—or, often more accurately, the elites who lead them—will claim to be the true defenders of the wider group's interests and aspirations, and will seek to portray other factions as weak or even treacherous. To match and surpass the claims made by its rivals, each faction must take an increasingly uncompromising stance. Claim and counterclaim result in a bidding war that leads even moderate factions to adopt an increasingly hardline stance.[45]

In practice, 'outbidding' is a nuanced and variegated phenomenon.[46] Factions may have different aims or reasons for engaging in it: for example, one faction may be seeking the complete collapse of a constitutional settlement whereas another may be seeking nothing more than to revise an aspect of it. On the other hand, factions may employ different tactics: for example, one faction may threaten the use of violence, whereas another may rely on nothing more than rhetoric and innuendo. Yet whatever form it takes, the outbidding thesis predicts that the arguments to which ordinary group members are exposed will become more and more extreme. Since all groups are subject to this same internal dynamic, the prospects for meaningful intergroup deliberation can look extremely bleak.

Again, it should be said that 'outbidding' is not unique to conflict societies. In many developed democracies, for example, mainstream elites and parties have been driven to voice more extreme (or at least less flexible) arguments for fear of being undercut by populist rivals on their left or right.[47] In conflict

[44] Adeno Addis, 'Deliberative Democracy in Severely Fractured Societies' (2009) 16(1) Indiana Journal of Global Legal Studies 59, 64; Sujit Choudhry, 'Building Comparative Politics and Comparative Constitutional Law: Constitutional Design in Divided Societies' in Sujit Choudhry (ed), *Constitutional Design for Divided Societies: Integration or Accommodation* (OUP 2008) 3.

[45] Brian Barry, 'Political Accommodation and Consociational Democracy' (1975) 5(4) British Journal of Political Science 477, 505; Cathy Gormley-Heenan and Roger MacGinty, 'Ethnic Outbidding and Party Modernization: Understanding the Democratic Unionist Party's Electoral Success in the Post-Agreement Environment' (2008) 7(1) Ethnopolitics 43; Donald Horowitz, *Ethnic Groups in Conflict* (University of California Press 1985) 349–60; Alvin Rabushka and Kenneth Shepsle, *Politics in Plural Societies: A Theory of Democratic Instability* (Charles E. Merrill 1972) 86. While outbidding can have dire consequences, some scholars take a more ambivalent view: eg, Geoffrey Evans, Brendan O'Leary and Paul Mitchell, 'Extremist Outbidding in Ethnic Party Systems is Not Inevitable: Tribune Parties in Northern Ireland' (2009) 57(2) Political Studies 397.

[46] Gavin Moore and others, 'Winning Peace Frames: Intra-Ethnic Outbidding in Northern Ireland and Cyprus' (2014) 37(1) West European Politics 159.

[47] See, eg, Christopher Hare and Keith T Poole, 'The Polarization of Contemporary American Politics' (2014) 46(3) Polity 411.

societies, however, the effects of outbidding can be far more severe, ranging from the derailment of a peace process to a return to full-scale war. Dramatic effects of these sorts have been witnessed in, among other places, Cyprus, Sri Lanka, and Sudan.[48]

(iv) Group targeting: Conflict societies' laws can seek to disadvantage and invidiously target minority (and sometimes, as in apartheid South Africa, majority) groups. This also occurs in relatively peaceful democracies where, for example, referendums meant to outlaw same-sex marriage have been common. However, in conflict societies such group-targeting can be more severe and sustained: legal and policy attacks can be aimed at multiple dimensions of the group's identity (eg, its cultural and religious practices, including dress codes) as well as at its social and economic opportunities (eg, in employment, housing, and education). Most concerning of all, group targeting in conflict societies can more readily lead to violence, and more deeply aggravate a sense of physical or status insecurity among members of the targeted group (arguably itself a form of violence).

Though problematic in themselves, these effects are also barriers to deliberation if they mean that intergroup relationships are characterized not by reasoned argument but chiefly by coercion and inequality. To discriminate against others on the basis of their group identity is to treat them as less worthy of concern and respect.[49] Such unequal treatment is inimical to deliberation, and destructive of the respectful, other-regarding attitudes and dispositions on which deliberation depends.

While no two conflicts are the same, at a general level 'all aggravated grievances can be subsumed under two headings—neglect and discrimination, or [in other words] a distributional element and an identity element'.[50] Without a distributional element (eg, a struggle over housing, jobs, or access to education) there may be no occasion for conflict; but without an identity element (eg, the denigration of an entire group of people as worthless or inferior) there

[48] Moore and others (n 46); on Sri Lanka, see Neil DeVotta, 'From Ethnic Outbidding to Ethnic Conflict: The Institutional Bases for Sri Lanka's Separatist War' (2005) 11(1) Nations and Nationalism 141; on Sudan, see Horowitz, *Ethnic Groups in Conflict* (n 45) 358.

[49] Charles Taylor, 'The Politics of Recognition' in Amy Gutmann (ed), *Multiculturalism: Examining the Politics of Recognition* (Princeton University Press, 1994) 25.

[50] William Zartman, 'Dynamics and Constraints in Negotiations in Internal Conflicts' in William Zartman (ed), *Elusive Peace: Negotiating and End to Civil Wars* (Brookings Institute 1995) 5. See also Nancy Fraser, *Justice Interruptus: Critical Reflections on the 'Postsocialist' Condition.* (Routledge 1995). Focusing on distribution reveals some ambiguities in definitions of 'conflict'. Alhough we have described conflicts as conscious, collective campaigns of violence, we acknowledge that legal and social discrimination can also passively enable mass intergroup violence: Catharine MacKinnon, 'Women's September 11th: Rethinking the International Law of Conflict' (2006) 47 Harvard International Law Journal 1, 2.

can be no sense of one group against another. This is not to suggest that conflict always has its roots in targeted discrimination—for example, in the struggle between Serbs and Albanians over the status of Kosovo, economic issues were relatively unimportant.[51] But there is a wealth of evidence to suggest that targeted discrimination is often an important part of the story.[52]

(v) Uneven deliberative commitments: Not all people deliberate to the same extent or in the same way. Mixed deliberative commitments—of those primed and wishing to deliberate, and also those who reject deliberative ideals in favour of a competitive struggle for power and resources—are present in every society.[53] On top of that, some people might be better than others at giving reasons for their political claims and responding to others' reasons in return, partly as a function of socio-economic position and partly as a function of their own psychological dispositions.[54] To call a society 'deliberative' is therefore always a matter of degree, and implicitly an assessment comparative to other societies.

Two questions that uneven commitments to deliberation raise for deliberative democracy are: first, whether institutional design can encourage more people to deliberate (or deliberate better), and second, how to accommodate democratically the inevitable hard core of individuals who will refuse to deliberate under any circumstances. These questions are especially relevant for conflict societies. As Dryzek asserts, 'mutual acceptance of reasonableness is exactly what is lacking in divided societies. . . . [O]penness to persuasion by critical argument . . . is in fact not widely held, and explicitly rejected by' some.[55] Uneven commitments to deliberation are in turn complicated by the fact that, while some people are predisposed to deliberate, others first meta-deliberate about whether deliberation in the present case is worthwhile. This gives rise to a prisoner's dilemma as meta-deliberators are willing to deliberate, but only after it becomes evident that other people are too.[56]

[51] Milton Esman, *An Introduction to Ethnic Conflict* (Polity 2004) 79; Mark H Ross, 'Psychocultural Interpretations and Dramas: Identity Dynamics in Ethnic Conflict' (2001) 22(1) Political Psychology 157, 166.

[52] For an extended discussion, see Horowitz, *Ethnic Groups in Conflict* (n 45) 95–288.

[53] Steiner and Jaramillo (n 27).

[54] See, eg, Michael Neblo and others, 'Who Wants To Deliberate—And Why?' (2010) 104(3) American Political Science Review 566; Ian O'Flynn and Gaurav Sood, 'What Would Dahl Say?: An Appraisal of the Democratic Credentials of Deliberative Polls and Other Mini-Publics' in Kimmo Grönlund, André Bächtiger and Maija Setälä (eds), *Deliberative Mini-Publics: Involving Citizens in the Democratic Process* (ECPR Press 2014) 46–47. Specifically on conflict societies, see Ugarriza and Nussio (n 10) 160; Carolyn Hamilton, 'Uncertain Citizenship and Public Deliberation in Post-Apartheid South Africa' (2009) 35(2) Social Dynamics 355, 359.

[55] Dryzek, 'Deliberative Democracy in Divided Societies' (n 10).

[56] John S Dryzek and Christian List, 'Social Choice Theory and Deliberative Democracy: A Reconciliation' (2003) 33(1) British Journal of Political Science 1, 11. See also Robyn Dawes, Jeanne McTavish and Harriet Shaklee, 'Behavior, Communication, and Assumptions About Other

(vi) Violence and reaction: Perhaps the most serious impediment to deliberation amid conflict is violence. Instead of the force of the better argument, what prevails is the force of arms. Active violence magnifies each of the problems and dilemmas outlined above. Violence inspires visceral responses that may cut short good faith attempts to engage in deliberation.[57] For instance, even in predominantly peaceful societies, legislative responses based on immediate reactions to terroristic carnage tend to call for restrictive and punitive responses, without necessarily taking account of the potential for backlash against these very responses and for more violence.[58] The responses often bypass careful legislative procedure and may fail to achieve reasonable balance in policymaking. National security matters 'can elicit highly emotional reactions because of fears about safety and security, anger over perceived transgressions, and desires for vengeance'.[59] Vocal advocacy for immediate punitive responses to violence is common, even among citizens who at other times may be open to deliberating. However, in peaceful societies, the hope is that constitutional or cultural constraints will curb the worst excesses of such responses and ground a more principled approach. In conflict societies, the same hope may have less bearing on reality.

III. Referendums in Conflict Societies

The impediments just listed show the uncertain prospects for deliberation in conflict societies. But they generally do not address the comparative institutional question of whether deliberation can be better promoted by a referendum or by an entirely elite-controlled settlement process. Conflict theorists often conclude that representative or other elite leadership is preferable to more diverse and unpredictable popular participation.[60] In democratic theory—including deliberative democratic theory—referendums and other forms

People's Behavior in a Commons Dilemma Situation' (1977) 35(1) Journal of Personality and Social Psychology 1.

[57] See, eg, Rajat Ganguly, 'Sri Lanka's Ethnic Conflict: At a Crossroad Between Peace and War' (2004) 25(5) Third World Quarterly 903.

[58] See, eg, Brian Blankenship, 'When do States Take the Bait? State Capacity and the Provocation Logic of Terrorism' (2018) 62(2) Journal of Conflict Resolution 381; Kyle Welch, 'The Patriot Act and Crisis Legislation: The Unintended Consequences of Disaster Lawmaking' (2015) 43 Capital University Law Review 481.

[59] Mary Derosa and Milton Regan, 'Deliberative Constitutionalism in the National Security Setting' in Ron Levy and others (eds), *The Cambridge Handbook of Deliberative Constitutionalism* (CUP 2018).

[60] See, eg, Arend Lijphart, *The Politics of Accommodation: Pluralism and Democracy in the Netherlands* (2nd edn, University of California Press 1975) 111; O'Leary, 'Debating Consociational Politics' (n 8) 10.

of direct democracy are habitually understood as democratic ideal types, set aside in practice due to their assumedly inferior deliberative quality.[61] This assumption often overlooks contrary evidence and fails to spell out the range of circumstances in which it holds.

For instance, the social, political and economic divisions that can stymie deliberation across groups or factions can manifest in referendum processes; but they can also manifest, and may even manifest more strongly, in elite-led processes. Works by Kahan and other social psychologists suggest that group polarization can especially characterize decision-making by elites, many of whom are a society's most highly educated citizens. Superior formal learning makes elites especially prone to using new knowledge to reconfirm what they already believe.[62] Whether by cherry picking or applying logical sophistry, they are best equipped to choose and bend information to match pre-existing assumptions aligning with their own polarized positions.[63] Partisan polarization is often a problem not of low information, but of excessive mutual familiarity and long-developed animus. While 'motivated reasoners' may be well apprised of the other side's views they may still be driven to force what they learn into existing polarized frames, and may seldom pause to reconsider matters afresh from first principles.[64]

In addition, the risk of group targeting may be no greater amid referendums than amid other forms of institutionalized decision-making. Commentary on this point often neglects to examine it as a comparative matter, and one of degrees of difference.[65] Though a referendum is a majoritarian event, this does not necessarily make it a tool of minority coercion. A referendum in which minority interests are at stake (eg, a referendum to recognize indigenous peoples in a constitution) can symbolize, at opposite extremes, either a dangerous submission of minority interests to majority will and whim, or an attempt to fairly advantage the group.[66] Which expressive direction the referendum actually

[61] Richard Posner, *Law, Pragmatism, and Democracy* (Harvard University Press 2005) 167. Though the recent interest in 'democratic innovations' may change all of this: see, eg, Graham Smith, *Democratic Innovations: Designing Institutions for Citizen Participation* (CUP 2009); Stephen Elstub and Oliver Escobar (eds), *The Handbook of Democratic Innovation and Governance* (Edward Elgar 2019).

[62] Dan M Kahan, 'Ideology, Motivated Reasoning, and Cognitive Reflection: An Experimental Study' (2012) 8 Judgment and Decision Making 407, 416–18; Matthew S Nurse and Will J Grant, 'I'll See It When I Believe It: Motivated Numeracy in Perceptions of Climate Change Risk' (2020) 14(2) Environmental Communication 184; Jonathan Haidt, *The Righteous Mind: Why Good People are Divided by Politics and Religion* (Pantheon 2012).

[63] Kahan (n 62) 417–18.

[64] ibid 408.

[65] For similar observations see, eg, Tierney, 'Using Electoral Law' (n 25) 511; Céline Colombo, 'Justifications and Citizen Competence in Direct Democracy: A Multilevel Analysis' (2018) 48(3) British Journal of Political Science 787.

[66] See, eg, Larissa Behrendt, 'The 1967 Referendum: 40 Years On' (2007) 11 Australian Indigenous Law Review 12; Seraina Pedrini, André Bächtiger and Marco Steenbergen, 'Deliberative Inclusion of

takes depends partly on elite leadership of the referendum campaign. Even absent a referendum, governmental leaders often engage in the same invidious rhetoric expected of referendums. In non-conflict societies the comparative record on invidious lawmaking via legislatures and referendums is mixed.[67] As we will see in this book, in at least some conflict societies (where, admittedly, the record is less complete), there is even more reason to suspect that the deliberative advantage favours non-elites.

None of this is to deny the real weaknesses of referendums, at least in their standard (ie, non-deliberative) forms, in both relatively peaceful societies and societies beset by conflict. In the chapters to follow, we will canvass occasional faults such as non-representative population samples, divisive campaign rhetoric, simplification of issues, low levels of voter information, and much else. These are among the reasons why, comparatively speaking, like many other scholars of democracy, deliberative democrats tend to favour representative lawmaking over referendums.

More specifically, deliberative democrats tend to think about decision-making in terms of a division of labour. While non-elites rarely become involved in actual lawmaking, they are responsible for highlighting issues and bringing them to public attention. To that end, they engage in deliberation about the broad and foundational values, interests, principles, ideologies, and worldviews that inform their policy preferences.[68] By contrast, elites, and especially governmental actors and policy experts, engage in relatively structured and detailed deliberation, focusing on drafting laws or policies in order to apply broad concepts in specific terms.[69] The assumption that non-elites are unsuited to these more technical forms of deliberation is at least partly justified. After all, ordinary citizens generally do not have the time to develop

Minorities: Patterns of Reciprocity Among Linguistic Groups in Switzerland' (2013) 5(3) European Political Science Review 483. For discussion see, eg, Arend Lijphart, 'Constitutional Design for Divided Societies' (2004) 15(2) Journal of Democracy 96, 106; Tierney, *Constitutional Referendums* (n 23) 52.

[67] Daniel C Lewis, 'Bypassing the Representational Filter? Minority Rights Policies under Direct Democracy Institutions in US States' (2011) 11(2) State Politics and Policy Quarterly 198, reviewing conflicting studies. Mixed results obtain even for that most feared of referendum types, the citizen-initiated referendum: Zoltan L Hajnal, Elisabeth R Gerber and Hugh Louch, 'Minorities and Direct Legislation: Evidence from California Ballot Proposition Elections' (2002) 64(1) Journal of Politics 154.

[68] In deliberative democratic theory the two main division-of-labour conceptualizations are, first, a 'two-track' model in which parliamentary elites launder or filter non-elite preferences and values into coherent and informed law or policy; and second, a more diffuse model in which large sets of expert and non-elite individuals, groups and bodies contribute towards what is, on the whole, a functioning 'deliberative system': see, respectively, Jürgen Habermas, *Between Facts and Norms: Contributions to a Discourse Theory of Law and Democracy* (William Rehg tr, MIT Press 1996) 304–08; and John Parkinson and Jane Mansbridge (eds), *Deliberative Systems: Deliberative Democracy at the Large Scale* (CUP 2012) 1–26.

[69] Habermas, *Between Facts and Norms* (n 68) 304–08.

specialized knowledge about the procedures and substantive detail of law- and policymaking. In the ideal case, however, what results from a deliberative division of labour is (to adopt another metaphor) a virtuous democratic cycle between elites and non-elites.[70] Non-elites thus transmit their issues and concerns to governmental elites, who in turn publicly justify or account for the decisions they have made. But, for this cycle to work, elites must be responsive to the views and opinions of non-elites. They must also think of themselves as accountable.

And yet, even in this relatively benign form, a deliberative division of labour giving key roles to elites can sometimes become problematic. Its assumptions about the relative deliberative capacities of elites and non-elites, and hence their respective contributions to democratic decision-making, should raise particular doubts when the subject is *constitutional reform*. In this book, as noted, we will contend that non-elites (voting in referendums) are generally better than elites at key constitutional forms of deliberation needed for peacemaking. This argument ultimately will depend on a close examination of the relative deliberative abilities of elites and non-elites in the context of constitutional settlement.

We will also describe our argument's limitations. And, in turn, we will stipulate some of the institutional conditions necessary—if not always sufficient—to lessen these limitations in practice. Crucially, while most critiques of referendum deliberation have some basis in past experience, they do not often account for the possibility of reform of the referendum process itself. Yet this is our main subject. The design features of a deliberative referendum—or, in a conflict setting, of a DPR—are specifically geared to problems of deliberation in referendums. Any comprehensive account of referendums' prospects for peacemaking—or, more broadly, of the referendum as a lens through which peacemaking might be viewed—must be alive to the institutional varieties of referendums. It should also notice how assorted varieties can influence the nature and effectiveness of constitutional settlement. We will set out at length how a DPR can offer institutional assistance to such a settlement.

That said, like others who provide institutionalist accounts in deliberative democracy, our aim will be 'not at institutional rupture but at incremental improvement in a deliberative direction'.[71] Throughout this book, then, we will from time to time remind the reader of our comparative and incremental aims.

[70] ibid.
[71] Archon Fung, 'Deliberation Before the Revolution: Toward an Ethics of Deliberative Democracy in an Unjust World' (2005) 33(3) Political Theory 397, 403.

Our discussion of the possibilities of DPRs will remain focused on degrees of change: not a claim that referendums can yield ideal deliberation but, just a little more modestly, that when carefully designed they may improve on peace referendums of the past.

IV. The Plan of this Book

The book will have three parts after this one. Part II will lay out the bulk of our theoretical and empirical argument, along with a broadly applicable ('generic') suggested institutional design for DPRs. Part III will then apply these broad themes and designs to particular kinds of conflict. And Part IV will offer a brief summation.

A. Part II, Foundations

Part II opens with Chapter 2, which will focus on the first of two principal rationales supporting the use of peace referendums, namely *settlement achievement*. The chapter will start by locating the argument of the book in the public reason tradition, and specifically in the work of John Rawls. The chapter will identify how public values often feature in crucial, if generally under-appreciated, ways in peace agreements—not just as lofty aspirations but as powerful normative constraints on the content of particular constitutional clauses. With this much in place, the chapter will then defend the claim that non-elites may be as, or even more, adept than some classes of elites (such as governmental, ethnic, or secessionist leaders) at deliberating about those values. We accept that constitutional settlements often contain a great deal of institutional detail; and we also accept that elites are usually better placed to deliberate about that detail. Yet we explain why the comparative advantage may rest with non-elites when it comes to deliberating about general public values. All of this is contingent on robust deliberative institutional supports being in place, both in the course of the referendum campaign and at the final vote.

Chapter 3 will outline how we envisage a generic DPR could look. We will introduce some key innovations here, such as a modestly coercive referendum ballot design that encourages public-value based deliberation. We will also point to more established institutional options (eg, mini-publics) and where they could fit in the course of a DPR process. By describing the model here as 'generic', we intend to make clear that it should be open to modification, and especially to adaptation to the particular aims and constraints that assorted conflicts may raise. But we will leave our discussion of institutional variations to the next part of the book.

Chapter 4 will describe settlement endurance, which as noted is a further rationale supporting the use of peace referendums. As also noted, even a brief popular act of entrenchment, in a well-designed referendum enjoying popular perceptions of legitimacy, may solidify into a lasting constitutional settlement. We will focus on the capacity of DPRs, in particular, in this regard. (We will also look to other 'sources' of constitutional legitimacy—eg, ideas of legal pedigree—and notice how a DPR may enliven these as well.) A particular claim in this chapter will be that a DPR, drawing on its institutional supports for deliberation, may expose a broad but latent constitutional agreement that may have existed at the popular (but not the elite) level in a conflict society. The DPR may also clarify the reasons upon which an agreement rests, and hence deepen the sense of legitimacy that attaches to it.

Yet, as we have said, these and other expectations may depend on the kind of conflict that a referendum seeks to address, and on the kind of referendum. In certain circumstances, we may need to vary our DPR recommendations from the generic model.

B. Part III, Variations

Chapter 5 will discuss a key type of conflict that centres on group sovereignty. Here two or more identity-based groups compete for political dominion within a specific territory. In this chapter, we will introduce group sovereignty in broad terms as a concept in political and constitutional theory. We will also offer some initial suggestions for the design of a DPR taking account of group sovereignty elements in conflict. We will contend that this element cannot be ignored or wished away, but must be accommodated—for instance, by means of a rule of 'concurrent consent' in the referendum. Such a rule requires a majority vote within each of the distinct groups in conflict. A critical question raised, however, is the degree to which deliberation is feasible when we give group identity (the root cause of many deliberative pathologies, as we saw above) a robust role in the DPR.

Within the broad category of conflict over group-sovereignty, there are further (and sometimes overlapping) sub-types. Our focus will be on two subtypes: secession conflicts and indigenous-settler conflicts.

In Chapter 6 we will focus on conflicts in which members of a group pursue their group's legal and political separation from a sovereign state of which the group has been an integral part. Often this entails the establishment of a new sovereign state meant to enjoy international legal status on a par with other states in the international system. As we will see, secession is essentially unilateral: the decision to secede from an existing state rests ultimately with the seceding group. Consequently, the idea that secession referendums should be based on concurrent consent will be out of place. Yet while the consent of the existing state may not be formally required, the degree to which the seceding group seeks to include the existing group in its deliberations may make an important difference to how the legitimacy of the referendum is perceived—domestically, regionally, and internationally.

In secession conflicts, therefore, DPR design must reflect both the unilateral nature of the decision and the need to reach out to individuals in the existing state, the wider region, and the international community. To this end, we will consider (among other matters) both the structure of the ballot and the potential role of mini-publics. However, before we do so, we will discuss a prior question. Various legal and political philosophers disagree about when secession is justified. Some argue that secession cannot be sensibly justified on self-determination grounds. By corollary, they argue that the referendum should play no part in thinking about secession conflicts. Against this view, however, we will argue that the right to self-determination is an important public value of the sort that Rawls describes. Like all such values, it needs to be weighed in the balance against other, competing public values—which is to say that it can and should be tested through a DPR.

Finally, in Chapter 7 we will discuss indigenous-settler conflicts, in which the roots of the conflicts lie in historical acts by which colonizing powers asserted their own sovereignties over or in place of those of existing peoples in the same territories. Here, conflict may be the long-term consequence of an act of conquest. Not all indigenous-settler states experience overt conflict, but those that do sometimes share certain characteristics, such as experiences of '[d]ispossession of land, incorporation and subalterneity within the institutional structure of a state, and cultural assimilationist policies'.[72] This presents an especially formidable obstacle to deliberation about public values. Adequate DPR design may require a preliminary period in which comprehensive and detailed changes to policies and laws are used to address political and economic

[72] Martin Hébert, 'Indigenous Spheres of Deliberation' in André Bachtinger and others (eds), *The Oxford Handbook of Deliberative Democracy* (OUP 2018).

inequalities in the interim—and a delay in the running of the DPR for years, or even decades.

Moreover, while structural inequalities are not unique to indigenous-settler societies, we must also consider whether a further, distinctive feature in these societies will significantly draw down deliberation in a DPR. Several authors have explored the sharp divergences between the normative views (including views about group sovereignty itself) of indigenous and settler populations, which may make remote the prospect of deliberation about public values. Hence indigenous-settler conflicts will be among the conflict subtypes that most significantly challenge our conception of deliberative peacemaking within the DPR.

C. Part IV, Conclusions

In this final chapter we will reprise the book's content by offering several key take-aways. We will also proffer predictions about where future work may take studies of deliberative design for peace referendums. As noted, DPRs (in the full sense) are novel, and hence generally untried. Consequently, in this largely normative book we will have to rely on at best partial past cases, where a peace referendum possessed only some of the features of a deliberative referendum. We will also engage in speculation informed by what we do know about the faults of standard peace referendums in the past, as well as their strengths and popular appeal.

As we have noted, referendums are now part of very many peacemaking efforts. We expect referendums to continue to be used this way. But when this occurs, the success of peace referendums—particularly their capacity to achieve and secure the endurance of constitutional peace settlements—may turn largely on whether institutional supports for deliberation are in place. Of course, even under ideal institutional conditions, a DPR, like any other referendum, will always risk misfiring—for instance, becoming a catalyst for further conflict over the immediate or the long term. Yet our aim ultimately is to outline how the design of referendums can by degrees be improved to enhance, though in all likelihood never to perfect, the practice of peacemaking by referendum.

PART II

FOUNDATIONS

2

Settlement Achievement

I. Introduction

In this chapter we contend that referendums may, at least in some cases, prompt the parties in a conflict to achieve a constitutional settlement meant to manage or end the conflict. There are two key elements to this argument. First, settlement achievement may follow from a deliberative process that encourages the parties to endorse certain public values that are shared between them. And second, ordinary voters may be more effective, as compared with many types of 'elites',[1] at deliberating about such shared public values. Together these elements point to peace referendums as useful tools for settlement achievement.

We will develop—but also critique—these positions across two main sections. In Section II we will locate the foundations of our argument in John Rawls's theory of public reason. That theory is concerned with the question of how citizens holding very different moral, philosophical, or religious worldviews—or 'comprehensive doctrines', as Rawls calls them—can live together peaceably and on just terms. In essences, the answer that Rawls gives is that they should justify their political claims and proposals in terms of public values—that is, values like freedom and equality that all democratic citizens can reasonably be expected to endorse. In theory, therefore, public reason holds out the prospect of deliberation from common ground. But the discussion here will not only be theoretical; we will also observe how deliberation over public values can in practice be a feature of deliberation that leads to the achievement of a constitutional settlement. Peacemaking should often, in the first instance, centre on public-value deliberation, rather than leaping straight to the details of a settlement. Public-value deliberation may be more likely to yield a constitutional settlement, and in some cases may even be a practical requirement before a settlement can be reached.

In Section III we will query which classes of people—whether political leaders and other elite figures, or else non-elites—are best placed to deliberate about public values. By concluding that non-elites may have the better claim

[1] See definition in Chapter 1.

Deliberative Peace Referendums. Ron Levy, Ian O'Flynn, Hoi L Kong, Oxford University Press (2021). © Ron Levy, Ian O'Flynn, and Hoi L Kong. DOI: 10.1093/oso/9780198867036.003.0002

here, we will confront entrenched doubts about the deliberative capacities of ordinary people. We will also challenge the widely held assumption that such people are best kept out of peace processes. Yet we will nuance our discussion by considering not only whether, but also under what general circumstances, referendums can aid deliberation about constitutional settlements. This discussion will be comparative as between referendums and more standard, elite-dominated efforts at peacemaking.

We will conclude that whether, in practice, peace referendums reliably promote settlement achievement depends largely on whether the referendums provide institutional support for deliberation. Thus in general terms only a weak case can be made in favour of pursuing peacemaking through referendums: certain common and formidable deliberative faults mean that referendums will frequently fall short of our expectations. This will set up our discussion in Chapter 3, in which we will outline a set of institutional prescriptions for deliberative peace referendums (DPRs) that, when added to our comparative assessment, point to a far stronger case for peace referendums.

II. Public Reason and Conflict

A. Deliberating about Public Values

Theories of public reason suppose that, in order to be legitimate, important decisions of law and policy must be publicly justifiable to all those who stand to be bound by them.[2] There are different views on what exactly this entails, but in this section we focus on the account offered by Rawls.[3] We do so for three reasons. First, Rawls has had a tremendous influence on the development of deliberative democratic theory generally; his work has served as an essential reference point for, among others, Joshua Cohen, and Amy Gutmann and Dennis Thompson.[4] Second, his work on the idea of public reason specifically

[2] See, eg, Amy Gutmann and Dennis Thompson, *Democracy and Disagreement* (Harvard University Press 1996) 50, 55.

[3] John Rawls, *Political Liberalism* (Colombia University Press 1996); John Rawls, 'The Idea of Public Reason Revisited' (1997) 64(3) University of Chicago Law Review 765. See also, eg, Gerald F Gaus, *The Order of Public Reason: A Theory of Freedom and Morality in a Diverse and Bounded World* (CUP 2011); Stephen Macedo, *Liberal Virtues: Citizenship, Virtue and Community in Liberal Constitutionalism* (Clarendon Press 1990); Charles E Larmore, *The Morals of Modernity* (CUP 1996); Jeremy Waldron, 'Theoretical Foundations of Liberalism' in Jeremy Waldron (ed), *Liberal Rights: Collected Papers 1981–1991* (CUP 1993) 35–62.

[4] Joshua Cohen, 'Deliberation and Democratic Legitimacy' in Alan Hamlin and Philip Pettit (eds), *The Good Polity: Normative Analysis of the State* (Blackwell 1989) 17–34; Gutmann and Thompson,

is not only the best known treatment of that idea but also the most exhaustively criticized. We cannot hope to cover each and every criticism here, but what we can do is address those that we think are most relevant to the project of this book—in particular, the charge that public reason is (1) exclusionary and (2) unrealistic (or perhaps even hopelessly utopian). Finally, Rawls's account is limited in scope to what he terms 'constitutional essentials and matters of basic justice'—to questions concerning how government is structured, how elections are conducted, how important social and material resources are distributed, how the economy is organized, and so forth.[5] His account thus matches this book's overarching concern with constitutional settlement.

The starting point for Rawls's account is the fact of pluralism—the fact that, in modern democratic societies, people adhere to different and conflicting comprehensive doctrines or worldviews, religious, moral, or philosophical.[6] This circumstance is not merely an unfortunate feature of our modern world. Rather, it is a natural consequence of the use of reason in circumstances of freedom, particularly given the 'burdens of judgement' (the burdens of reasoning under conditions of incomplete information, moral uncertainty, limited time, and so forth).[7] Since reasonable people will recognize that everyone is subject to the same burdens of judgement, Rawls views it as important to distinguish the mere fact of pluralism from the fact of *reasonable* pluralism.[8]

This distinction implies that some disagreement will not belong to reasonable disagreement. But Rawls clearly thinks that most will—that reasonable disagreement is a perfectly proper and normal feature of human life in a liberal society with a plural culture,[9] and is therefore a feature that just institutions should take into account. We should not seek to remove reasonable disagreement nor should we see it as a matter for regret.[10] Nevertheless, reasonable pluralism presents a serious challenge. A liberal society will leave as much room as possible for people to pursue their own comprehensive doctrines or worldviews, free from external interference. Yet to ensure that one person's pursuit does not unfairly infringe upon another's, there have got to be some

Democracy and Disagreement (n 2). See also Antonio Floridia, *From Participation to Deliberation: A Critical Genealogy of Deliberative Democracy* (ECPR Press 2017) ch 11.

5 Rawls, *Political Liberalism* (n 3) 227–29.

6 ibid 3–4. A doctrine is 'comprehensive' in the sense that its principles and injunctions reach into or govern life in general.

7 ibid 56.

8 ibid 37, 54–6, 61 .

9 In Chapter 3, we will consider the complication that many conflict societies are in some respects illiberal.

10 Rawls, *Political Liberalism* (n 3) 245–46.

generally applicable ground rules. Moreover, those rules have got to be generally agreed to. But if, in pluralistic societies, agreement cannot be found at the level of (reasonable) comprehensive doctrines, how else might 'constitutional essentials' be grounded?[11]

Rawls's answer to this question is public reason. A person engages in public reason 'when he or she deliberates within a framework of what he or she sincerely regards as the most reasonable political conception of justice'.[12] All reasonable conceptions conceive of society as a cooperative endeavour among free and equal citizens. Yet since values like cooperation, freedom, and equality can be interpreted in different ways, what result are different views on how constitutional essentials should be arranged.[13] For example, liberals and libertarians share a commitment to individual freedom. However, liberal interpretations of that value, and the conditions necessary to secure it, may lead to precisely the sorts of arguments for progressive taxation that libertarians disavow. Nevertheless, the fact that liberals and libertarians share a commitment to individual freedom means that they are at least deliberating from common ground. And since they are deliberating from common ground, it is in principle possible for them to reach an agreement that is publicly justifiable to all.[14]

Thus, public reason requires us to focus on broadly generalized values that can be agreed to, after some discursive back-and-forth, by members of a democratic society.[15] In turn, that requirement can be viewed as an expression of the principle that one must be reciprocally willing to be held to any reasonable obligation that one sees as fit to impose on others.[16] We will use the term 'public-value deliberation' to describe that aspect of public reason that invokes such generalized values. In short, in seeking to resolve or manage disagreements about the basic constitutional structure of a democratic society, the members of that society should appeal not to their own comprehensive doctrines but to more broadly applicable public values: again, to political considerations that any democratic citizen (*qua* democratic citizen) might reasonably be expected to endorse.

The intuition behind the idea of public reason is easy to appreciate. Since a constitutional settlement will have a major bearing on people's lives, the

[11] ibid 100, 146.
[12] Rawls, 'The Idea of Public Reason' (n 3) 773.
[13] ibid 774.
[14] See also Ronald Dworkin, *Is Democracy Possible Here?: Principles for a New Political Debate* (Princeton University Press, 2006).
[15] ibid; Rawls, *Political Liberalism* (n 3) 223–27.
[16] Rawls, 'The Idea of Public Reason' (n 3) 770.

reasons for that settlement should be broadly accessible and acceptable to all. As Charles Larmore puts it, '[i]f the principles of political association are to be rooted in a commitment to equal respect, they must be justifiable to everyone whom they are to bind'.[17] Or to quote Gutmann and Thompson, '[b]ecause the results of democratic deliberation are mutually binding, citizens should aspire to a kind of political reasoning that is mutually justifiable'.[18] That is because (and here their indebtedness to Rawls is clear) 'the principles of democracy must provide some guidance for living with fundamental moral disagreement, not simply resolving it'.[19]

In short, public reason does not try to deal with the fact of reasonable pluralism directly through democratic deliberation but instead leaves that fact in place and provides for political arrangements that are independent of it. Public reason does not compete with citizens' comprehensive doctrines but instead seeks to show how citizens who possess different and conflicting comprehensive doctrines might live together peaceably and on equal terms within a common democratic framework.[20] It enables individuals and groups to reach an agreement on a framework of constitutional essentials that leaves each of them equally free to pursue their own comprehensive worldview. As we will see in later chapters, we now have empirical evidence from social psychology experiments to support the validity of these key propositions under certain circumstances.

B. Public-Value Deliberation amid Conflict

We argue that notions of public reason are often especially applicable and useful to constitutional settlements in conflict societies. We are not the only ones to have made this argument, though more unique, we think, are the institutional and other implications that we will identify further on. Placing public values at the centre of discussion is potentially advantageous if it helps to manage conflict, rather than seeking to eliminate all disagreement. Public reason does not seek to resolve conflicts between comprehensive doctrines, but instead focuses

[17] Larmore (n 3) 141.

[18] Gutmann and Thompson, *Democracy and Disagreement?* (n 2) 53.

[19] ibid 54–55.

[20] Though Rawls was later to say things that muddied the waters, public reason is in our view best conceived as a 'discontinuous' rather than 'continuous' strategy for dealing with pluralism or diversity. For this terminology, see Ronald Dworkin, 'Foundations of Liberal Equality' in Grethe Peterson (ed), *The Tanner Lectures on Human Values, XI* (University of Utah Press 1990) 16–22.

on forms of disagreement that might be more realistically addressed. In deliberation over public values, even groups in conflict may find it possible to reach a mutual accommodation.

Importantly, though the point usually goes unnoticed, public values are already habitual parts of successful peace agreements. As Christine Bell observes, '[i]n peace processes, ceasefires are rarely just about ceasefires. . . . [T]hey often have constitutional dimensions and implications'.[21] Settlements thus frequently implicate not merely short-term acts (eg, monetary reparations), but also second-order norms—norms that are 'constitutional' by virtue of 'regulat[ing] matters that are in some sense more fundamental than others'.[22] In intra-state conflicts, workable long-term arrangements must be found in relation, for example, to power sharing, the conduct of elections, the distribution of powers of revenue, cultural self-determination, and military and security apparatuses. Conflicts of other types may also implicate second-order norms, including territorial boundaries and the establishment or enforcement of human rights.

Therefore many norms of settlement—the various rules or principles that a conflict settlement sets out—either directly describe public values, or can be made sense of only as relatively direct expressions of such values. Questions concerning public value are at least the implicit subjects of many settlement debates. But in some cases the questions are explicit. For example, in the case of the 1988 Belfast Agreement, British unionists' and Irish nationalists' acceptance of the principle of 'parity of esteem' formed a significant part of the basis of the power-sharing arrangement on which the parties were finally to agree: it is reflected, for example, in the Agreement's dual premiership, communal designation, proportionality rules and mutual vetoes.[23] As well, top of the agenda for mediators in Tanzania seeking an end to the three-year Rwandan Civil War

> was the establishment of the rule of law based on national unity, democracy and respect for human rights. Tanzanian mediators saw an agreement on these broad principles as a way to commit the parties to an 'ideological

[21] Christine Bell, 'Lex Pacificatoria Colombiana: Colombia's Peace Accord in Comparative Perspective' (2016) 110 American Journal of International Law 165, 170.

[22] Jon Elster, 'Forces and Mechanisms in the Constitution-Making Process' (1995) 45 Duke Law Journal 364, 366.

[23] Brendan O'Leary, 'The Nature of the Agreement' (1999) 22 Fordham International Law Journal 1628, 1638–39.

> set of values' that would form the basis for negotiating the details of power-sharing procedures within the framework of a broad-based transitional government.[24]

As one would expect, there is variation from case to case. But values relevant to conflict settlement typically include, to provide just a partial list, peace, stability, democracy, the rule of law, mutual toleration, non-violence, human rights, human dignity, anti-domination, cultural recognition, and fairness in resource distribution. All of these values, if adopted, may give general direction to a conflict society's decisions and deliberations about a range of narrower cases (eg, when and where a human right applies or how a natural resource is to be shared or distributed).

An alternative strategy to achieve settlement could be to remain mostly silent about values—to 'incompletely theorize' in order, it may be hoped, to reach an agreement without the need to lay bare deeper and assumedly more intractable divisions.[25] Looking at US (non-conflict) examples, Cass Sunstein describes the reasons for such a strategy as follows:

> When people disagree or are uncertain about an abstract issue . . . they can often make progress by moving to a level of greater particularity. They attempt a *conceptual descent*. This phenomenon has an especially notable feature: It enlists silence, on certain basic questions, as a device for producing convergence despite disagreement, uncertainty, limits of time and capacity, and heterogeneity. In short, silence can be a constructive force. Incompletely theorized agreements are an important source of successful constitutionalism and social stability.[26]

We think Sunstein's observations are astute and valuable. Their value is partly in the descriptive claim that, when different people support the same concrete decision, but for a plurality of reasons, this joint support offers a reprieve from discord.[27]

[24] Gilbert Khadiagala, 'Implementing the Arusha Peace Agreement on Rwanda' in Stephen Stedman, Donald Rothchild, and Elizabeth Cousens (eds), *Ending Civil Wars: The Implementation of Peace Agreements* (Lynne Rienner 2002) 471.

[25] Cass R Sunstein, 'Incompletely Theorized Agreements' (1995) 108(7) Harvard Law Review 1733.

[26] Cass R Sunstein, *Conspiracy Theories and Other Dangerous Ideas* (Simon and Schuster 2014) 189 (emphasis in original).

[27] See similarly John Dryzek, *Deliberative Democracy and Beyond: Liberals, Critics, Contestations* (OUP 2000) 170; John Dryzek, 'Democratization as Deliberative Capacity Building' (2009) 42(11) Comparative Political Studies 1379, 1391.

However, especially amid conflict, a *complete* (or near-complete) absence of theorization would potentially be unsuitable. Maintaining a focus on value content can obviate some of the need for ordinary citizens to engage in difficult social learning about myriad legal and institutional details. For once we veer too far into the realm of factual argumentation, we are potentially prone to a suite of deliberative problems. Voters who feel ill-informed, when the issues discussed in a referendum are excessively technical, are more likely to vote negatively in a referendum—that is, against a peace settlement or peacemaking. 'Don't know, vote no' is an important, telling slogan in referendum campaigns around the world.[28] Voters hesitate to endorse reforms whose details are complex and thus, to them, obscure (and, one might add, who could blame them?). This effect may be pronounced when, as in at least some conflict societies, social trust in the elite authors of the reform text is lacking.[29] Some information deficiencies even result from the intentional choices of elites, as referendum questions and campaign materials confuse voters by design.[30]

Moreover, a campaign excessively focused on deliberation about particulars can commit the bulk of the campaign to the cat-and-mouse game of presenting and countering factual and legal claims and misrepresentations.[31] Many settlement processes (including peace referendums) indeed involve tendentious empirical assumptions or scare campaigns that are misleading yet persuasive. Even when misleading claims can in theory be falsified with other evidence, amid the din of competing claims there may be no opportunity to right the record in a convincing way.[32] Focusing on public-value deliberation may to some extent prevent the peace process from becoming derailed by factual claims, counterclaims, and misinformation. (We will return to this point later and some difficulties that it raises.)

More fundamentally, a key problem with trying to commit a peace process to factual and legal particulars is that asking participants to avoid parsing an agreement's guiding principles may be unrealistic and, in any event, misguided. Such avoidance is unlikely to happen because when (as may be inevitable) the

[28] Ron Levy, '"Deliberative Voting": Realising Constitutional Referendum Democracy' (2013) Public Law 555, 555–56.

[29] ibid; Lawrence LeDuc, 'Referendums and Deliberative Democracy' (2015) 38 Electoral Studies 139, 143–44.

[30] Ethan J Leib, 'Can Direct Democracy Be Made Deliberative?' (2006) 54 Buffalo Law Review 903, 907–08.

[31] For more on this see Ron Levy, '"Shotgun Referendums": Popular Deliberation and Conflict Settlement in Conflict Societies' (2018) 41(3) Melbourne University Law Review 1237, 1253–54.

[32] Stephen Tierney, 'The Scottish Independence Referendum: A Model of Good Practice in Direct Democracy?' in Saskia P Ruth, Yanina Welp, and Laurence Whitehead (eds), *Let the People Rule? Direct Democracy in the Twenty-First Century* (ECPR Press 2017) 90.

parties wonder about the scope and implications of the agreement, they first need to know what the core of the agreement stipulates, including its reasons or purposes. At the same time, the ultimate causes of a conflict cannot be ignored; any agreement is likely to be understood as a response to those causes. Peacemaking focused on particulars would require the parties to will themselves to suspend any examination of the underlying clashes of value that drove them to contemplate violence in the first place (eg, incompatible group claims to legitimate occupation of the same territory, or fundamental disagreement about the locus of political authority). These value clashes organize and motivate the conflict. Even if only implicitly, the parties' rhetoric and concerns keep coming back to them, and they remain obstacles to settlement.

For instance, Thomas Hennessey notes that for many years in Northern Ireland '[n]either Unionists nor Nationalists could comprehend the other'.[33] Efforts at settlement yielded little progress as leaders focused on constitutional options to distribute power post-conflict, without working through more fundamental questions of value. In particular, neither side 'really accepted the legitimacy of the other'.[34] And sections of both sides 'were prepared to aggressively demonstrate the righteousness and moral superiority of their worldview' through the use of violence.[35] In conflict societies, each side may have 'an all too vivid sense of what the other side wants but not see how it could reasonably want it. In Rawlsian terms, they may have trouble viewing each other as reasonable people engaging in reasonable disagreements'.[36] Hence constitutional solutions such as power sharing, along with quasi-confederal systems involving the Ireland and the UK, had for decades been proposed to address the violence.[37] The parties made these solutions the immediate subjects of their debates. Yet for decades they were simply unable to agree, in no small part because the underlying issues remained unsettled.[38]

To reuse our language from Chapter 1, the solutions long mooted were specific and applied; yet, what more basic content were the solutions intended to apply? When genuine progress towards a settlement finally came in the mid-1990s, a key reason was the acceptance of the principle of plural claims to

[33] Thomas Hennessey, *The Northern Ireland Peace Process* (Gill & Macmillan 2000) 7–9.

[34] ibid 9.

[35] ibid 10.

[36] Robert Luskin and others, 'Deliberating across Deep Divides' (2014) 62(1) Political Studies 116, 116.

[37] Hennessey (n 33) 9.

[38] Seamus Mallon, deputy leader of the nationalist SDLP, described the Belfast (Good Friday) Agreement as 'Sunningdale for slow learners', referring to a similar power-sharing deal that collapsed soon after its inception in 1974. See Mary Holland, 'A Very Good Friday' *The Observer* (London, 12 April 1998) [7].

national recognition. The two parties' grudging (and even then not universal) adoption of a bi-national conception of Northern Ireland, which better tolerates distinct identities, geography and power, helped to impel the settlement process. The document that ordinary people eventually ratified in a referendum adopted the language of public values. In particular, the 'Declaration of Support' with which the Agreement begins is couched in the language of (*inter alia*) 'reconciliation', 'tolerance', 'mutual trust', 'human rights', 'partnership', 'equality', 'mutual respect', and 'exclusively democratic and peaceful means'.[39] Public values such as these can also conflict. Yet in principle they permit agreement from common ground in ways that non-public values, such as absolutist claims to one group's sovereign status within a territory, do not.

To be clear, we do not mean to say that participants in peacemaking must agree on precisely the same public values before they can move forward. Sometimes agreements that do not principally rest on particulars nevertheless may rest on not one, but a few public values. Sunstein also contemplates this possibility (again in non-conflict contexts). He suggests that constitutional agreement may be reached not after complete conceptual descent, but based on incomplete descent that still leaves the parties focused on abstractions. Thus it may be relatively easy to find 'agreement about abstractions amid disagreements or uncertainty about the particular meaning of those abstractions'.[40] For example, constitutional guarantees can elide several reasons why people in a pluralistic society might favour abortion rights.[41] In this vein Sunstein points obliquely to a role for public values—including equality, privacy, respect for judicial precedent, and wariness of public roles for religion.

These points are important because, even if we seek reasons based on public values, people will almost inevitably invoke more than one public value or more than one reading of the same public value, though they may support the same constitutional settlement. Some of these values may bear a family relation to one another (eg, 'toleration' and 'mutual respect'). And some may be more or less particular versions of the same value (eg, 'non-domination' and 'non-interference'). Below we will see Michael Walzer's criticism that such interpretive variety can make public values themselves the subjects of sharp disagreement. Yet, in our view, an incomplete conceptual descent—from a more generalized value to a slightly less generalized value—may still

[39] '*Belfast Agreement*, Britain-Northern Ireland-Government of Ireland, signed 10 April 1998, No 50 (2000) Cm 4705 (entered into force 2 December 1999) Preamble paras 1–6.

[40] Cass R Sunstein, *One Case at a Time: Judicial Minimalism on the Supreme Court* (Harvard University Press, 2001) 11.

[41] Sunstein, *Conspiracy Theories* (n 26) 191.

allow public-value deliberation to go ahead, and on the basis of more flexible requirements.

Another clarification is that focusing on public values means, in effect, that the parties must defer the settlement of certain particulars. Hanna Lerner argues that deferring resolution of some matters (eg, about which laws to adopt regarding official languages or the civil legal code) can be helpful in deeply divided societies.[42] She contemplates a relatively drawn out, or even arrested, constitutional reform process, rather than a discrete reform moment. We do not advocate quite so piecemeal a process, as will become clear. Yet we think Lerner is right to suggest putting off some discussions about thorny applied issues that may frustrate agreement. In Northern Ireland, the parties chose to defer a number of important practical matters, including policing and the decommissioning of paramilitary weapons.[43] The parties thus reached an agreement on overarching values without clarifying every detail, which may help to explain the agreement's (qualified) success. Admittedly, while these issues have today been successfully addressed, they did haunt the settlement process for several years. However, there is a good case for arguing that no agreement could have been reached without setting them to one side, to be addressed at a point when circumstances became more propitious.

We raise the Northern Irish example's successes not to suggest that its lessons are universally applicable, but as a stepping-off point for our remaining discussion. The example's lesson is that, in at least some conflicts, bypassing efforts to mitigate differences of value might only delay or derail settlement. As William Zartman puts it, '[i]ndividual notions of justice act as a substantive veto on agreement, and must be coordinated and accepted as the first stage of negotiation'.[44] A great many writers on conflict societies, particularly those influenced by rational choice theory, tend to view peace agreements in terms of strategic bargaining. As Donald Horowitz puts it, the 'tacit assumption has been that, if the parties agree and can live with the agreement, they must have arrived at something like the market-clearing price'.[45] Typically, however, elites cannot begin to bargain seriously about specific issues until the 'rules of the game' have been agreed. In particular, little progress can be made until guiding

[42] Hanna Lerner, *Making Constitutions in Deeply Divided Societies* (CUP 2011).

[43] Arthur Aughey, *The Politics of Northern Ireland: Beyond the Belfast Agreement* (Routledge 2005) 143–51.

[44] Ira William Zartman, *Negotiation and Conflict Management: Essays on Theory and Practice* (Routledge 2008) 83.

[45] Donald Horowitz, *A Democratic South Africa? Constitutional Engineering in a Divided Society* (University of California Press 1991) 153.

norms and principles have been accepted by all sides, which, as should be clear by now, will normally require deliberation.[46]

As one of us has previously observed, if settlements 'are to provide a platform for sustainable peace, they must . . . reflect a commitment to basic principles'.[47] In at least some conflict situations, deliberating over underlying public values is a step towards the common ground needed for conflict settlement. It may be a way of working through conflict, in the sense of reorienting public attention to where the parties can find basic shared values between them. Some conflict settlement indeed may *only* succeed if such key values are agreed upon—or at least if interpretations of values are sufficiently reconciled.

III. Comparing Deliberative Capacities

A. The Terms of Comparison

We have argued that deliberation about public values is, though a hard labour, sometimes indispensable—or, better, fundamental—to conflict settlement. Absent this kind of deliberation, settlements may fail to get off the ground. What we now want to argue is that, under some conditions, non-elites can be more adept at public-value deliberation than elites. The sum of our arguments will be that efforts to achieve a constitutional settlement can benefit from public-value deliberation conducted substantially by non-elites, especially in and around referendums.

This argument may jar with some. In the conflict literature, it is widely assumed that ordinary people should be kept out of any deliberative process for fear of heightening the risk of violence. Ordinary people are said to lack the temperament for deliberation: they are likely to be badly informed, insecure, and mutually suspicious. Consequently, commentators view attempts to practise direct democracy in a deliberative democratic mode as futile, supposing that ordinary voters are not up to the required deliberative tasks.[48]

[46] Ian O'Flynn, 'Pulling Together: Shared Intentions, Deliberative Democracy and Deeply Divided Societies' (2017) 47(1) British Journal of Political Science 197–98.

[47] Ian O'Flynn, 'Divided Societies and Deliberative Democracy' (2007) 37 British Journal of Political Science 731, 741. See similarly Adeno Addis, 'Deliberative Democracy in Severely Fractured Societies' (2009) 16(1) Indiana Journal of Global Legal Studies 59, 64.

[48] John McGarry and Brendan O'Leary, 'Power Shared after Deaths of Thousands' in Rupert Taylor (ed), *Consociational Theory: McGarry and O'Leary and the Northern Ireland Conflict* (Routledge 2009). For similar views with respect to stabler societies see, eg, James Fishkin, *Democracy and Deliberation: New Directions for Democratic Reform* (Yale University Press 1993); Claus Offe, 'Referendum vs. Institutionalized Deliberation: What Democratic Theorists Can Learn from the 2016 Brexit Decision' (2017) 146(3) Daedalus 14.

Many referendums indeed validate the worst fears of critics. Some of the anti-deliberative features of conflict societies in general, which we canvassed in Chapter 1, are particularly features of referendums (even if not exclusively so). For example, voters may have uneven levels of commitment to deliberating in the referendum. Or those who do want to deliberate may be vulnerable to the polarizing effects of intra-group outbidding and the uncompromising rhetoric that normally accompanies it. Moreover, occurrences of violence during the campaign may mean that those who are otherwise primed to deliberate lack safe spaces within which to do so. Thus, referendums may encounter or even magnify many of the elite and non-elite deliberative faults that ordinarily arise in conflict societies.

This is a serious worry. But the charge that some people may struggle to engage in deliberation is an empirical claim; how well supported is it? Critics of non-elite decision-making do not always back their assertions up with comparative and contextualized evidence. To assess criticisms of peace referendums, we need to be clear about what kinds of evidence and argumentation the critics are offering, and what kinds might instead be more relevant. Our focus is on four kinds that, where available, are particularly relevant:

(i) *Public-value deliberation:* For reasons that we have explained, we will mostly look for evidence of capacities for deliberation about *public values*. Is it necessary to restrict such deliberation to elites? Or might ordinary people be adept at public-value deliberation?

(ii) *Comparative:* Adopting a comparative view, we focus on the capacities of non-elites to engage in public-value deliberation in referendums while acknowledging that there are no absolute measures of deliberative capacity to which we might appeal. High and low are inevitably relative terms and matters of degree.[49] The relevant question then becomes whether ordinary citizens are really all that much worse than elites at public-value deliberation in conflict settings. As we will see shortly, non-elites are indeed often better at such deliberation, and particularly less prone to catalysing or prolonging conflict.

(iii) *Institutional:* Any comparison of deliberative capacities ultimately depends on the institutions within which deliberation takes place.[50] By

[49] John Dryzek, 'Theory, Evidence, and the Tasks of Deliberation' in Shawn Rosenberg (ed), *Deliberation, Participation and Democracy* (Palgrave Macmillan 2007) 244.

[50] John Parkinson, 'Legitimacy Problems in Deliberative Democracy' (2003) 51 Political Studies 180, 186–87; Céline Colombo, 'Justifications and Citizen Competence in Direct Democracy: A Multilevel Analysis' (2016) 48 British Journal of Political Science 787, 790, 801.

the end of this chapter, our comparative claims favouring peace referendums will have to remain tentative. We will only be able make them in stronger terms once certain institutional requirements for referendums come into view—especially in Chapter 3's account of the DPR model. Whether efforts at conflict settlement include institutional support for deliberation, as well as the form that support actually takes, should affect our assumptions about who is best placed for public-value deliberation.

(iv) *Empirical:* In practice DPRs have yet to run in full form. Therefore no peace process has yet had what we assume would be the benefit of all of the institutional prescriptions for DPRs to be laid out in Chapter 3. This makes empirical assessment of DPRs difficult. But normative theories require at least some empirical verification. What we have said about Rawls's conception of public reason—and, equally, what we will say about Rawls's critics below—takes for granted the plausibility or implausibility of certain kinds of deliberation in the real world. Similarly, the Habermasian notion of two-track deliberation, as we said in Chapter 1, sees a division of deliberative labour between elites and non-elites as justified in light of elites' presumed greater capacities for applied deliberation.[51] Other authors also advocate elite leadership based on the assumption that elites will 'be more competent to make enlightened decisions because of their personal characteristics (eg, their moral dignity or their intelligence)'.[52] These positions rest on empirical assumptions about elite and non-elite capacities for deliberation.

Again, are the assumptions accurate? One thing we know is that selective anecdotal claims that referendums of the past have demonstrated poor deliberation are contradicted by other anecdotal cases yielding opposite conclusions. As we will see, some referendums seem to have served effectively as crucibles for public deliberation about public values. Since there have been no genuine uses of purpose-designed DPRs in practice, some of what we will say must be speculative. Keeping in mind our four parameters, in the rest of this chapter we

[51] Jürgen Habermas, *Between Facts and Norms: Contributions to a Discourse Theory of Law and Democracy* (William Rehg tr, MIT Press 1996). Habermas does not attempt to delimit non-elite deliberation to public values; indeed, his conception of public reason is broader than Rawls's: Jürgen Habermas, 'Reconciliation Through the Public Use of Reason: Remarks on John Rawls's Political Liberalism' (1995) 92 (3) Journal of Philosophy 109. For a discussion, see J Donald Moon, 'Rawls and Habermas on Public Reason: Human Rights and Global Justice' (2003) 6 Annual Review of Political Science, 257.

[52] Discussed in Maija Setälä, 'On the Problems of Responsibility and Accountability in Referendums' (2006) 45 European Journal of Political Research 699, 700.

will assess what is already known about the relative deliberative capacities of referendums as against wholly elite-led peacemaking. We will also aim to provide an account of how people might deliberate, should institutional prescriptions for DPRs be adopted.

B. Non-Elite Advantage: Key Factors

Once we conceptually separate public-value deliberation from other sorts of deliberation (eg, about facts or specific legal applications), and especially once we stipulate that public-value deliberation is our main focus, then the elite deliberative advantage likely diminishes. Let us now consider, in outline, why the advantage in public-value deliberation may belong to non-elites, and how those who originate and sustain intergroup polarization are more often elites. Later, in Section C, we will nuance these introductory points by considering criticisms against them, as well as rejoinders and institutional responses to the criticisms.

A persistent assumption in work on direct democracy is that voters tend to have low levels of knowledge and formal education, which may affect their deliberation. Debate on this point is ongoing.[53] But works taking specific account of public-value deliberation (or cognate notions) offer compelling evidence that this debate often rests on unfounded assumptions or asks the wrong questions. For instance, many surveys focus on 'factual political-knowledge questions on generic aspects of national politics, such as the names of certain officeholders'.[54] Others resist falling into this trap. Céline Colombo's wide study of Swiss referendums is of the latter kind. She examines voters' 'level of justification' (ie, whether they provide reasoned arguments for their choices),[55] and finds that education exerts 'a surprisingly small effect [on levels of justification] given that education has traditionally been treated as the principal determinant of political knowledge'.[56] Meanwhile, 'elite polarization has a negative (statistically significant) effect on' levels of justification.[57] Stephen Tierney similarly

[53] See, eg, John Matsusaka, 'The Eclipse of Legislatures: Direct Democracy in the 21st Century' (2005) 124(1–2) Public Choice 157; Elisabeth Gerber and others, 'Minorities and Direct Legislation: Evidence from California Ballot Proposition Elections' (2002) 64(1) Journal of Politics 154.

[54] Colombo (n 50) 789.

[55] ibid 787–806.

[56] ibid 795–97. See also Christopher Johnston and others, *The Ambivalent Partisan: How Critical Loyalty Promotes Democracy* (OUP 2012).

[57] Colombo (n 50) 787–806, 795–96, 789. Colombo does not distinguish between the deliberation of elites and non-elites here, but does find levels of deliberative justification lower in a context of elite polarization over an issue: at 798. See also Dennis Thompson (2008) 'Who Should Govern Who Governs?'

observes that 'the empirical data on the behavior of elected representatives in many legislatures around the world display high levels of ignorance, pathologies of venal self-interest and submission to the pressures of the party whip'.[58] Tierney concludes that 'the contrast between an ignorant electorate and an enlightened parliament acting as the conduit for informed and disinterested public reasoning simply does not match reality'.[59]

This does not of course establish that non-elites are better deliberators in all settings.[60] But the data should prompt a shift in assumptions about the relative advantages of elites and non-elites at deliberating in a public-value key. The reasons behind the data are not hard to fathom. Despite their great diversity of vocations and educational achievement, ordinary people may be adept at deliberation about public values. Few if any people lack value commitments. Values are 'abstract trans-situational goals that serve as guiding principles in people's lives'.[61] One cannot organize a life or form even rudimentary preferences without them.[62] In this light it is unsurprising to find empirical studies in non-conflict contexts showing many non-elites' substantial self-confidence in their own capacities to decide largely value-based matters, including matters that are broadly moral in kind. In Australia and Ireland, matters such as same-sex marriage and physician-assisted suicide were widely considered to be intuitive and accessible by publics that were (or might in future be) asked to vote upon them.[63] By contrast, non-elite citizens tended to think that technical or applied matters, such as specific power-sharing federal arrangements, should be handled by governmental insiders.[64]

in ME Warren and H Pearse (eds), *Designing Deliberative Democracy: The British Columbia Citizens' Assembly* (Cambridge University Press 2008) 20–49, 24.

[58] Stephen Tierney, 'Using Electoral Law to Construct a Deliberative Referendum' (2013) 12(4) Election Law Journal 508, 511.

[59] ibid.

[60] Studies of, eg, US direct democracy are sometimes less positive, though also widely variable: See, eg, Gerber and others (n 53); Cheryl Boudreau and Scott MacKenzie, 'Informing the Electorate? How Party Cues and Policy Information Affect Public Opinion about Initiatives' (2014) 58(1) American Journal of Political Science 48; cf Delli Carpini and Scott Keeter, *What Americans Don't Know about Politics and Why It Matters* (Yale University Press 1996).

[61] Gregory R Maio and others, 'Applying the Value of Equality Unequally: Effects of Value Instantiations that Vary in Typicality' (2009) 97(4) Journal of Personality and Social Psychology 598, 598.

[62] Charles Taylor, *Sources of the Self: The Making of the Modern Identity* (Harvard University Press 1989) pt I; M Rokeach, *The Nature of Human Values* (Free Press 1973); Shalom H Schwartz, 'Universals in the Content and Structure of Values: Theoretical Advances and Empirical Tests in 20 Countries' (1992) 25 Advances in Experimental Social Psychology 1.

[63] Paul Kildea and others, 'When Should the People Decide? Public Support for Direct Democracy in Australia' (2020) 73(4) Parliamentary Affairs (forthcoming); 'Republic of Ireland 2015' (2016) 31 Irish Political Studies 364, 384–85. See, similarly, Colombo (n 50) 797.

[64] Kildea and others (n 63).

Turning to conflict societies, social attitude surveys, where they are available, regularly suggest that non-elites lack their leaders' intensity of in-group feeling, and especially the willingness to express it through violent means.[65] Lacking elites' institutional, reputational, economic, and other incentives to maintain divisions and sustain conflict, non-elites may be better able to reconsider their own positions.[66] Non-elites may also be more eager to see the struggle conclude so that they may begin to lead less uncertain and anxious lives.[67] Non-elites can, of course, be caught up in violent struggles. But they often are motivated to do so only after incitement by elites purporting to represent the group (eg, promising to elevate or restore the group's status through projects of independence and nation-building).[68]

Those who exercise or seek public power are often the first-movers of conflict, and the main barriers to its resolution. This of course depends on the nature of the conflict in question. In some conflicts, such as the Colombian and South Sudanese wars, the struggles are largely among national or rebel armies, leaving the remaining population relatively uninvolved, except as the innocent victims of violence.[69] In other conflicts, such as that in Israel/Palestine, group antipathies seem to be more socially pervasive (though even here a sense of conflict being intractable does not pervade the population as much as may be assumed).[70]

Even on factual or applied matters, the elite deliberative advantage may be illusory. Possession of higher general knowledge might only give to certain elites an inflated sense of their own competency.[71] For example, they may be

[65] See, eg, Times Survey (2017). ARK. Northern Ireland Life and Times Survey, 2003; Palestinian Center for Policy and Survey Research and Tami Steinmetz Center for Peace Research, Tel Aviv University, 'The Palestinian-Israeli Pulse: A Joint Poll' (June-July 2017); cf McGarry and O'Leary, 'Power Shared' (n 48) 68.

[66] John S Dryzek and others, 'Turning up the Heat: Partisanship in Deliberative Innovation' (2007) 55 Political Studies 362.

[67] Denise Natali, 'The Kirkuk Conundrum' (2008) 7(4) Ethnopolitics 433, 438.

[68] John S Dryzek, 'Deliberative Democracy in Divided Societies: Alternatives to Agonism and Analgesia' (2005) 33(2) Political Theory 218, 226. For a psychological perspective on group status, see, eg, Mark Howard Ross, 'Psychocultural Interpretations and Dramas: Identity Dynamics in Ethnic Conflict' (2001) 22(1) Political Psychology 157, 157–78; Vamik Volkan, *Bloodlines: When Ethnic Pride Becomes Ethnic Terrorism* (Westview Press 1997).

[69] Abbey Steele, *Democracy and Displacement in Colombia's Civil War* (Cornell University Press 2017) 93; Øystein Rolandsen, 'Another Civil War in South Sudan: The Failure of Guerrilla Government?' (2015) 9(1) Journal of Eastern African Studies 163, 171; cf Phillip Naucke, 'The Memory of Resistance Historicity and Remembrance in a Colombian Peace Community' (2017) 61(2) The Latin Americanist 145, 148.

[70] See, eg, PCPSR and TSCPR, 'The Palestinian-Israeli Pulse' (n 65) (showing widespread preferences for peacemaking).

[71] Ron Levy and Graeme Orr, *The Law of Deliberative Democracy* (Routledge 2016) 47.

unschooled about the specific substantive reform models appearing on a referendum ballot, or about the constitutional reforms that elsewhere have been effective in the past.[72]

Moreover, recall that works by Kahan and others show how governmental or other elites often call on their educational and intellectual resources not in order to approach policy matters afresh, but to reinforce their own existing polarized opinions and allegiances.[73] We initially raised this point in Chapter 1, where we discussed evidence showing that many kinds of elites are 'motivated reasoners' uniquely capable of picking information and bending argumentation to serve fixed partisan positions. What this means is that, even in elite-dominated peacemaking deliberations that ostensibly focus on technicalia, underlying (if unspoken) clashes of value may still ultimately drive the positions of the various elites involved. This is so because elites' explicit appeal to general knowledge may have no direct bearing on the relevant technical questions, and the true bases for their positions are their unarticulated values; the technical terms of their claims thus provide cover for value positions over which they can claim no special competency.

Our observations so far suggest that, when public values are at issue, the assumption that elites are necessarily better able than non-elites to resolve conflict is questionable. This assumption is implicit, for instance, in the idea that referendums elevate the general voting population to a 'veto player' in the peace process—just another barrier to clear before peace can be achieved.[74] While this is potentially a real phenomenon (eg, the 2016 Colombian peace referendum saw a peace plan narrowly rejected), it is far from uniform. And it simply assumes that elites are the more rational and effective actors in peacemaking.[75] It does not account for a positive vote's potential catalytic effects on settlement (see more on this below and in later chapters). It also significantly

[72] Colombo (n 50) 787–806, 789; See also Martin Gilens, 'Political Ignorance and Collective Policy Preferences' (2001) 95(2) American Political Science Review 379.

[73] Dan M Kahan, 'Ideology, Motivated Reasoning, and Cognitive Reflection' (2013) 8(4) Judgment and Decision Making 407, 416–18; Matthew S Nurse and Will J Grant, 'I'll See It When I Believe It: Motivated Numeracy in Perceptions of Climate Change Risk' (2020) 14(2) Environmental Communication 184; Mason Richey, 'Motivated Reasoning in Political Information Processing: The Death Knell of Deliberative Democracy?' (2012) 42(4) Philosophy of the Social Sciences 511; Hugo Mercier and Hélène Landemore, 'Reasoning is for Arguing: Understanding the Successes and Failures of Deliberation' (2012) 33(2) Political Psychology 243.

[74] George Tsebelis, *Veto Players: How Political Institutions Work* (Princeton University Press 2002).

[75] For discussion and critique of this position in the ethnic conflict context see Stuart Kaufman, 'Symbolic Politics or Rational Choice: Test Theories of Extreme Ethnic Violence' (2006) 30(4) International Security 45.

overestimates the willingness of elites to engage in the kinds of deliberation that may lead to a conflict settlement.[76]

Many elites tend to have limited incentives to transcend or modify their own value commitments. Often the last people we should wish to see lead processes of peacemaking premised on public-value deliberation are the elite leaders whose careers, ideologies, and identities may be tied to the struggle with the other side. Many elites have had to rise to their positions through the professional or social ranks of party, ethnic or other group hierarchies, while proving and affirming their allegiance at each step.[77] Moreover, especially at the highest levels of power, many elites are insulated from the physical consequences of conflict, including violence, economic collapse, and forced migration.[78]

Conversely, conflict settlements can threaten the secure power positions of top political and military figures. The constitutional reforms that settlements require generally involve transfers of power, usually from one type of elite office holder to another.[79] According to Joanne McEvoy, 'elites may be more interested in securing their own self-interests including power and rent-seeking opportunities'.[80] 'Leaders' personal goals may even conflict with the groups' goals they purport to represent, given the incentives to avoid punishment ranging from "loss of power, exile, imprisonment, or death." '[81]

Elites poised to lose power after reforms may be especially likely to resort to the types of spoiler behaviours discussed in Chapter 1. Elites can draw from and instrumentalize divided feelings in conflict societies as bases for their own perceived authority—often the more so if they have served as military leaders or combatants themselves.[82] Such elites can become high-status figures by purporting to speak for an aggrieved group, and engaging in misinformation or incitement to violence to serve their own ends, or their own

[76] See similarly Jürg Steiner and Maria Clara Jaramillo, 'How to Arrive at Peace in Deeply Divided Societies? Using Deliberation to Refine Consociational Theory' (2019) 15(3) Journal of Public Deliberation Art 9, 5–6.

[77] See Brian Barry, *Culture and Equality: An Egalitarian Critique of Multiculturalism* (Polity 2001) 129.

[78] Michael J Brown and Marie-Joëlle Zahar, 'Social Cohesion as Peacebuilding in the Central African Republic and Beyond' (2015) 10(1) Journal of Peacebuilding and Development 10, 15–17; Guus Meijer, *Briefing: Crisis in the Central African Republic* (Conciliation Resources, 2013).

[79] Stephen John Stedman, 'Spoiler Problems in Peace Processes' (1997) 22(2) International Security 5, 5–12; Steiner and Jaramillo (n 76) 4–7.

[80] Joanne McEvoy, 'Letting "the People(s)" Decide: Peace Referendums and Power-Sharing Settlements' (2018) 25(5) Democratization 864, 867. See also Joseph Schumpeter, *Imperialism and Social Classes* (Meridian, 1955) 65.

[81] McEvoy (n 80) 867, citing Alyssa K Prorok, 'Leader Incentives and Civil War Outcomes' (2016) 60(1) American Journal of Political Science 70, 70.

[82] Terrence Lyons, *Demilitarizing Politics: Elections on the Uncertain Road to Peace* (Lynne Rienner Publishers 2005) 62, 66–71; Christel Lane, 'Legitimacy and Power in the Soviet Union through Socialist Ritual' (1984) 14(2) British Journal of Political Science 207.

aggrandizement, rather than the good of those they claim to represent.[83] Even those elites inclined to pursue a settlement will often find themselves undercut or squeezed out by hardline rivals from within their own group—a phenomenon that we described as 'outbidding' in Chapter 1.

A related observation is that elites' generally *elitist* attitudes towards non-elites may undermine their leadership of peacemaking. These attitudes call into question the empirical assumptions behind the division of deliberative labour in lawmaking. Even if it were normatively justifiable for elites to take primary carriage of constitutional reform, the division of labour would still require them to make good-faith efforts to gauge relevant public values. Many elites instead condescendingly assume that non-elites cannot be trusted to decide weighty matters, including public values.[84] As we have just seen, this is a doubtful assumption. But when elites drive constitutional reform, we often see ordinary voices excluded. This 'elite problem' sees empowered elites neglect to try to understand the values of non-elite citizens, and act instead according to their own fixed value preferences.[85]

All of this turns on its head the routine idea that it is the legislature's 'job' to decide contentious matters. In Maija Setälä's words,

> [a]ccording to . . . liberals and those deliberative democrats who emphasize representative mechanisms, accountability requires that representatives use their capacities and competence to make reflected and reasoned decisions. These theorists think that referendums may be harmful if the accountability of representatives is undermined.[86]

This criticism assumes that legislatures are freer to vindicate liberal-democratic interests when they do not have to consult a reactionary public. Yet, as we have seen, this gives unjustified credit to legislatures and other elite authorities. These elites often significantly lag behind their notional constituents, even after popular opinion crystallizes around the necessity of constitutional reforms.[87] While some elites have been protagonists, many others have

[83] Stedman (n 79).

[84] For a study and discussion of this phenomenon, see, eg, Lawrence C Walters, James Aydelotte, and Jessica Miller, 'Putting More Public in Policy Analysis' (2000) 60(4) Public Administration Review 349.

[85] Ron Levy, 'The "Elite Problem" in Deliberative Constitutionalism' in Ron Levy and others (eds), *The Cambridge Handbook of Deliberative Constitutionalism* (Cambridge University Press 2018) 351–69.

[86] Setälä (n 52) 709.

[87] Daniel Philpott, 'In Defence of Self-Determination' (1995) 105(2) Ethics 352, 380.

stood in the way of constitutional settlement (eg, in Israel/Palestine, France/Algeria, and South Africa).[88]

C. Criticisms

Now let us consider criticisms of our arguments up to this point. Earlier we foreshadowed the criticisms that public reason can be exclusionary or unrealistic. Applied to a peace referendum, however, the potency of these and other critical claims may vary depending on whether DPR design can provide at least partial answers to them.

(1) The exclusion objection

We have argued that constitutional settlement requires people to give priority to public values over non-public values. Rawls sets an admittedly high standard: in his view, anyone who rejects public values' priority runs 'the risk of being unjust, politically speaking'.[89] Yet a key worry is that this requirement may be too demanding in practice. 'Difference democrats' such as Lynn Sanders and Iris Marion Young suggest that such standards may disadvantage the inarticulate, or at least those who may not have access to a sophisticated political vocabulary.[90]

We can find similar criticisms dotted around the deliberative literature, including in the work of those who are sometimes doubtful of public-reason approaches. For instance, Dryzek claims that some 'deliberative democrats, especially those who traffic in public reason, want to impose narrow limits on what constitutes authentic deliberation, restricting it to arguments in particular kinds of terms'.[91] By contrast, in his view 'a more tolerant position would allow argument, rhetoric, humour, emotion, testimony or storytelling, and gossip'.[92] Sanders, Young, and Dryzek intend their criticisms of public reason to highlight the possible exclusionary effects of high deliberative demands.[93]

Yet, on our view, in the absence of such demands, the risk is that we may disadvantage the very minorities the authors are concerned about. Dryzek himself

[88] On Israel/Palestine, see again PCPSR and TSCPR, 'The Palestinian-Israeli Pulse' (n 65). On France/Algeria and South Africa, see Chapters 4 and 7.

[89] Rawls, *Political Liberalism* (n 3) 247.

[90] Lynn Sanders, 'Against Deliberation' (1997) 25(3) Political Theory 347; Iris Marion Young, *Inclusion and Democracy* (OUP 2000) 52–80.

[91] Dryzek, *Deliberative Democracy and Beyond* (n 27) 48.

[92] ibid.

[93] Young (n 90) 56.

also holds that 'any communication that cannot connect the particular to the general should be excluded'.[94] We would argue, like Dryzek, that people should be free to tell their stories but that ultimately those stories must clearly express or invoke a value, principle, or standard that any democratic citizen might reasonably be expected to endorse. Like him as well, we are concerned that absent this condition there may be no way of knowing whether storytelling and the like are not themselves vehicles of unjustified oppression or exclusion.[95]

These concerns apply to referendums. If voters are not required ultimately to justify their positions in terms of public values, then majorities may vote for outcomes that (inadvertently or otherwise) are hostile to the interests of marginalized or excluded populations. Majorities may fail to appreciate the narratives or stories minorities have to tell. They may fail to recognize the moral force of what minorities have to say or the universal justice of their claims. As a consequence, they may also see themselves as less accountable to others in society. Thus the irony of the difference democrats' position is that their criticisms may end up promoting greater minority exclusion if they lead us to drop any attempt to enhance public reason in the referendum. They could perhaps reply that no referendum should then run at all. Yet neither is cancelling the use of referendums necessarily an appealing solution to those who favour democratic inclusion.

The difference democrats' arguments would seem therefore to raise a dilemma. But we are not so sure. Recall the important goals that we set out above: weighing deliberative capacities comparatively, contextually, and with a focus on institutions and forms of deliberation. The difference democrats assume that elites of certain types are better positioned for public reason. For example, Sanders and Young associate speech that is rational and general with dominant groups in society (especially white, middle-class men).[96] Yet the assumption that non-elites engage poorly with public reason is empirically questionable (as we said above), and also fails to consider whether elites might encounter the same or different difficulties. We must remember that if non-elites are not at the centre of a constitutional settlement process—and if institutions are not designed to this end—then elites will be. To say that non-elites are flawed public-value deliberators is trivially true, but does not yet answer

[94] ibid 68; David Miller, 'Is Deliberative Democracy Unfair to Disadvantaged Groups' in David Miller (ed), *Citizenship and National Identity* (Polity Press 2000) 142–60.

[95] Dryzek, *Deliberative Democracy and Beyond* (n 27) 167–68. For discussion, see André Bächtiger and others, 'Disentangling Diversity in Deliberative Democracy: Competing Theories, Their Blind Spots and Complementarities' (2010) 18(1) Journal of Political Philosophy 32.

[96] See, eg, Sanders (n 90) 361, 370–71; cf David Miller (n 94) 153.

whether the alternatives are any better or whether more might be done to improve their (alleged) plight.

Ultimately, then, arguments about public-value deliberation's exclusionary effects rest upon or collapse into assumptions about the poor deliberative capacities of non-elites. While we presented perspectives contradicting this scepticism above, we must now also consider certain further claims. Most are variations on the possibility that public-value deliberation may not occur at all, or at least not in the ways that we imagine. Conceptual descent is always a possibility, due at least to the persistent roles of comprehensive doctrines, the varying degrees of generality of public values, and the often meagre quality or availability of relevant information. A further set of problems to be seen are specific to the institutional design challenges of referendums.

(2) Comprehensive doctrines and conceptual descent

Are public values simply too general or under-specified to guide the constitutional settlement process? Rawls himself suggests that a point may well be reached when public reason will run out of steam and we can no longer keep comprehensive doctrines out of political decision-making.[97] There is, then, the potential problem that deliberations may descend from public values into comprehensive doctrines.

Rawls has important responses here, some of which we also adopt. He argues that on a 'wide view' of public reason, comprehensive doctrines can still have an important role to play. By showing how our interpretation of a given public value is supported by our comprehensive doctrines, we can demonstrate to others the sincerity of our views. In doing so, we not only build mutual trust and confidence, but advance the ideal of public reason.[98] Yet while non-public reasons can therefore aid decisions about constitutional essentials, their use is subject to an important proviso:

> [R]easonable comprehensive doctrines, religious or non-religious, may be introduced in public political discussion at any time, provided that in due course proper political reasons—and not reasons solely given by comprehensive doctrines—are presented that are sufficient to support whatever the comprehensive doctrines introduced are said to support.[99]

[97] Rawls, *Political Liberalism* (n 3) 247–54.
[98] ibid 249; Rawls, 'The Idea of Public Reason' (n 3) 785.
[99] Rawls, *Political Liberalism* (n 3) 462.

In short, it must ultimately be possible to show that assertions grounded in non-public values support public values that all can share. Rawls thinks that this proviso is not the hurdle that it seems. In particular, he contends that comprehensive doctrines will often be congruent with public values, or will be only 'partially comprehensive' in that they have nothing to say on the matters with which the public values are concerned.[100] But even where they are not congruent, he supposes that citizens will be unhappy to adhere to doctrines that are inconsistent with values such as freedom and equality and so will modify or 'bend' their doctrines to remove any conflict. In other words, he supposes that their different views will overlap, or come to overlap, in supporting the same general agreement.[101]

Rawls gives the example of how Catholic notions of religious freedom shifted in more liberal-democratic directions.[102] Ultimately, public reason consists of reasons that the members of a plural society can share, as distinct from non-public reasons stemming from comprehensive doctrines that they do not share (and probably cannot share). As people come to recognize and accept the importance of public values in democratic life, and in particular in processes of constitutional change, over time they may accommodate their comprehensive doctrines to those values.

While we agree with the spirit of his approach, we will adopt a distinct view of what it may mean in practice. We have in mind not a process of gradual acculturation, but something more immediate. A DPR requires, at least of those who agree to participate, that they engage in public-value deliberation. In Chapter 3, we will examine the institutional particulars by which peacemaking deliberations may be channelled through a DPR so that discussions proceed in public-value terms to a greater extent (eg, by listing public values on the ballot). Our perspective is 'minimalist' in that it uses a DPR not to attempt broad cultural change, but for the most part only to *expose* existing normative common ground (based on public values) between the parties. The exposure need only be brief: just long enough to achieve a constitutional settlement, or to mandate negotiations toward the achievement of a settlement.

As the cases earlier in this chapter should have made clear, public values have previously been at the centre of some peace referendums that yielded constitutional settlements. We have already seen the example of Northern Ireland, where the positive referendum result in 1998 demonstrated a significant

[100] ibid 40, 246; Rawls, 'The Idea of Public Reason' (n 3) 780, 800, 803–04.

[101] Rawls, *Political Liberalism* (n 3) 246–47; Rawls, 'The Idea of Public Reason' (n 3) 781–82, 795, see n 51. See also TM Scanlon, *What We Owe to Each Other* (Harvard University Press, 1998).

[102] Rawls, 'The Idea of Public Reason' (n 3) 796, n 75.

meeting of minds across seemingly fixed sectarian boundaries. Similarly, as Loizides notes, the 1992 referendum in South Africa on constitutional change to end apartheid 'created new cross-cutting linkages, including a shared political vision of the future among supporters of the "yes" vote which transcended ethnic and communal boundaries'.[103] The referendum's endorsement of President De Klerk's reform policy

> added an element of responsibility among [African National Congress] elites; this later translated into creating a new common symbolic landscape of racial relationships in South Africa while maintaining and reinforcing the inclusion of whites within ANC and the governing structures of the country.[104]

Our own view of these cases is that political and constitutional linkages premised on common ground were largely, again, not created but exposed through the discussion of public values (alongside other matters) in the referendums. In general, although latent social agreement may exist about the need for a settlement, or even about some of the desired terms of a settlement, this may not be apparent until groups in conflict begin to talk about the issues between them differently. As we use the term, public-value deliberation mainly calls not for changes in the parties' positions, but for changes in the language and concepts by which they express those positions.

Running a referendum may help to reveal existing commonalities in the public values that various groups can endorse because, in comparison with elites, non-elites may hold each other in less contempt and better tolerate each other (as we said earlier). Often the more cynical elites in politics and the media obscure such common ground, by professing for instance to speak for wider populations—yet doing so based not on data, but on impressionistic readings of the *zeitgeist*.[105] Running a peace referendum may see non-elites nevertheless push onwards to expose agreement. A DPR, especially, should be designed to spotlight any common ground that the parties may already share, but that they may previously have failed to recognize. This will be one of the primary objectives of our account of the DPR in Chapter 3.

None of what we have said or will say is to suggest that debates in the past took place solely in public-value terms. But it is to suggest that the bar for entry into meaningful public-values deliberation may not be as high as critics imply.

[103] Neophytos Loizides, 'Negotiated Settlements and Peace Referendums' (2014) 53 European Journal of Political Research 234, 239.
[104] ibid.
[105] ibid. See also Chapter 4.

There is ample evidence of effective public-value deliberation in deeply divided and conflict societies.[106] There is even some (as we saw) in peace referendums. Notably, and encouragingly, the latter arose even without the benefit of the full suite of DPR features to be developed in Chapter 3.

(3) Partial descent

As mentioned earlier in this chapter, even if some deliberations remain focused on public values, a given public value may still be subject to interpretative dispute. According to Michael Walzer, while people may share the same values at a very general level, once we begin to ask them what they mean by these values we may soon find out that they attach very different (culturally, ethnically, ideologically, etc) specific meanings to them.[107] In conflict societies, such disputes may even precipitate a return to violence. People seeking to deliberate across deep religious, cultural, ethnic, national, or ideological divides may either fail to deliberate or deliberate but divide further.[108] Once people begin to drill down into terms like equality, freedom, free speech, due process, non-discrimination, or the rule of law, old wounds can be reopened, potentially deepening rather than ameliorating divisions, and raising the spectre of (further) violence.

One reason for interpretive disputes is that values can be generalized to varying degrees. An example is the value of non-domination,[109] a value that has the most purchase for the weaker parties in a conflict. A process of deliberation might only reveal, and perhaps entrench, different groups' readings of the same public value. Appeals to public values, or to specific readings of public values, may also mask calculations of private self-interest. For example, Jon Elster notes that since public values can be interpreted in different ways,

[106] M Lydia Khuri, 'Facilitating Arab-Jewish Intergroup Dialogue in the College Setting' (2004) 7(3) Race, Ethnicity and Education 229, 244; Luskin and others (n 36) 116; Alex Norman, 'The Use of the Group and Group Work Techniques in Resolving Interethnic Conflict' (1992) 14(3/4) Social Work with Groups 175; Margarita Orozco and Juan Ugarriza, 'The Citizens, the Politicians and the Courts: A Preliminary Assessment of Deliberative Capacity in Colombia' in Juan Ugarriza and Didier Caluwaerts (eds), *Democratic Deliberation in Deeply Divided Societies: From Conflict to Common Ground* (Palgrave 2014) 73–88; Didier Caluwaerts and Kris Deschouwer, 'Building Bridges Across Political Divides: Experiments on Deliberative Democracy in Deeply Divided Belgium' (2014) 6(3) European Political Science Review 427; Manlio Cinalli and Ian O'Flynn, 'Public Deliberation, Network Analysis and the Political Integration of Muslims in Britain' (2014) 16(3) British Journal of Politics and International Relations 428.

[107] Michael Walzer, *Thick and Thin: Moral Argument at Home and Abroad* (University of Notre Dame Press 1994).

[108] Brendan O'Leary, 'Debating Consociational Politics: Normative and Explanatory Arguments' in Sid Noel (ed), *From Power Sharing to Democracy: Post-conflict Institutions in Ethnically Divided Societies* (McGill-Queen's University Press 2005) 10–11; McGarry and O'Leary, 'Power Shared' (n 48) 68.

[109] Philip Pettit, *Republicanism: A Theory of Freedom and Government* (Clarendon Press, 1997) 51–79.

there is always the danger of strategic misrepresentation—that people will use them merely as covers for their own special interests.[110] Dryzek and Christian List similarly point out that a sceptic's take might be 'that invocations of generalizable interests are just rationalizations for self-interest'.[111]

Hence, in addition to the risk of descent from public values to comprehensive doctrines, there is also the subtler risk that some public values are more general than others and may appeal selectively to just one part of a conflict society. To be sure, some of Rawls's answers (and ours) to the former problem may apply again here. Just as comprehensive doctrines may motivate people to support certain public values, public reasons of varying levels of generality may perhaps do the same. We cannot guarantee this of course. But institutional design should bear it in mind as an objective. In Chapter 3, we will explore how public values listed on the referendum ballot can be framed with varying degrees of breadth. For instance, non-domination can be further generalized as a guarantee of non-interference. While both are generalized public values applicable to everyone, one is wider than the other: non-interference is more universally applicable, relevant to more groups, and potentially more likely to attract broad support when presented to voters on a DPR ballot. The most widely framed values may have the highest likelihood of drawing support across diverse groups, even if the reasons and nuances behind such support vary from group to group.

(4) Information and conceptual descent

Other potential causes of conceptual descent include failures to manage the information around public values adequately. Exposure to certain kinds of information, such as the historical, sociological, and legal specifics surrounding a conflict or suggested settlement, may be a condition-precedent for people to be persuaded to endorse particular public values. Yet, in conflict societies especially, there may be relatively limited access to formal education and other sources of relevant information.[112] This may, for instance, compromise understandings of the contexts surrounding specific public values—such as relevant

[110] See Jon Elster, 'Deliberation and Constitution Making' in John Elster (ed), *Deliberative Democracy* (CUP 1998) 101–05. Elster is careful not to overstate this risk: 'If nobody was ever moved by the public interest, nobody would have anything to gain by appealing to it. Self-serving appeals to the public interest are parasitic on genuine appeals': Elster, 'Forces and Mechanisms' (n 22) 380.

[111] John Dryzek and Christian List, 'Social Choice Theory and Deliberative Democracy' (2003) 33(1) British Journal of Political Science 16, citing as an example William H Riker, *Liberalism Against Populism* (WH Freeman 1982) 205.

[112] Chapter 1.

histories of dispossession accounting for a group's focus on values of non-domination or self-determination.

Reasoning can never be purely value-based. Without opportunities to acquire relevant and accurate information—that is, information relatively free from essential omissions or misrepresentations—one may simply know too little about people from other groups. It may be hard under such circumstances to see which values might be salient for members of those other groups. A still trickier problem is that people may be unaware of, or unwilling to credit, evidence of the faults or complicity of one's own group in creating some of the conditions for conflict.[113] Adequate information is, then, part of the background necessary for value generalization.

These considerations raise another key problem to be addressed in Chapter 3. However, note that they do not straightforwardly suggest a single institutional solution. Simply increasing access to the flow of information, on its own, may have unintended consequences for deliberation. Earlier in this chapter we presented one reason why this might be so. Peacemaking, we said, should often centre on public values, and downplay how those values might specifically apply in practice. Excessive focus on applied specifics could see peacemaking miss out on the various comparative benefits of public-value deliberation. The deliberative potential of non-elite citizens is (we said above) relatively high for matters of public value. Yet, for various reasons, people still tend often to engage with technicalities, even where these are of secondary importance in the referendum.[114] And referendum designers sometimes ask voters to endorse settlements that, when loaded with seemingly useful clauses, may make it difficult for ordinary people to recognize the essentials.[115] In the Colombian case, voters were asked to consent to a draft settlement with FARC rebels that buried broad political principles (eg, rural reform, the political status of former guerrillas, and transitional justice) inside 297 pages on implementation and 'issue-by-issue' detail.[116] This helped to thwart an affirmative referendum vote by making the content inaccessible to ordinary citizens.[117]

[113] See, eg, Eqbal Ahmad, *Terrorism: Theirs and Ours* (Seven Stories Press 2001).

[114] See, eg, Robert Young, 'Quebec 1995: The Rhetoric of the Referendum' in Gianluigi Galeotti, Pierre Salmon, and Ronald Wintrobe (eds), *Competition and Structure: The Political Economy of Collective Decisions: Essays in Honor of Albert Breton* (CUP 2000); Scott Bennett, 'The Politics of Constitutional Amendment' (Research Paper No 11, Parliamentary Library, Parliament of Australia, 2003); Cass Sunstein, 'Deliberation, Democracy, Disagreement' in Ron Bontekoe and Marietta Stepaniants (eds), *Justice and Democracy: Cross-Cultural Perspectives* (University of Hawai'i Press 1997) 95.

[115] See LeDuc (n 29) on the risks of 'deliberative overload' in referendums meant to endorse 'long and detailed' treaties: at 143.

[116] Bell (n 21) 166.

[117] ibid.

Exposure to information may also backfire if a decision-making process is poorly structured. Absent opportunities for reflection and other deliberative procedures, information may be too overwhelming to be parsed effectively,[118] or too incomplete or selective. The provision of information should instead contribute towards a fair and inclusive account of context. A good deal of research on the informational conditions for robust deliberation centres on mini-publics (on which we too will focus in part of Chapter 3). These mainly non-elite bodies often successfully demonstrate open-minded and flexible deliberation based on diverse (but not excessive) information—including in divided and conflict societies.[119] But larger-scale deliberations, including referendums, have also managed to get the kinds and amounts of information approximately right. As we saw earlier, in some cases the focus of a peace referendum was not only on technical arcana, such as the costs of independence or the precise forms of consociation, but also on the wider principles underlying decisions at hand.[120] Constitutional technicalia frequently resurfaced, but public debate focused in large part on broad values and issues.

An important lesson from such cases is that it is far from clear, as some might have expected, that elites of various kinds are best at handling information effectively. Here even a political neophyte's deliberative capacities can sometimes exceed those of the political veteran (eg, a partisan legislator), given the right institutional setting. Elites do not necessarily enjoy the deliberative advantage in accessing and using information. We have already seen Colombo's important dismissal of general political knowledge (to which elites may have greater access) as largely irrelevant to the specific decisions at hand in referendums.[121] Moreover, it is notable that a conflict society's sharp lines of division, which can send deliberation into isolated enclaves, may particularly aggravate informational deficiencies among elites. More extensive formal education does not

[118] For an overview, see Selen A Ercan, Carolyn M Hendriks, and John S Dryzek, 'Public Deliberation in an Era of Communicative Plenty' (2019) 47(1) Policy & Politics 19.

[119] Didier Caluwaerts and Min Reuchamps, 'Does Inter-Group Deliberation Foster Inter-Group Appreciation? Evidence from Two Experiments in Belgium' (2014) 34(2) Politics 101; Luskin and others (n 36) 116; cf Juan E Ugarriza and Enzo Nussio, 'There is no Pill for Deliberation: Explaining Discourse Quality in Post-Conflict Communities' (2016) 22(1) Swiss Political Science Review 145.

[120] For similar findings around non-conflict referendums, see, eg, Simon Hug and Pascal Sciarini, 'Referendums on European Integration: Do Institutions Matter in the Voter's Decision?' (2000) 33(1) Comparative Political Studies 3, 6–8; John Parkinson, 'Ideas of Constitutions and Deliberative Democracy and How They Interact' in Levy and others (eds), *Cambridge Handbook* (n 85) 254; Johan Elkink and others, 'Understanding the 2015 Marriage Referendum in Ireland: Context, Campaign, and Conservative Ireland' (2017) 32(3) Irish Political Studies 361, 364–65, 377; Hoi L Kong and Ron Levy, 'Deliberative Constitutionalism' in André Bächtiger and others (eds), *The Oxford Handbook of Deliberative Democracy* (OUP 2018) 629–32, 634.

[121] Colombo (n 50) 789.

necessarily mitigate, and may in some cases deepen, the problems of enclave learning first discussed in Chapter 1. Whether schools promulgate the kinds of information necessary to develop wider or more tolerant values depends on the nature of the education (eg, whether secular or parochial, ethnically streamed or pluralistic).[122]

In addition, and consistently with what we said earlier about motivated reasoning, greater familiarity with one's rivals does not necessarily breed political acceptance or recognition. As we have seen, political sophistication does not rule out confirmation bias, but in fact increases its risk.[123] Elites' knowledge of others can be abundant, but incomplete or skewed: often self-focused and distorted by hostility towards perceived enemies. To give just one example, on the negotiations towards the Oslo peace accord between Israelis and Palestinians, Shimon Peres (Israel's Foreign Minister during the negotiations) recalled an aide observing: 'while we kn[e]w everything about the Palestinians, it seemed we understood nothing'.[124] This comment is remarkable for its self-awareness and self-critique, though the limitations to which it refers are common enough.[125]

(5) Institutional context

Until now, we have asked in generic terms whether non-elites are more, or perhaps less, capable of deliberating about public values than are elites. But we have said relatively little about how the institutional features of referendums colour and channel the deliberation of non-elites (who make up the vast bulk of referendum voters). Some institutional effects on deliberation are positive, but others are likely to inhibit deliberation—unless they can be addressed through refinements to institutional design.

(i) Binary reduction: Referendums may distort deliberation by neglecting the full range of perspectives lying beyond the single point of view of the voter, or beyond two 'sides' of a conflict. As Roger Mac Ginty argues,

122 Amy Gutmann, *Democratic Education* (Princeton University Press, 1999) 50–51.

123 Mason Richey, 'Motivated Reasoning in Political Information Processing: The Death Knell of Deliberative Democracy?' (2011) 42(4) Philosophy of the Social Sciences 511, 526; Charles Taber and Milton Lodge, 'Motivated Skepticism in the Evaluation of Political Beliefs' (2006) 50(3) American Journal of Political Science 755, 767. More generally, see James Druckman, Erik Peterson, and Rune Slothuus, 'How Elite Partisan Polarization Affects Public Opinion Formation' (2013) 107(1) American Political Science Review 57; David Stasavage, 'Polarization and Publicity: Rethinking the Benefits of Deliberative Democracy' (2007) 69(1) Journal of Politics 59; Thompson, 'Who Should Govern' (n 57) 24.

124 Shimon Peres, *No Room for Small Dreams* (Weidenfeld & Nicolson 2017) 161 (quoting Uri Savir).

125 See also, eg, Jonathan Powell, *Great Hatred, Little Room: Making Peace in Northern Ireland* (Vintage 2009).

> the principal problem with referendums in situations of profound ethnonational conflict is that they are zero-sum, creating winners and losers. Simple majoritarian devices do little to help manage the complexity of conflict. Instead they validate the position of one side and reject that of another. Often, they do little other than delimit and quantify division.[126]

Standard two-option ('yes'/'no') referendums can indeed diminish the space for deliberation about complex issues or set up binary contests between groups in ways that only deepen intergroup ignorance and polarization. The pressure to win (or not lose) may be deliberatively debilitating. Our discussion of DPR design in Chapter 3 will address this.

(ii) Elite manipulation: The referendum is also occasionally an instrument wielded, by elites especially, in ways that actually do violence to democratic and deliberative norms. For instance, fear and intimidation during the campaign can result in entire groups failing to participate in referendums, with the vote and campaign then dominated by exclusive segments of the population.[127] Relatedly, referendum designers may manipulate questions to support their own 'side'—a phenomenon even in non-conflict settings.[128] They may also hold and manipulate referendums to give cover to illegal constitutional changes.[129]

Referendums might also target vulnerable minorities. To be sure, this criticism has been called into question in certain cases (eg, Zoltan Hajnal and his colleagues suggest that ballot initiatives in California do not in general reflect attempts to target unpopular minorities or exclude them from public life).[130] But one cannot deny that minority targeting has sometimes occurred. And, as mentioned earlier, the persuasive power of misleading or demagogic elite speech may be heightened during referendums. While the referendum enhances the voices of non-elites, it also focuses a population on a given issue, giving elite or other spoilers a broader platform and enhanced attention for speech that is demagogic, misleading, and worse. The DPR must also seek to head off such efforts.

[126] Roger Mac Ginty, 'Constitutional Referendums and Ethnonational Conflict: The Case of Northern Ireland' (2003) 9(2) Nationalism and Ethnic Politics 1, 3.

[127] Ashish Chaturvedi, 'Rigging Elections With Violence' (2005) 125(1–2) Public Choice 189, 189–91; Paul Collier and Pedro Vicente, 'Votes and Violence: Evidence From a Field Experiment In Nigeria' (2014) 124(574) The Economic Journal 327, 330.

[128] Paul Howe, 'Rationality and Sovereignty Support in Quebec' (1998) 31(1) Canadian Journal of Political Science 31, 34.

[129] See, eg, Stephen Tierney, 'Sovereignty and Crimea: How Referendum Democracy Complicates Constituent Power in Multinational Societies' (2015) 16(3) German Law Journal 523.

[130] Gerber and others (n 53).

(iii) Unequal influence: The influence of wealthy and out-of-jurisdiction actors may give some people more influence than is arguably fitting by permitting them to fund one side in a referendum campaign.[131] It may be possible to legislate against this problem. But whether it is indeed a problem is a question that calls for case-by-case judgement. If their influence is largely deliberative—in that outside voices present cogent arguments—then the influence of outside groups may in some respects be unproblematic. Moreover, what counts as an 'outside group' itself can be contentious. As we will see in Chapter 5, particularly hard problems arise in conflicts that have spawned large diaspora populations.

(iv) Acontextual deliberation: Referendums can see participants 'deliberat[e] out of context' by addressing 'one set of interests without adequately . . . considering the costs or any countervailing interests'.[132] In one research survey illustrating the problem, US respondents were asked whether they agreed with two policy propositions: that taxes should decrease, and that the provision of public services should increase. In the result, large majorities preferred both,[133] suggesting that many non-elites fail to connect benefits to costs. In this regard legislatures, including power-sharing legislatures in conflict societies, might enjoy a comparative deliberative advantage as they typically must engage in balancing and horse-trading over diverse social interests over time. By contrast, non-elites may struggle to generate an holistic view of the trade-offs in a constitutional settlement. DPR design must also address this issue.

(v) Initiating the referendum: Finally, buy-in by at least some governmental leaders may be required before a referendum can be held at all. Given the noted elite incentives and tendencies towards polarization, winning broad elite support for holding a DPR can seem unlikely. It may be more likely that elites will prevent any peace referendum from running in the first place. Under conflict conditions elites may not feel compelled to call a referendum. This is a variant of the criticism of referendums as 'hegemonic'—as mere empty shows of popular (or, indeed, populist) legitimation that are ultimately under the sway of elites who call referendums.[134]

Yet we must place such worries in context. The referendum has entered into more or less constant use in the field of peacemaking. Some referendums, we

[131] OECD, *Financing Democracy: Funding of Political Parties and Election Campaigns and the Risk of Policy Capture* (OECD Publishing 2016) 23.

[132] Finance and Public Administration Legislation Committee, Australian Senate, *Debate on the Citizen Initiated Referendum Bill 2013*, Melbourne, 29 April 2013, 16–17; see also Leib (n 31) 908.

[133] Katherine Gregory and David Hetherington, 'Public Attitudes towards Taxation and Government Expenditure' (2010) Per Capita Tax Survey 3–5, 15.

[134] Arend Lijphart, *Democracies: Patterns of Majoritarian and Consensus Government in Twenty-One Countries* (Yale University Press 1984) 203–04; Markku Suksi, *Bringing in the People. A Comparison of the Constitutional Forms and Practices of the Referendum* (Martinus Nijhoff Publishers 1993) 160;

have said, provided only cover for constitutional or military *faits-accomplis*. But in practice, elites have often initiated peace referendums based on (it seems) genuine desires for peacemaking. Though nearly impossible to universalize to all cases, a range of factors might convince empowered elites of the wisdom or necessity of holding a referendum. For instance, in Papua New Guinea, a promise to hold a referendum on the constitutional status of Bougainville was a condition insisted upon by Bougainvillean leaders before a peace treaty could be concluded to end a long and destructive conflict.[135] Thus governments may wish to call referendums to help resolve divisive issues that have reached an impasse.[136] Alternatively, popular endorsement via a referendum may be 'politically necessary' when a government itself wishes to move forward on key reforms.[137] Another possibility is that a deliberative and popular assembly (eg, Ireland's substantively open-ended Constitutional Convention) might 'force the hand' of some reluctant leaders to hold a referendum.[138]

It is also worth noting that a popular vote might arise not with the blessing of national governing elites, but as a result of an informal mass mobilization (and perhaps also international pressure). An extra-governmental, or 'rogue', body might administer a referendum (properly a 'plebiscite') even without the formal authority to do so. This was the case in Hong Kong amid the abortive 'Umbrella'/'Occupy' movement of 2014, during which a privately-organized online poll of the territory's people may have helped to forestall the implementation of measures broadly understood as illiberal. In other cases, such as the Kurdistan region in Iraq or the Catalonia region in Spain, sub-national governments initiated votes for independence, even though these moves apparently lacked legality. These examples are instructive. They illustrate how at least some of the intended effects of a peace referendum—especially that of giving popular legitimacy and momentum to a constitutional reform—might still result from a vote that is held without elite authorization. We will return to this discussion in Chapter 6.

cf Mads Qvortrup, 'Research Note: Are Referendums Controlled and Pro-hegemonic?' (2000) 48(4) Political Studies 821.

135 Ron Levy and others, 'Designing Referendums for Peacemaking: The Case of Bougainville' (2018) 33(1) Australasian Parliamentary Review 6.

136 Ron Levy, 'The Deliberative Case for Constitutional Referenda' (2017) 16(2) Election Law Journal 213, 219–20; LeDuc (n 29) 140.

137 LeDuc (n 29) 140.

138 Elkink and others (n 120) 364.

IV. Conclusion

It is no longer realistic to idealize the deliberation that occurs among elites (if it ever was), especially given the polarization and deadlock that are often endemic in conflict societies. Elites of various kinds are, in many cases, only more likely to conform to or aggravate political divisions than to legislate based on generalized notions of the collective good.

We have seen that referendums do not always offer the straightforwardly better alternative. But the criticisms that we have seen of referendums (including peace referendums) are so far inconclusive. Most of the criticisms assume a continuing reliance on standard referendum models. Yet as Parkinson observes, 'it is not that ordinary people cannot deliberate, but that existing liberal democratic structures do not allow them the chance to develop those deliberative capacities'.[139] With new institutional conditions in place, we may be able to improve, at least by increments, non-elite deliberation. In the following chapter, we will discuss DPR innovations with this object in mind.

[139] Parkinson, 'Legitimacy Problems' (n 50) 186–87. For an early, seminal statement of this view, see Cohen (n 4) 26.

3

Designing a Deliberative Peace Referendum

I. Introduction

Deliberative Peace Referendums (DPRs) are designed to be more deliberative than standard peace referendums. DPRs provide specific opportunities for people to deliberate amid both the referendum campaign and the vote itself. In this chapter we will detail a set of designs for a generic model of DPR. Some are established, others still speculative. In outlining a generic model we will set aside, but only for the moment, any modifications needed to suit particular conflict types. (We will consider such variations in Part III of this book.)

In Section II, we will outline the main features of our generic DPR model. Many of the features will respond to the need, mentioned in the last chapter, to provide institutional support for non-elite (including referendum) deliberation. Our main prescription will be the *public-value ballot*, meant to promote public-value deliberation. On a DPR ballot, the first questions should ask voters to endorse certain widely applicable public values. (An independent, largely non-elite body should have earlier agreed on which public values will appear on the ballot.) Farther down on the ballot, there should be at least one other question: whether voters endorse a *mandate* for peace negotiations. In such a 'mandate referendum',[1] the expectation is that elite negotiators will eventually take over the final and detailed drafting of the terms of a settlement (eg, the metes and bounds of a new international frontier). Sequencing deliberation in this way aims to sideline elites, as much as possible, until the referendum has concluded. This is an important objective given our claim in the last chapter that non-elites may have greater capacity for public-value deliberation.

In Section III, we will raise criticisms of our generic DPR proposal and also describe how it departs from past deliberative democratic projects. Of course, in spite of best efforts, DPRs will occasionally misfire. We will draw one criticism out in particular: that by reframing deliberation in generalized public-value terms, DPRs may be too coercive of voters—or too 'paternalistic', in the

[1] Neophytos Loizides, 'Negotiated Settlements and Peace Referendums' (2014) 53 European Journal of Political Research 234, 237.

Deliberative Peace Referendums. Ron Levy, Ian O'Flynn, Hoi L Kong, Oxford University Press (2021). © Ron Levy, Ian O'Flynn, and Hoi L Kong. DOI: 10.1093/oso/9780198867036.003.0003

language of liberal political theory. Yet we judge the coercions involved to be modest and, on balance, warranted if they can aid the achievement and endurance of constitutional settlement.

II. Generic DPR Model

We propose that the DPR should incorporate at least four general features. These four have not previously been tried as a unit, and some have not been tested at all. Hence the combined effects of these features remain speculative. Their effectiveness in practice will be contingent on adequate funding, publicity, and a host of other practicalities. Yet we focus here, in broad and idealized terms for the moment, on how DPRs might improve on the deliberation witnessed in standard peace referendums.

A. Public-Value Ballot

The referendum ballot should feature an initial segment in which voters are asked to consider a set of *public values*. As we saw in the last chapter, public values are 'public' in the sense of being broadly shared by, or acceptable to, all democratic citizens *qua* democratic citizens. The aim here is to clarify what exactly voters think is, or ought to be, foundationally at stake in the peace process. Public-value choices should be organized in a multi-option ballot asking voters to rank a set of public values listed on the ballot.

The listed values should be clearly cast in generalized terms: in language indicating that these are public values and that, as such, they are widely shared, not reducible to any particular comprehensive doctrine. The referendum ballot should ask voters not about their own interests—for example, what they want to win out of a settlement—but what general values, applying to all sides in a conflict, should drive the settlement. The ballot therefore should present voters with value options such as 'All groups should enjoy equal protection against violence'. Another version of this statement is more explicit: 'Community *X* should enjoy protection against violence and community *Y* should also enjoy protection against violence.' In either case, voters can only select the entire compound proposition, rather than make a more limited choice to favour such a value just in relation to their own community.

As we will see later on, in a second segment of the ballot, there should be a *mandate question*: a question asking voters to endorse the general proposition that peacemaking negotiations should commence and proceed in good faith. While our preference is for a mandate referendum, the second segment of the DPR ballot can, as an alternative, ask voters to endorse an already-concluded draft settlement.

If the DPR runs as a mandate referendum, then a third and final, and optional, segment of the ballot could present concrete, but still broad, questions about constitutional *reform outcomes* (eg, whether voters favour adopting a new consociational system, federalism, independence, etc).

But we focus for the moment on the public-value segment of the ballot. This approach has never occurred in peacemaking in quite the ways suggested here. We previously saw that express invocations of public values have been indirectly part of peace referendums, most clearly in the 1998 vote to endorse the Belfast Agreement.[2] Yet our proposed method, which would recast peacemaking in public-value terms more directly and expansively, may have several benefits for peacemaking:

(1) Exposing agreement under conditions of minimalism

Public-values balloting seeks to fast-track a process that is central to some ideals of deliberative democracy: acknowledging views beyond one's own non-public interests and perspectives (eg, comprehensive doctrines premised on particular religious or nationalist perspectives). Public values are, as we have seen, generalized values that bracket differences based on preferences or interests that could not reasonably be defended to differently situated others. This shift to a more generalized perspective may help conflicting parties to stake out common ground between them.

Notably, however, recall that we mostly do not expect a DPR to encourage fundamental changes in voters' views. Instead the chief aim is to recast these views, reframing them in terms around which agreement is more likely. We previously called this 'exposure' of shared values. As discussed, achievement of settlement is more likely when it emerges that the parties had already agreed with each other in certain areas (public values), even though they may not have recognized it. Ultimately, the DPR can probably aim to do little more than draw upon voters' existing, latent capacities for agreement. The referendum result can prominently and formally highlight any existing intergroup agreement based on public values.

Of course, the obverse is also a possibility. Normally, if results from each community are published, then one would expect the DPR's tally of public-value

[2] Chapter 2.

votes to highlight certain value differences as well. These differences may not be extreme, and they may be overshadowed by points of agreement. But there is always the worry that stark value differences will emerge.[3] These might then become the focus of the rhetoric of elite and other spoilers opposed to peacemaking, deployed as evidence of intractable differences or of the futility of the peacemaking effort. However, below we will stipulate the use of mini-publics to determine which values should be included in the ballot, and we will explain that these bodies may minimize value differences in referendum results. The mini-public is likely to design a ballot to include only those values that are generalized and public, and in practice already widely shared between communities. To make sure of this, we will also suggest supermajority or near-consensus voting within the mini-public.

These considerations bring us to a *minimalist proviso.* The DPR's objective should be to see voters endorse certain limited areas of common ground between groups in conflict. The results of public-values voting may be a clear identification of the main values on which the parties are agreed. The DPR should not aim to manage or resolve any non-public disagreement, nor any value differences tangential to the conflict. The kind of minimalism that we have in mind here anticipates that particular institutions might prompt a momentary meeting of minds between disparate groups on the basis of just a small set of public values.[4] Voters need only deliberate under these controlled and time-limited circumstances—just long enough to expose agreement and perhaps to mandate negotiations.

This minimalist approach is not as onerous as seeking to improve social deliberation broadly across a range of subjects.[5] In this way we depart from earlier commentators. For example, Bora Kanra stresses the benefits for settlement when deliberative democracy involves a process of broad and unforced general social learning.[6] And Adeno Addis argues for deliberation 'through which the identities of the participants, not just the policies and institutions of the polity, are constructed and transformed'.[7] Both, therefore, address deliberative

[3] Joanne McEvoy, 'Letting "the People(s)" Decide: Peace Referendums and Power-Sharing Settlements' (2018) 25(5) Democratization 864, 866.

[4] The concept of minimalism here is distinct from that of legal theorists such as Sunstein: see, eg, Cass R Sunstein, *One Case at a Time: Judicial Minimalism on the Supreme Court* (Harvard University Press 2001).

[5] But cf Rawls on the distinction between 'constitutional consensus' and 'overlapping consensus': John Rawls, *Political Liberalism* (Colombia University Press 1996) 158–68.

[6] Bora Kanra, *Islam, Democracy and Dialogue in Turkey: Deliberating in Divided Societies* (Ashgate 2009).

[7] Adeno Addis, 'Deliberative Democracy in Severely Fractured Societies' (2009) 16(1) Indiana Journal of Global Legal Studies 59, 82. Addis imagines this happening over time at a social level. However, he also advocates a form of minimalism ('incompletion') by cautioning that constitutions should not seek to settle all contentious issues at once: 76–77.

conflict settlement as a widespread and long-term process. Indeed, we previously saw some of Rawls's own language consistent with a drawn-out form of public reason.[8] Yet, while a gradual movement towards wider trust, learning, shared values, and perhaps even shared identity may be welcome, often it will be unrealistic. There is no expectation that a DPR will develop and expand such capacities. To be sure, it may be that a DPR can only achieve its limited objectives once there is at least a basic core of people able and willing to deliberate.[9] Yet we previously saw that such conditions are not uncommon, even amid conflict.[10]

Minimalist approaches may help to address key criticisms from the last chapter: especially that public reason makes excessive demands on deliberators and can be exclusionary or unrealistic. Notably, our concept of deliberative minimalism does not require flexibility as to the boundaries of one's identity. Substantial abstraction from one's own identity-based group (eg, adopting perspectives that deny the salience or unique perspectives of groups) is not likely, and neither is it necessary. Minimalist public-value deliberation imposes requirements nowhere near as exacting as this. Again, what is required is only that groups reach a limited form of common ground between them, based on values such as equality, fairness, and mutual toleration.

The values on the public-value ballot should include, at a minimum, some form of constitutional recognition of the legitimacy and status claims of all relevant groups.[11] More wholesale changes may not be required. In the Northern Irish settlement, for instance, there was no expectation of the two communities' becoming closer in identity. Nor did they need to be more politically accommodating *as a general matter*, or more committed to leading lives characterized by deliberation. The endorsement of the settlement in that case required just a focused, and time-limited, broadening of attitudes—a limited reconsideration of the kinds of group identities understood as legitimate (effectively, the Belfast Agreement recognized Northern Ireland as bi-national), as well as the order of priority between such identitarian debates and needs for stability and physical security. (We will have more to say on these points in Chapter 5.)

[8] Chapter 2.

[9] Hennessey thinks that attempts to achieve peace in Northern Ireland in the early 1970s faltered because social attitudes had yet to progress towards greater social acceptance of the legitimacy of other communities: Thomas Hennessey, *The Northern Ireland Peace Process* (Gill & Macmillan 2000) 18. See also Chapter 7.

[10] Chapter 2.

[11] See Chapter 5 on the 'boundary problem' this raises.

(2) Public values and persuasion

As we have explained, our expectation is that a DPR may expose existing value-based agreements. Admittedly, however, it would be an oversimplification to assume that voters possess fixed and straightforward opinions about peacemaking—a set of latent views readily revealed as soon as the right institutions come along. In reality, an agreement may to some extent need to be coaxed out of voters who, for instance, may not trust the referendum process or the good faith of other voters. Many voters will also remain open to non-public, and more generally non-deliberative, forms of speech (eg, divisive and misleading claims). An element of persuasion is probably therefore required, even when the focus of a DPR is on fulfilling voters' latent aptitudes for agreement.

Some deliberative democrats have reasoned that arguing in generalized terms is more persuasive than the alternatives. When we engage in deliberation, we seek to persuade others that our position is superior to theirs—that the stronger reasons are on our side. To make out our case, we cannot simply appeal to our own interests in the matter since appeals of that kind normally fall on deaf ears. Hence the wish to persuade others obliges us to present our position in more generalized terms.[12] In so doing, we broaden both our position and its appeal. Dryzek and List describe the point this way:

> Deliberation may rule out arguments that cannot withstand deliberative scrutiny. Deliberative theorists often stress the invocation of interests 'generalizable' to deliberators, and to their society. Arguments couched in such terms are more persuasive than those couched in terms of the interests of some subgroup, which in turn are more persuasive than those couched in terms of the interests of specific individuals. Preference orderings denying the personal integrity and political equality of other actual or potential deliberators are not easily sustained, for participation in deliberation has to bring to mind the interests of these others.[13]

The broad point here is that those who initially reason from non-public positions may be compelled, by the force of better and more generalized reasons, to abandon relatively unsupportable self-interested arguments.[14]

[12] Jon Elster, 'Deliberation and Constitution Making' in Jon Elster (ed), *Deliberative Democracy* (CUP 1998) 100–05, 111; Bernard Manin, 'On Legitimacy and Political Deliberation' (1987) 15(3) Political Theory 338, 358–59.

[13] John Dryzek and Christian List, 'Social Choice Theory and Deliberative Democracy' (2003) 33(1) British Journal of Political Science 1, 15.

[14] See also Jon Elster, 'Deliberation and Constitution Making', in Jon Elster (ed), *Deliberative Democracy* (CUP 1998) 97–122.

One aim of public-value balloting is to make generalized reasons more prominent. After bringing public values to the fore, a DPR may challenge voters' relatively self-interested interpretations of values. Widely-generalized public values on the ballot may expose other values or interpretations as arbitrarily narrow, or at least make the voter do some conceptual work to justify continuing to hold the narrower position.[15] For example, values such as mutual respect and mutual toleration are highly generalized. Any reasons that lead a voter to reject these generalized values starkly stated on the ballot may not be easily defended. Of course, voters in fact may turn to motivated logical sophistry, or just lazy reasoning, to continue justifying non-public values or interpretations.[16] But, when generalized values are presented to them, they may be less likely to invoke reasons in terms of their own sub-group's interests. If Dryzek and List are right, then in the competition between widely-generalized and narrower values, the former are likely to be more dominant and persuasive.

What do we know about these kinds of predictions in practice? Many experiments in social psychology show the influence on opinion poll responses of what is called value 'priming'. This refers to the framing of discussions according to a stated set of values, which encourages reasoning in line with those values. Priming may prompt respondents to construe later information in ways that are compatible with earlier information to which they were intentionally exposed;[17] a meta-value of consistency—of avoiding dissonant positions—seems to be at work.[18]

Priming with certain values can prompt intergroup agreement, whereas other values often have the opposite effect. The experiments noted particularly distinguish between values of universalism, equality, and benevolence on the one hand, and values including power, status, influence, achievement, and wealth on the other.[19] The former are more generalized and broadly applicable, and could readily be described in Rawlsian terms as public. They are also, in practice, 'self-transcendent' and consistent with agreement between people (or between groups).[20] In terms of these values' priming effects, as Gregory Maio and his colleagues explain:

[15] David Miller, 'Deliberative Democracy and Social Choice' (1992) 40 Political Studies 54 (supplementary volume 1).

[16] See Chapter 2.

[17] Gregory R Maio and others, 'Changing, Priming, and Acting on Values: Effects Via Motivational Relations in a Circular Model' (2009) 97(4) Journal of Personality and Social Psychology 699, 700–02, 713.

[18] MJ Ferguson and JA Bargh, 'Liking is for Doing: The Effect of Goal Pursuit on Automatically Activated Attitudes' (2004) 87 Journal of Personality and Social Psychology 557.

[19] Maio and others (n 17) 700–01.

[20] ibid 699, 701–02.

> if the value of equality expresses a universalist motive . . . then any event that causes individuals to increase the importance of equality should cause them to increase the importance of other values that similarly promote universalism (e.g., a world at peace). At the same time, such an event should decrease the importance of values (e.g., wealth) that express opposing motives, such as power and achievement . . . .[21]

When poll participants are exposed to information that 'makes them feel dissatisfied with the extent to which one of their values fulfills their self-conceptions of competence or morality, . . . they reduce this self-dissatisfaction by changing their value priorities'.[22] Notably, '[n]umerous experiments have used [this] procedure to modify values, attitudes, and behavior that are often regarded as being resistant to change'.[23] Other researchers have come to very similar conclusions.[24] For our purposes, the studies are especially illuminating as they show us the effects of generalized values on the behaviours of opinion-poll respondents—just a step (albeit a significant one) removed from the 'poll' of the referendum. Interestingly, though such empirical work seldom finds any reference in theories of public reason (and vice-versa), the assumptions of public reason theory may help to explain the experimental results.[25]

(3) Purposive and holistic deliberation

We have argued that public-value questions at the top of the ballot can be persuasive in the sense that voters may be willing to endorse them. Yet public-value questions early on may also affect how a voter reasons about the peacemaking

[21] ibid 701. These two sets of values are positioned on opposite sides of a 'circular model of values'; additional, orthogonal values (eg, tradition, self-direction, and freedom) are not directly opposite to, nor in competition, with the values in the first two sets.

[22] ibid, citing Joel W Grube and others, 'Inducing Change in Values, Attitudes, and Behaviors: Belief System Theory and the Method of Value Self-Confrontation' (1994) 50(4) Journal of Social Issues 153; M Rokeach, 'Long-term Value Change Initiated by Computer Feedback' (1975) 32(3) Journal of Personality and Social Psychology 467.

[23] Maio and others (n 17) 701, referring to Robert A Chernoff and Gerald C Davison, 'Values and Their Relationship to HIV/AIDS Risk Behavior Among Late-Adolescent and Young Adult College Students' (1999) 23(5) Cognitive Therapy and Research 453; Patricia G Devine and others, 'Breaking the Prejudice Habit: Progress and Obstacles' in Stuart Oskamp (ed), *Reducing Prejudice and Discrimination* (Lawrence Erlbaum 2000) 185; Joel W Grube and others, 'Predicting Adolescent Drinking From Alcohol Expectancy Values: A Comparison of Additive, Interactive, and Nonlinear Models' (1995) 25(10) Journal of Applied Social Psychology 839; Mayton II Grube and Ball-Rokeach (n 22); Shalom H Schwartz and Netta Inbar-Saban, 'Value Self-Confrontation as a Method to Aid in Weight Loss' (1988) 54(3) Journal of Personality and Social Psychology 396.

[24] See, eg, Kennon M Sheldon and others, 'Americans Recommend Smaller Ecological Footprints When Reminded of Intrinsic American Values of Self-Expression, Family, and Generosity' (2011) 3(2) Ecopsychology 97.

[25] Recall that Rawls supposes that, when citizens' comprehensive doctrines conflict with public values, they will adjust or 'bend' their comprehensive doctrines to make them better fit: see Chapters 1 and 2.

mandate or broad institutional options farther down the ballot. The early questions may encourage *purposive* deliberation by encouraging a consideration of the objectives behind the mandate or institutional options.[26] Evidence from the area of survey design shows that posing preliminary, broadly-based questions can indeed prompt respondents' more extensive engagement with later questions.[27] Similarly, voters may notice how the concrete ballot questions at the bottom of the DPR ballot relate to the public values that they selected earlier on. One result may be to reinforce conceptual ascent from particular concerns to public values.

Purposive voting may also prompt voter reasoning that is relatively *holistic*. The act of ranking values at the top of the ballot necessitates trading values (or other considerations) off against each other. This may mitigate the tendency, noted previously, of voters to make decontextualized selections that do not weigh costs against benefits (eg, favouring, at once, both tax cuts and public spending increases).[28]

In an existing referendum model called the 'scaled referendum' or 'structured value referendum', voters expressly choose from a range of concrete options (eg, different waste treatment procedures) on a ballot that clearly identifies each option's costs and benefits (eg, environmental and economic).[29] This model's aim is to generate an holistic view of policymaking. However, the scaled referendums trialled so far have invoked roughly objectively quantifiable costs and benefits (eg, the price of each option shown as a monetary figure). By contrast, for much constitutional reform the 'costs and benefits' involved are contested matters of value. These intangible values cannot be reduced to simple numeric figures on the ballot.

Public-values balloting may provide a partial answer to this problem. Here voters themselves decide on the relative weightings of each value. As mentioned, the values portion of the ballot should require voters to rank values, an act that necessarily involves comparison. That several values appear on the ballot, and that voters are compelled to choose among them, indicates the

[26] One of the objectives of deliberation is greater 'inter-subjective consistency'—that is, 'more consistent connections between particular subjective positions and corresponding preferences': Simon Niemeyer and John Dryzek, 'The Ends of Deliberation: Meta-Consensus and Inter-Subjective Rationality as Ideal Outcomes' (2007) 13(4) Swiss Political Science Review 497, 501.

[27] Fritz Strack, '"Order Effects" in Survey Research: Activation and Information Functions of Preceding Questions' in Norbert Schwarz and Seymour Sudman (eds), *Context Effects in Social and Psychological Research* (Springer 1992) 23–34.

[28] Chapter 2.

[29] Ron Levy, 'Deliberative Voting: Realising Constitutional Referendum Democracy' (2013), July, Public Law 555, 570–71; Timothy McDaniels, 'The Structured Value Referendum: Eliciting Preferences for Environmental Policy Alternatives' (1996) 15(2) Journal of Policy Analysis and Management 227.

complex trade-offs underlying institutional choices. For instance, in a secession referendum, values of political autonomy and economic cooperation or efficiency might appear on the ballot.

Note that it sometimes may be thought desirable to hold a referendum with values alone appearing on the ballot. This could give broad direction to elites, who would then decide whether or how to start negotiating. But such an approach would give up any chance to use the referendum to endorse a negotiating mandate as well, and thus to give impetus to peacemaking where some elites are reluctant negotiators. Moreover, on their own value questions may generate less robust voter engagement. As AV Dicey observed, '[d]ebates which are indecisive can never possess the full importance, or interest, attached to discussions which result in final decisions'.[30]

(4) Reducing polarities

Simply having a segment of the ballot present three or more options to voters (ie, several public values to be ranked) may decrease the polarization and hardening of positions that is always a risk, especially, with two-option referendums.[31] The Venice Commission on referendums, which we previously criticized for its inattention to deliberative values, views the binary Yes/No referendum as best-practice in referendum design; the Commission favours the simplicity and clarity of binary questions.[32] However, far more convincing in our view is Lawrence LeDuc's argument in favour of multi-option referendums, which prioritize '*voice* over *votes*, in part by lowering the stakes of partisan political interests in the outcome'.[33] Deliberating over several options in a referendum could uncouple decision-making from fixed and polarized categories of policy reasoning.[34] This would be useful in any referendum, but especially so in a peace referendum where polarized positions and mutual antipathies may be even more firmly rooted. However, our observations here are subject to the 'minimalist' proviso noted above. Ballot questions and officially disseminated information should be confined to the small set of generalized public values that are most relevant to a conflict; an overbroad

[30] AV Dicey, 'Ought the Referendum to be Introduced into England?' (1890) LVII Contemporary Review 502, cited in Mads Qvortrup, 'AV Dicey: The Referendum as the People's Veto' (1999) 20(3) History of Political Thought 531, 541.

[31] Chapter 2.

[32] European Commission for Democracy Through Law (Venice Commission), *Guidelines for Constitutional Referendums at National Level* (11 July 2001) COE Doc CDL-INF (2001) 010, [II], E 2.a.

[33] Lawrence LeDuc, 'Referendums and Deliberative Democracy' (2015) 38 Electoral Studies 139, 141 (emphasis in original).

[34] See similarly Ron Levy, 'Regulating Impartiality: Electoral-Boundary Politics in the Administrative Arena' (2008) 53 McGill Law Journal 1, 42.

deliberation—one with too many options—may be unworkable and may expect too much of voters. It may also detract from the clarity of any intergroup agreement exposed in a referendum.

B. Elite Roles and Restraints

We previously noted that neither elite nor applied deliberation is, relatively speaking, conducive to agreement.[35] Yet elite negotiations over settlement details cannot be avoided: only elites can finalize the applied specifics of an agreement (eg, constitutional structures, legal drafting, apportionment of debts after secession, metre-by-metre delineations of borders, and military deployment areas). Thus as noted, following the public-value segment, the ballot should ask voters to endorse a mandate for elite-led peace negotiations leading to a final settlement. Such a question may be phrased in terms such as: 'Should [*x* government or other leadership] negotiate to conclude a lasting peace settlement with [*y* government or other leadership]?'.

Often, in a conflict with sharp divisions based on distinct group identities, a rule of *concurrent consent* should also apply: published tallies should indicate how many people in each group endorse the mandate. The mandate should be considered passed only if a majority in each community votes in its favour.[36] (We will explore this option, especially, in later chapters and consider where concurrent consent rules may or may not be appropriate.)

Instead of a mandate approach, a DPR can alternatively endorse an existing peace plan. But this is less ideal. A DPR conducted as a mandate referendum may give 'early approval for the nascent agreement'[37] and may help to impel elites to sit down together to begin negotiations. It is occasionally the case (eg, in the referendums in France/Algeria in 1961 and South Africa in 1992) that a significant majority of people, bucking some of their more intransigent leaders, support peacemaking.[38] A referendum's signalling of a popular mandate may instigate negotiations, and perhaps even carry them through to successful completion.

[35] Chapter 2.

[36] On deliberative effects and risks of veto, see Anna Drake and Allison McCulloch, 'Deliberative Consociationalism in Deeply Divided Societies' (2011) 10(3) Contemporary Political Theory 372, 385–86.

[37] Loizides (n 1) 237.

[38] See generally Loizides (n 1). De Gaulle also notoriously used the referendum as a referendum on his own authority. Consistently enough, when he lost a referendum in 1969, he resigned.

As we saw in earlier chapters, elites have outsized influence in public discourses—especially amid conflict, where they may draw on the apparent moral authority of, for example, their roles as ethnic representatives or military leaders. We also saw that (some) elites can both benefit from continued conflict and derail peacemaking efforts. But when a referendum runs, the relative speech roles of elites may diminish if the referendum dominates a public discourse. The referendum potentially draws on the perceived democratic legitimacy of the people themselves to exert an influence that may rival or eclipse that of elites (a point explored in the next chapter). The referendum may be one of the few effective counterweights to elite authority. In this sense, the potential to lessen the relative voices of elites is inherent to any referendum.

But merely running a referendum may not be enough. Rules—either agreed to by elite parties, or if necessary legislated—may be required to restrain certain elite roles until after the referendum vote concludes and elite negotiations begin (assuming a mandate referendum). Some elites should have few if any roles in designing the referendum, dictating the content of the ballot, or writing the officially promulgated information. Empowered elites (eg, members of the elected, administrative, judicial, and military wings of the state; and leaders of separatist or other insurgent militias), especially, should be excluded from these leadership roles. This can be a challenge: there is always the risk that excluded elites will seek to spoil the process from the outside. They may question its legitimacy, spread misinformation, or engage in scare tactics.

Yet if we assume a scenario in which the different sides to a conflict have already arrived at a 'mutually hurting stalemate' (where the costs of continuing with a conflict seem to outweigh the costs of settlement),[39] then the parties may be seeking a way out. There can be no guarantee that spoilers can be contained. But moderates from each side to the conflict may be able to support a mandate referendum that both gives them the authority to negotiate and serves as a bulwark against the machinations of other, less scrupulous elites who have interests in destabilizing the process.

Of course, a mandate referendum will not run itself. It must be organized and funded. It must be fairly conducted and its results must be counted with integrity. Consequently, some empowered elites with specific expertise must still be included in the design and running of the DPR (eg, electoral commissioners and advisors). While trying to avoid prejudging outcomes, various elites must at a minimum guide the overall process, assign roles to particular

[39] Ira W Zartman, 'The Timing of Peace Initiatives: Hurting Stalemates and Ripe Moments' (2001) 1(1) The Global Review of Ethnopolitics 8.

groups and individuals in the mini-public, and facilitate mini-public deliberations. Relatively neutral international personnel may be useful in these roles.

At times it may be appropriate for laws actively to bar wider sets of elites—including members of the media, or influential ethnic, military, or religious leaders—from publicizing statements that stoke either violence or intergroup animus in the course of the referendum campaign. While we cannot realistically exclude elites from using their own means (eg, the media, or the pulpit) to influence a referendum, we can at least limit the kinds of these interventions. Globally, the legality and propriety of hate speech limitations are generally well established (outside of the outlier United States).[40] Below, as well, we will address laws prohibiting false information. However, legal prohibitions against most other types of referendum expression—that is, against any direct argument for or against propositions on the ballot—would be more controversial and also less workable, especially where the internet can be widely accessed.

Limiting elite involvement is clearly, then, a tenuous prospect. Legal or self-imposed restraints may reduce the risk of spoiler behaviour by elites—and by others too—but can never eliminate the risk. A complete ban on elite engagement could backfire. Some, accustomed to the honour of being formally consulted by their community, may begrudge being silenced. Indeed 'a wholly non-elite process could be culturally unsuitable'.[41] Some may also contest the justice of the exclusionary measures themselves. Empowered elites may after all have useful perspectives, for instance as representatives of aggrieved groups and as experts on the groups' circumstances and needs. Hence such elites should be able to exercise some substantive influence in the process, but only (or at least largely) *indirectly* via an institution providing for deliberative decision-making. For example, some may be included as expert witnesses within mini-publics (more on which below). Such bodies typically hear from an array of speakers with intimate knowledge of the issues. On the other hand, empowered elites should be wholly excluded, even from this measured role, if they have historically peddled demagogic or hateful speech or speech that incited violence. These kinds of contributions would directly contradict the bodies' aims. (Admittedly, we are asking here for very delicate judgement calls.)

As noted, following the mandate question on the ballot, there is also an option to include specific constitutional reform options. For instance, voters in a

[40] Michel Rosenfeld 'Hate Speech in Constitutional Jurisprudence: A Comparative Analysis' (2003) 24(4) Cardozo Law Review 1523.

[41] Ron Levy and others, 'Designing Referendums for Peacemaking: The Case of Bougainville' (2018) 33(1) Australasian Parliamentary Review 6, 32.

secessionist region can be presented with options such as 'full independence', 'an autonomous region within a federation', or maintenance of the constitutional status quo. Whether such substantive questions should be included in a referendum will vary from case to case. On its face, this method detracts from our main proposal that the referendum remain predominantly public-values focused. However, in some cases, referendums can also include substantive questions so long as the questions remain broad rather than detailed. Such questions might be legally required.[42] Or they may have some other instrumental use. For instance, voters' answers to specific reform questions might constrain the negotiating freedom of elites—a potentially useful function in cases where some elites are reluctant peacemakers and, if given to much negotiating freedom, may seek to scuttle a constitutional settlement.

At the elite negotiating stage, there are a variety of ways—some more deliberative than others—by which the finalization of a settlement can be conducted. Negotiators cannot rely wholly on public-value deliberation, but must engage in detailed discussions of applied constitutional, economic, geographic, and other matters. Inevitably, negotiations will involve disagreements. But ideally the negotiations may still remain deliberative in certain respects. Jane Mansbridge and others describe a range of possibilities for deliberation in negotiating arenas.[43] One such possibility would see negotiators settle on terms of agreement that have win-win effects.[44] In the conflict settlement context, this might for example mean territorial swaps in which each side receives a tract of land that it values more than the tract it has to relinquish. Negotiation may also involve more indissoluble issues, where win-win solutions are unavailable and all of the parties stand to lose something significant (even if they gain something as well). For instance, in the apportionment of debts after the secession of a territory, each side may argue for taking on a relatively small share of the debt. These are clearly harder cases. Yet negotiation may still involve inclusive and respectful deliberative processes. As well, the settlement in substance should be as fair as possible, in that it minimizes disadvantages to each party.[45]

These settlement processes and outcomes are plainly challenging to achieve. However, a negotiating mandate emerging from a DPR may make negotiations

[42] See, eg, *Constitution of the Autonomous Region of Bougainville 2004* pt 17.

[43] See, eg, Jane Mansbridge and others, 'The Place of Self-Interest and the Role of Power in Deliberative Democracy' (2010) 18(1) Journal of Political Philosophy 64, 69–72.

[44] ibid.

[45] ibid 72; Mark Warren and Jane Mansbridge, 'Deliberative Negotiation' in Jane Mansbridge and Cathy Jo Martin (eds), *Negotiating Agreement in Politics* (American Political Science Association 2013) 97.

more likely to be conducted in a deliberative mode. This may be the case if the outcome clearly indicates a popular agreement that the conflict should be settled, and settled fairly. The mandate of negotiators is then to act promptly and in good faith to settle contentious issues whichever way they can. A mandate referendum may help to motivate elites to reach a settlement by 'offering advice, direction, and more importantly, a mandate to negotiating leaders'.[46] Mandate referendums may also provide 'feedback' to leaders who later undertake negotiations, specifically by indicating which values and institutional options should most drive discussions.[47] A mandate for settlement may also reduce the incentive or space for intra-community outbidding, and dampen the opposition of some who are inclined to play spoilers.[48] Though of course there are no guarantees here, elite negotiators can generally be expected to heed the referendum's democratic expressions, knowing that ignoring the considered preferences of their constituents can erode their own popular support.[49]

C. Deliberative Mini-Publics

As noted, some of the features that we propose for a DPR already are familiar and well-tested. One such option is the routine mini-public model (eg, citizens' jury, citizens' assembly, or deliberative poll), whose members are (in the ideal case) randomly selected and hence demographically and attitudinally representative of the broader public. A mini-public ideally should help to lead the DPR process. Many studies confirm the ability of mini-publics to work as effective deliberative bodies,[50] and even to prompt better (eg, more informed, cooperative, and inclusive) deliberation among wider populations in subsequent referendums.[51] A mini-public's small membership (eg, 20–200) permits more

[46] Loizides (n 1) 237.

[47] ibid. In Loizides's description, but contrary to our proposals, leaders are also responsible for formulating the initial options presented to voters.

[48] Stephen John Stedman, 'Spoiler Problems in Peace Processes' (1997) 22(2) International Security 5.

[49] Public opinion clearly can drive public policy: see, eg, Paul Berstein, 'The Impact of Public Opinion on Public Policy: A Review and an Agenda' (2003) 56(1) Political Research Quarterly 29. In Chapter 4, we will see how this phenomenon is not necessarily diminished in authoritarian societies.

[50] Robert S Ratner, 'British Columbia's Citizens' Assembly: The Learning Phase' (2004) 27(2) Canadian Parliamentary Review 20.

[51] Fred Cutler and others, 'Deliberation, Information and Trust: The British Columbia Citizens' Assembly as Agenda-Setter' in Mark E Warren and Hilary Pearse (eds), *Designing Deliberative Democracy: The British Columbia Citizens' Assembly* (CUP 2008) 168–70; Michael MacKenzie and Mark Warren, 'Two Trust-Based Uses of Minipublics in Democratic Systems' in John Parkinson and Jane Mansbridge (eds), *Deliberative Systems: Deliberative Democracy at the Large Scale* (CUP 2012); Brian Tobin, 'Marriage Equality in Ireland: The Politico-Legal Context' (2016) 30(2) International Journal of Law, Policy & The Family 115, 123–24; Johan Elkink and others, 'Understanding the 2015

sustained and extensive deliberation than is possible for an entire public.[52] (In the larger mini-publics, such as deliberative polls or citizens' assemblies, the participants are themselves randomly assigned to small discussion groups, each of which is moderated by a trained, neutral facilitator.)

In some mini-public designs, participants learn extensively from experts with diverse views (eg, in plenary sessions where participants can question or hear from government officials, business leaders, trade unionists, scientists, etc) before tackling a contentious policy problem and ultimately issuing a reform recommendation. That recommendation in some cases is then put to voters in a referendum. Mini-publics can also have a hand in writing, or at least vetting, campaign materials distributed to voters (eg, pamphlets or the tutorials described below).[53]

Even in conflict societies such as Colombia, Israel/Palestine, and Northern Ireland, experimental mini-publics have been effective at prompting their members to become well-informed about the issues at stake and about other participants' perspectives.[54] Though these studies are still relatively few, and include outliers,[55] the balance of empirical evidence thus far suggests that citizens in conflict jurisdictions can deliberate effectively under the right institutional conditions.[56] A focused deliberative setting can 'foster more positive inter-group attitudes' among participants, including 'mutual respect and the acknowledgement of the validity of others' claims, indicating that ordinary

Marriage Referendum in Ireland: Context, Campaign, and Conservative Ireland' (2017) 32(3) Irish Political Studies 361, 369–72.

[52] For a general overview and evaluation, see Ian O'Flynn and Gaurav Sood, 'What Would Dahl Say? An Appraisal of the Democratic Credentials of Deliberative Polls and Other Mini-Publics' in André Bächtiger, Kimmo Grönlund, and Maija Setälä (eds), *Deliberative Mini-Publics: Practices, Promises, Pitfalls* (ECPR Press 2014).

[53] Katherine Knobloch and others, 'Vicarious Deliberation: How the Oregon Citizens' Initiative Review Influenced Deliberation in Mass Elections' (2014) 8 International Journal of Communication 62.

[54] M Lydia Khuri, 'Facilitating Arab-Jewish Intergroup Dialogue in the College Setting' (2004) 7(3) Race Ethnicity and Education 229, 244; Robert Luskin and others, 'Deliberating across Deep Divides' (2014) 62(1) Political Studies 116; Alex Norman, 'The Use of the Group and Group Work Techniques in Resolving Interethnic Conflict' (1992) 14(3/4) Social Work with Groups 175; Margarita Orozco and Juan Ugarriza, 'The Citizens, the Politicians and the Courts: A Preliminary Assessment of Deliberative Capacity in Colombia' in Juan Ugarriza and Didier Caluwaerts (eds), *Democratic Deliberation in Deeply Divided Societies: From Conflict to Common Ground* (Palgrave 2014) 73–88. Similarly, on Belgium, a deeply divided society but not a conflict society, see, eg, Didier Caluwaerts and Kris Deschouwer, 'Building Bridges Across Political Divides: Experiments on Deliberative Democracy in Deeply Divided Belgium' (2014) 6(3) European Political Science Review 427.

[55] See, eg, Magdalena Wojcieszak, 'On Strong Attitudes and Group Deliberation: Relationships, Structure, Changes, and Effects' (2012) 33(2) Political Psychology 225 (finding that some participants in deliberation merely reconfirm strongly-held prejudices).

[56] Ian O'Flynn and Didier Caluwaerts, 'Deliberation in Deeply Divided Societies' in André Bächtiger and others (eds), *The Oxford Handbook of Deliberative Democracy* (OUP 2018) 747–749.

citizens' views on divisive issues may be less intractably conflicting than expected'.[57]

If running a mini-public is not feasible due to cost, organizational, integrity, or safety concerns, then an international independent agency should write the ballot questions and neutral information materials—though, so far as possible, this should still aim to include broad public consultation to gauge which values are relevant to each community. National electoral commissions can be controversial, their neutrality not always a given. But their work can either be supervised or assumed in its entirety by international experts from neutral third countries, independent non-governmental bodies (eg, the International Institute for Democracy and Electoral Assistance), or international bodies (eg, the Organisation for Security and Cooperation in Europe and, where it is trusted by the parties, the United Nations). These organizations regularly supervise voting around the world.

If a mini-public or similar body takes the lead, there remains the question of whether they can improve deliberation in the wider referendum campaign. Referendums inevitably involve more chaotic deliberation than a mini-public. Yet, in comparison with many other forms of debate in the public sphere, referendums are themselves time-constrained and substantively limited to just a few topics. This may help to make them more amenable to institutional design meant to enhance deliberation. For instance, studies in non-conflict societies indicate that mini-publics held prior to referendums can serve as trusted proxies for ordinary citizens during the referendum campaign. The mini-publics can be trusted to set cues about the subjects and styles of deliberation that referendum campaigns might follow, and also to ensure that the information made available to voters is balanced and accurate.[58] Better wide-scale deliberation is hardly guaranteed, but past cases suggest that mini-publics at least make it more likely.

As mentioned, mini-publics should be charged with articulating a set of values to be placed on the ballot. They may do so by a majority or, ideally, supermajority vote among members at the end of their deliberations. These and other decision rules are often strong predictors of deliberative quality.[59]

[57] ibid 748.

[58] Cutler and others (n 51) 168–70. See also Jane Suiter and Theresa Reidy, 'Does Deliberation Help Deliver Informed Electorates: Evidence from Irish Referendum Votes' (2019) Representation 1; Mark Warren and John Gastil, 'Can Deliberative Minipublics Address the Cognitive Challenges of Democratic Citizenship' (2015) 77(2) The Journal of Politics 582; Knobloch and others (n 53).

[59] Caluwaerts and Deschouwer, 'Building Bridges' (n 54); cf James Fishkin and Robert Luskin, 'Experimenting with a Democratic Ideal: Deliberative Polling and Public Opinion' (2005) 40(3) Acta Politica 284.

The closer the mini-public's final vote comes to consensus on which values should be included on the ballot, the less likelihood there is of referendum proposals being adopted over the objections of a group that is in a minority position. The values that the mini-public adopts are likely to be public in the sense of being acceptable to reasonable individuals in each community in conflict. The mini-public approach is also particularly useful because, due to random sampling, its deliberations tend not to be characterised by elite polarization (eg, ordinary people tend not to be affiliates of political parties).[60] This may give a mini-public insight into the values that matter to people in each community, and that are in principle generalizable across all of the communities.

An important proviso is that, in a conflict setting, it may be useful to depart from mini-publics' usual proportionate representation approach. Randomized, mini-publics are often demographically stratified to reflect various identity groups in rough proportion to their population numbers. However, since the experience of conflict may be such that vulnerable minorities may lack the critical mass and hence the confidence to voice their own concerns, rough parity of numbers in a mini-public may be more appropriate (eg, 1:1 in a two-sided conflict, 1:1:1 in a three-sided conflict, etc). This modification is more likely to see deliberations yield genuine public values that are generalized and applicable to all. Democratic inclusivity pursues the 'epistemic function of democracy': broad and equal participation has the benefit of accessing the bulk of useful information that a population possesses.[61] Take, for instance, a conflict society where only 3 per cent belong to one group, but where the conflict is nevertheless two-sided. Here, given a 97:3 ratio of mini-public members, the smaller mini-public contingent could struggle to get everyone else to hear and heed their views.

Deliberative democracy is not anti-majoritarian per se, but is egalitarian to the extent that it leaves greater room for minority perspectives to be aired—and even to win the day, should the better arguments be on the minority's side. Deliberative democracy is thus sometimes perceived as 'the weapon of the weak'.[62] Its institutions seek to ensure all social perspectives are considered

[60] But cf the Irish Constitutional Convention on marriage equality, which included 33 politicians (alongside 66 randomly selected citizens). For a discussion, see Elkink and others (n 51).

[61] Iris Marion Young, 'Difference as a Resource for Democratic Communication' in James Bohman and William Rehg (eds), *Deliberative Democracy: Essays on Reason and Politics* (The MIT Press 1997) 400–01; Hélène Landemore, *Democratic Reason: Politics, Collective Intelligence, and the Rule of the Many* (Princeton University Press 2012).

[62] Amy Gutmann and Dennis Thompson, *Democracy and Disagreement* (Harvard University Press 1996) 57–59, 110–19.

on equal terms according to their merits. Empirical studies establish the effectiveness of mini-publics, even on a proportionate representation model, at prompting participants' open-minded engagement with, and learning from, people who have identities and views different from their own.[63] Yet particularly where one group in a conflict is particularly small, or if it resists engaging in deliberation of the kinds recognized in the broader population (see Chapter 7), it may be appropriate to increase their representation.[64]

Finally, a mini-public can generate high quality deliberation through the use of trained facilitators. The purpose of facilitation is to ensure mini-publics conduct proceedings in line with deliberative procedural principles such as respectful listening and dialogue, diverse sources of expert testimony, and the airing of various perspectives. Consistent with the argument that we are advancing here, facilitation can also readily include a stipulation that the values adopted for inclusion on the ballot should reflect not just a single community's interests, but a set of values applicable and acceptable to all the communities.

To the best of our knowledge, no mini-public has ever expressly specified the use of public reason. But such a specification would be useful, and in keeping with established mini-public procedures. Public-value deliberation should be made an explicit part of the mini-public process, and should be the mini-public's chief method. This proposal does not exclude more informal modes of communication or reason-giving of the kind discussed in Chapter 2; indeed, far from it. Informal modes such as narrative and storytelling can play an important role in preparing the ground for more formalized deliberation. They can help make more vivid the experiences and daily realities of different voters. They can also allow people to get things off their chests. However, for all the reasons that we have already given, both here and in earlier chapters, public-value deliberation should be made an explicit, and indeed central, part of the mini-public process.

[63] For a recent major statement, see James Fishkin, *Democracy When the People are Thinking: Revitalising Our Politics Through Public Deliberation* (OUP 2018); see also Christopher Karpowitz and Chad Raphael, *Deliberation, Democracy and Civic Forums: Improving Equality and Publicity* (CUP 2014).

[64] Consider Eritrea's use of a Constitutional Commission (which was not a mini-public) in designing materials to allow a platform for public debate: Bereket Selassie, 'Creating a Constitution for Eritrea' (1998) 9(2) Journal of Democracy 164, 166–67. A conscious decision was made to staff the commission with 'Eritrea's ethnic groups, religious persuasions, and professions': 168–70.

D. Managing Information

A DPR should also provide information, as well as interactive 'instruction', on perspectives relevant to the referendum campaign. Official information should be disseminated during the campaign in the forms of pamphlets, media advertisements, and computer tutorials. To promote neutrality, a mini-public could design the materials (with expert facilitation). For instance, in the 'citizen initiative review' model pioneered in Oregon, the findings of a mini-public are included in the information booklet that is sent to voters in advance of the referendum.[65] More uniquely, just before casting their votes voters should ideally be required to engage with an interactive informational tutorial online or at voting stations.[66] (Where infrastructure is limited, often only in-person tutorials held earlier during the referendum campaign will be feasible.[67])

Crucially, the included information should focus in large part on defining and explaining, in simple terms, the public values listed in the ballot. Applied rather than public-value information should have a limited role in any officially promulgated information. However, as we first mentioned in Chapter 2, not all of the information and discussion in a referendum can be value-focused. The DPR should rely on balanced, independently-verifiable information to counter, to some degree, general informational deficiencies among those who vote. Tutorials should thus include both value and closely related non-value materials. While the materials should omit excessive detail,[68] they can include information about the major parties to a conflict—especially their histories, anxieties, and aspirations. Some applied information can serve to illustrate value propositions (eg, a group's history of social exclusion explaining why members favour group equality protections). In addition, there may be background information relevant to the referendum itself that voters should know. Such background might include information on voting integrity or on what the result of a given vote would be (eg, explaining the mandate for negotiation.

Care must be exercised to ensure that the materials are reasonably comprehensive, clearly and evocatively presented, and expressly even-handed. Preliminary instruction can inform voters well only to the extent that it is comprehensive rather than selective (a concern first discussed in Chapter 2).

[65] Knobloch and others (n 53).

[66] There is a very large literature on the design, and on the trust and trustworthiness, of online democracy: see, eg, Lyria Bennett Moses and others, 'No More Excuses: Automated Synthesis of Practical and Verifiable Vote-Counting Programs for Complex Voting Schemes' in *International Joint Conference on Electronic Voting* (Springer International Publishing 2017) 66–83.

[67] Levy and others, 'Designing Referendums for Peacemaking' (n 41) 33–34.

[68] LeDuc (n 33) 143.

Materials should illustrate trade-offs (eg, among values, short- and long-term consequences, social interests, economic costs and benefits) in clear and simple terms. Additionally, the interactive aspect of tutorials (eg, involving multiple choice questioning) can be an important feature to help avoid mere passive and superficial engagement.[69]

Granted, requiring voters to engage with a tutorial for a prescribed length of time, such as ten minutes, risks turning some voters away. The willingness of voters to engage with the materials may diminish with the length and complexity of instruction, or where the matters at issue are not easily accessible. In short, a key normative question is whether this modest requirement is on balance justified in light of its potential to enhance deliberation and, it is hoped, at least marginally to improve the prospects of a settlement; or whether it is unjustly coercive (see this concern again in Section III).

One answer is that voting on a weakly deliberative basis—for example, based on minimal or unbalanced information about the relevant perspectives of others—is a relatively low-utility democratic act. As one of us has previously argued, for any matter of law reform that is constitutional or otherwise significant, there is a convincing normative argument that popular participation alone is insufficient to legitimate the reform.[70] Effort must also be invested in making the campaign and the vote itself as informed and deliberative as is feasible—without turning away too many voters. It may be appropriate to insist on voters' responsibilities to deliberate about the effects of the vote prior to voting, or at least to agree to receive some basic information about the vote and its stakes. The alternative is to accept that voting should be a mere formal act, not an act of *informed* consent.[71] But this approach is unjustified if something better, like the DPR, appears to be plausibly within reach.

Beyond preliminary instruction, efforts to increase voters' exposure to diverse information can also involve hearing from all sides of a conflict by directly connecting mini-public deliberations to wider public deliberations. Mini-public can be 'integrated'[72] or 'open',[73] in the sense that they welcome broad television or internet audiences into at least some parts of their deliberations. In addition, members of mini-publics can engage in formalized

[69] Levy, 'Deliberative Voting' (n 29) 569–70.
[70] ibid 555–56.
[71] On informed consent in law, see, eg, *Scanlon v American Cigarette Co (Overseas) Pty Ltd (No 3)* [1987] VR 289.
[72] Levy, 'Deliberative Voting' (n 29) 572–74.
[73] Hélène Landemore, *Open Democracy: Reinventing Popular Rule for the 21st Century* (Princeton University Press, 2020) 218–19.

discussion tours to consult with and inform voters.[74] Of course, in conflict societies concerns about security may temper this suggestion, and require that lay members only tour virtually online, or that they stay physically within their own communities.

A final, relatively contentious proposal is to enact laws against misinformation.[75] Political misinformation laws can prevent elites, and potentially others using popular media, from uttering clearly false statements that are likely to misinform and mislead voters.[76] As we have noted, misinformation is a recurring problem in conflict societies.[77] Robust misinformation laws might have provided a check against brazen misstatements in some historical referendum campaigns, in conflict and non-conflict societies alike.[78] Such laws are employed, for instance, in South Africa[79] and Australia.[80]

Some such laws have been subject to challenges under constitutional free speech and communication guarantees.[81] But judges have sometimes upheld the laws in light of the benefits to voters of relying on accurate information. Granted, among many other complications, these laws require trustworthy electoral commissioners or judges to issue fair judgments about factual truth and falsity. Yet certain subtler legal methods do not ban speech outright, but rather replace cacophonies of privately—and often unequally—funded speech in a campaign with free television broadcast time to allow a more complete and balanced airing of political platforms.[82]

The DPR's informational conditions should generally aim to increase access to accurate information about diverse citizen interests and points of view (eg, about how a peace proposal affects disparate sub-populations). According to Young, broad inclusivity of ordinary people and their perspectives in a

[74] British Columbia Citizens' Assembly on Electoral Reform, *Making Every Vote Count: The Case for Electoral Reform in British Columbia, Final Report* (2004) 12.

[75] Ron Levy and Graeme Orr, *The Law of Deliberative Democracy* (Routledge 2016) 104–08.

[76] ibid 104–08.

[77] Barbara Walter, 'Bargaining Failures and Civil War' (2009) 12(1) Annual Review of Political Science 243. See also David Lake and Donald Rothchild, 'Containing Fear: The Origins and Management of Ethnic Conflict' (1996) 21(2) International Security 41; Barry Posen, 'The Security Dilemma and Ethnic Conflict' (1993) 35(1) Survival 27. See also Chapter 1.

[78] An obvious example is the Brexit public vote of 2016: Alan Renwick, Michela Palese, and Jess Sargeant, 'Discussing Brexit—Could We Do Better?' (2018) 89(4) The Political Quarterly 545.

[79] *Electoral Act* (South Africa) ss 89, 99 and Sch 2 'Code of Conduct', read down but not struck down in *Democratic Alliance v African National Congress* [2015] 2 SA 232. See also *Electoral Commission of South Africa v Democratic Alliance* (Supreme Court of South Africa, pending, SCA Case No: 1068/2019) on the breadth of the Code of Conduct applying to political parties and their supporters.

[80] See, eg, *Electoral Act 1985* (SA) s 113; *Electoral Act 2004* (NT) ss 268, 271(2).

[81] See, eg, *Cameron v Becker* (1995) 64 SASR 238 (South Australia); *Australian Capital Television Pty Ltd v Commonwealth* (1992) 177 CLR 106 (Australia); *Rickert v Washington Public Disclosure Commission*, 168 P 3d 826 (Wash, 2007).

[82] Levy and Orr (n 75) 132–35.

deliberative process also potentially 'neutralizes the ability of powerful interests to distort discussion with threats or coercion'.[83] Again, we do not want to sideline all elites all of the time; some have a positive role to play in organizing information and advocating for positions on the part of people who might otherwise have no one to speak for them. However, enhancing the quality of information may fill some of the informational vacuum in a peace referendum and perhaps dampen the roles of demagogic elites, including elite spoilers, in a peace process.

III. DPRs as Distinctive in Deliberative Democracy

Before we close the present chapter we wish to take stock of how the DPR model is distinctive as a deliberative-democratic institution, and the reasons why the exceptional context of conflict may call for some of the DPR's unique features.

A. Deliberative Voting

DPRs seek, in part, to enhance deliberation in the final stage of the referendum, that is, in the act of voting itself. Most deliberative democrats instead conceive of deliberation as a collective communicative endeavour that can inform voting but is nevertheless distinct from it.[84] Granted, the secret nature of the ballot means that voters are still generally unable to engage in face-to-face deliberation with each other when they cast their votes. But they can engage in 'deliberation within', as Robert Goodin terms it.[85] What is particularly distinctive about our proposed model is that it suggests how internal reflection might be encouraged, and offers institutional recommendations to that end.

In standard referendum models, voting usually requires no more than a simple 'X', or at best a ranking from a list of reform options. Voters are expected to make their minds up in advance and hence to cease deliberating about the choice or choices they confront. DPR voting calls for something more. Voters

[83] Young (n 61) 400–01; cf David Sanders, 'The Effects of Deliberative Polling in an EU-wide Experiment: Five Mechanisms in Search of an Explanation' (2012) 42(3) British Journal of Political Science 617.

[84] See, eg, Robert Goodin, 'First Talk, Then Vote' in Robert Goodin, *Innovating Democracy: Democratic Theory and Practice After the Deliberative Turn* (OUP 2008) 108–09, quoting Joshua Cohen.

[85] Robert Goodin, 'Democratic Deliberation Within' (2000) 29(1) Philosophy & Public Affairs 81.

not only tick a box or rank options, but think about the implications of one choice upon another—consciously working their way through the ballot paper by relating one question to the rest. Voters should be encouraged to see the act of voting itself as a reasoned, cognitively-demanding process, rather than one that merely facilitates going through the motions. Thus by prompting voters to deliberate about the values behind their votes, and to do so independently at the final stage, the public-value ballot challenges the standard 'deliberate, then vote'[86] account of what voters do.

To be sure, the specialized ballot designs of our proposed model of DPR may also generate deliberative and collective debate earlier, during the referendum campaign. If public-value options are publicized in advance, then we expect that many voters will discuss them with each other. The specialized ballot may, therefore, improve the chances that public-value deliberation will both commence during the referendum campaign and continue to the voting booth (or computer station).

B. Population-Wide Deliberation

A DPR seeks to achieve deliberation, if only briefly, across the whole of a population (or populations). This, too, marks a sharp turn away from previous deliberative democratic instruments. For instance, James Fishkin opines that, while the deliberativeness of referendums can be marginally improved, it is better to invest effort in deliberation within a mini-public *prior to* a referendum.[87] His own deliberative polling methods stress the importance of scientific random sampling to constitute a mini-public, and the provision of balanced briefing documents presented in advance to mini-public members. Random sampling ensures representativeness while the briefing materials ensure that any changes in the views of mini-public members are information-driven.[88]

While a mini-public based on scientific random sampling gives us some sense of what an entire population would think if it had been put through the same deliberative process, the fact remains that any changes that occur inside a mini-public are not necessarily mirrored in a population at large. Fishkin notes (rightly) that a mini-public is far likelier to be induced to improve its

[86] Discussed in Simone Chambers, 'Deliberative Democracy Theory' (2003) 6(1) Annual Review of Political Science 307, 308; LeDuc (n 33) 139–40.

[87] Fishkin and Luskin, 'Experimenting' (n 59).

[88] James Fishkin, *Democracy When the People are Thinking* (n 63).

deliberation than is the population at large.[89] Thus the use of mini-publics represents one answer to the 'hard choice . . . between debilitated but actual opinion, on the one hand, and deliberative but counterfactual opinion, on the other'.[90] But a DPR takes the opposite tack. There is little question but that a DPR is unlikely to achieve the kind of deliberation that we tend to see in a well-run mini-public. However, there are exceptional benefits to holding a referendum, which no mini-public can claim on its own. Foremost of these is the potential for a population(s)-wide deliberative democratic event to legitimate and help entrench an enduring constitutional settlement—as we will argue in Chapter 4.

C. Deliberative Systems and Referendums

Our understanding of referendums also differs sharply from past works that rely on deliberative systems theory in relation to referendums.[91] The deliberative systems approach illuminates how the interlaced elements of public decision-making (eg, parliament, courts, the media, civil society organizations) can be understood, collectively, as deliberatively democratic, even if individual elements fall short.[92] A number of past contributions view referendums as democratic but non-deliberative inputs ('necessary evils') in a system that is otherwise, on balance, deliberative.[93] These sources generally deal with referendums merely tangentially and, as Alice el-Wakil notes, endorse referendums, if at all, only as adjuncts to mini-publics.[94]

[89] But cf Bruce Ackerman and James Fishkin, *Deliberation Day* (Yale University Press 2004), calling for multiple, society-wide mini-publics in the run-up to general elections.

[90] James Fishkin, *When the People Speak: Deliberative Democracy and Public Consultation* (OUP 2009) 13.

[91] See especially John Parkinson, 'The Roles of Referendums in Deliberative Systems' [2020] Representation 1.

[92] Jane Mansbridge and others, 'A Systemic Approach to Deliberative Democracy' in John Parkinson and Jane Mansbridge (eds), *Deliberative Systems: Deliberative Democracy at the Large Scale* (CUP 2012) 3.

[93] Alice el-Wakil, 'The Deliberative Potential of Facultative Referendums: Procedure and Substance in Direct Democracy' (2017) 4(1) Democratic Theory 59, 60; citing Mansbridge and others, 'A Systemic Approach' (n 92). See also John Dryzek, 'Symposium Commentary: Reflections on the Theory of Deliberative Systems' (2016) 10(2) Critical Policy Studies 209, 211–12; Nicole Curato and Marit Böker, 'Linking Mini-Publics to the Deliberative System: A Research Agenda' (2016) 49(2) Policy Sciences 173, 175; Andrea Felicetti, Simon Niemeyer, and Nicole Curato, 'Improving Deliberative Participation: Connecting Mini-Publics to Deliberative Systems' (2016) 8(3) European Political Science Review 427, 440; John Parkinson, 'Democratizing Deliberative Systems' in John Parkinson and Jane Mansbridge (eds), *Deliberative Systems: Deliberative Democracy at the Large Scale* (CUP 2012) 162.

[94] el-Wakil, 'The Deliberative Potential' (n 93).

We do not dispute that the theory of deliberative systems can help to justify the use of referendums. Our point instead is that referendums—at least when they are reconceived as deliberative referendums, including as DPRs—may be more than just weak nodes in a deliberative democratic system, to be tolerated and ideally offset in other parts of the system. In this chapter we have focused squarely on what may be done to make referendums themselves more deliberative.

D. Coercion

A final distinction between our proposed DPR model and some other deliberative democratic institutions is the (modestly) coercive nature of our approach. The DPR aims to bring parties in conflict to the point of being able to conclude a settlement. To do so, the ballot and related public information intentionally influence substantive outcomes of the referendum by reorienting voting around generalized, public-value propositions.

In past work, one of us has described this as a 'shotgun' feature of a DPR—a term that denotes a forced, but fair, settlement.[95] The term comes from commercial law, in which 'shotgun buy/sell' clauses in incorporation or partnership agreements specify a self-help method to resolve disagreements or deadlocks between the principals of a company. The result of triggering the clause is that one principal party proposes to buy out another's share in the company at a specified price; the second party can then either agree to sell at that price, or choose instead to buy the company at the same price.[96] This kind of clause creates a useful uncertainty: the proposed price must be fair, because the first party cannot know at the outset whether it will end up as the buyer or seller. This is an example of a 'veil of ignorance rule',[97] which seeks to operationalize Rawls's famous metaphor of a group of constitutional founders oblivious to their own identities.[98] Veil of ignorance rules, more generally, induce participants to take positions that abstract from their own presumed

[95] Ron Levy, '"Shotgun Referendums": Popular Deliberation and Constitutional Settlement in Conflict Societies' (2018) 41(3) Melbourne University Law Review 1237.

[96] Holger Fleischer and Stephan Schneider, 'Shoot-Out Clauses in Partnerships and Close Corporations' (2012) 9(1) European Company and Financial Law Review 35; Jason M Hoberman, 'Practical Considerations for Drafting and Utilizing Deadlock Solutions for Non-Corporate Business Entities' [2001] Columbia Business Law Review 231.

[97] Adrian Vermeule, 'Veil of Ignorance Rules in Constitutional Law' (2001) 111(2) Yale Law Journal 399.

[98] John Rawls, *A Theory of Justice* (Harvard University Press 1971) 136–42.

interests and preferences, in favour of generalized norms fair to all. A referendum geared to public-value deliberation aims for similar effects, yet by different means.

Whatever the merits of this approach, the 'shotgun' moniker implies coercion of the parties to cause them to come together on common ground. At least on the surface, this raises a dilemma for deliberative democracy.[99] A venerable assumption in the field is that coercive force is to be avoided.[100] Persuasion by the force of argument is preferable to coercion by, for example, legal fiat, deceit, violence or threats of violence, and unequal power arrangements. Unwarranted coercion can involve a rule or a person simply imposing a set of substantive positions (eg, an orthodox theology), and cutting short what otherwise might have been a more robust and open deliberative democratic process—one that seeks to justify decisions on terms acceptable to all who stand to be bound by them.

But while the DPR is coercive, again it is only modestly so. Voters may abstain on a given question. And they may neglect to vote at all; to minimize coercion, DPR voting should remain voluntary. Moreover, though generalized value choices present a narrow set of options to voters in a referendum, this is not in itself unique: all referendum ballots involve design choices that constrain voter choices in one way or another. The use of multi-option voting in the DPR ballot (as opposed to binary 'yes/no' questions) also avoids unduly narrowing the options put to voters.

Despite these mitigating points, the DPR is still in part distinguished by the particular forms of coercion that it employs. Most of all, the DPR predicates democratic participation on voting about value statements that are structured to be public. The DPR ballot obligates voters to interpret values more broadly than they otherwise might, and hence inhibits them from interpreting values in more narrowly self-interested terms. This amounts to a relatively direct influence on the substantive results of decision-making. (The coercion here may even run afoul of the Venice Commission's warning against 'leading

[99] See, eg, Francis Cheneval and Alice el-Wakil, 'The Institutional Design of Referendums: Bottom-Up and Binding' (2018) 24(3) Swiss Political Science Review 294, 295–96 (stressing the need for 'outcome neutrality'); but cf Simone Chambers, 'Making Referendums Safe for Democracy: A Call for More and Better Deliberation' (2018) 24(3) Swiss Political Science Review 305, 305–07 (noting 'outcome neutrality' may not be compatible with deliberative democratic benchmarks of legitimacy).

[100] Jürgen Habermas, *The Structural Transformation of the Public Sphere: An Inquiry Into a Category of Bourgeois Society* (Thomas Burger tr, MIT Press 1989) 202. The coercion we have in mind here takes place in the course of deliberation towards a decision. This is distinct from the coercion that occurs once a decision has been taken; at this latter stage, deliberative democrats would seem to agree that the decision should bind in the form of a coercive norm such as a law: eg, Jürgen Habermas, *Between Facts and Norms: Contributions to a Discourse Theory of Law and Democracy* (William Rehg tr, MIT Press 1996) 188–89.

questions'.[101]) Even though all democratic procedures leave their marks on substantive outcomes, many of these effects are relatively indirect, unintended, or unpredictable. The criticism of public-value balloting as unduly coercive is thus at least superficially compelling.

Yet despite its bad name, coercion is already pervasive and inevitable in institutional design for deliberative democracy. Acknowledging this, Habermas offers one early and nuanced take on the presumption against coercion. He recognizes how such a presumption could potentially tie the hands of institutional designers, and addresses the paradox that to be an uncoerced participant in deliberative democracy, one must somehow be induced to adopt and internalize norms of reasoning conducive to deliberation.[102] Habermas thus holds that coercive interventions should be permitted, up to a point. They should be used to establish a deliberative democratic process and encourage participants to internalize norms of deliberation; but thereafter democratic participants should be free to deliberate by their own lights on the matters put to them. Designers might otherwise be powerless to create and structure deliberative democratic institutions if the use of binding laws and other rules were considered out of bounds.

Habermas gestures here at a more fundamental notion: that sometimes coercion can counter coercion. As Archon Fung says, 'widespread inequality and failures of reciprocity can justify nonpersuasive, even coercive, methods for the sake of deliberative goals'.[103] Hence the

> scope of permissible nonpersuasive action grows as the conditions for deliberation deteriorate. . . . Sometimes, forces more compelling than the better argument are necessary to establish fair and inclusive deliberation or the conditions that support such deliberation. . . . Persuasion will seldom be sufficient to effect deep institutional transformation.[104]

[101] Venice Commission (n 32).

[102] Habermas, *Between Facts and Norms* (n 100) 67–69. On the apparent infinite regress here, see Frank Michelman, 'Constitutional Authorship' in Larry Alexander (ed), *Constitutionalism: Philosophi cal Foundations* (CUP 1998) 91. For Habermas's own response, which views constitutional history as a 'self-correcting learning process', see Jürgen Habermas, 'Constitutional Democracy: A Paradoxical Union of Contradictory Principles?' (2001) 29(6) Political Theory 766, 774. See also Habermas, *Between Facts and Norms* (n 100) 128.

[103] Archon Fung, 'Deliberation Before the Revolution: Toward an Ethics of Deliberative Democracy in an Unjust World' (2005) 33(3) Political Theory 397, 399.

[104] ibid 400–04.

Mansbridge and her co-authors also reach this conclusion,[105] noting that in some cases 'coercion, fairly exercised, promotes the purposes of deliberation'.[106] They endorse what they call deliberative self-defence: 'Deliberative democrats should not be expected to cleave to the norms of deliberation when opposing parties do not meet those norms.'[107] Similarly, given the generally poor conditions that we are faced with when we seek to use a referendum to mitigate conflict, and also the uncommonly high stakes of the attempt, we think that the coercions of the public-value ballot are generally justified.

Coercion can ultimately be enabling—which is an idea embedded in liberal theory, and a practical feature of laws, institutions, and social rules (eg, criminal and tort laws, principles of grammar, formal rules of poetics) that constrain some conduct in order to preserve valuable forms of social activity.[108] In a related vein, legal and institutional interventions may channel, constrain, and direct deliberation, yet also in the process may facilitate deliberation. Prevailing political and social conditions may have suppressed deliberation, and may themselves need to be countered or contained. For instance, Habermas notes that the high status of some speakers may be coercively persuasive, rather than persuasive as a consequence of the cogency of the speakers' arguments. '[S]ocial power' and the 'strength of privileged interests' can give rise to 'illegitimate interventions' in deliberation.[109] More generally—and most relevantly for our purposes—deliberation can be inhibited by violence, polarization, or any of the other deliberative pathologies of conflict societies that we previously observed.[110]

Our preferred conceptualization therefore understands coercion *in net*, as a compound of cross-cutting coercive and/or deliberative vectors. The question becomes whether, in practice and on balance, an institution's rules and processes offer people the freedom and capacity to deliberate better.[111] This

[105] Mansbridge and others, 'The Place of Self-Interest' (n 43) 82–83, citing Jon Elster, 'The Market and the Forum: Three Varieties of Political Theory' in Jon Elster and A Hylland (eds), *Foundations of Social Choice Theory* (Cambridge University Press 1986) 116, 119.

[106] Mansbridge and others, 'The Place of Self-Interest' (n 43) 82.

[107] ibid 83.

[108] See, eg, Jean-Jacques Rousseau and Gita May, *The Social Contract: And, the First and Second Discourses* (Yale University Press, 2002); and JS Mill, 'On Liberty' in John M Robson (ed), *Collected Works of John Stuart Mill: Volume III.* (University of Toronto Press 1977) 213–310.

[109] Habermas, *Between Facts and Norms* (n 100) 150. See similarly Seyla Benhabib, 'Liberal Dialogue Versus a Critical Theory of Discursive Legitimation' in Nancy L Rosenblum (ed), *Liberalism and The Moral Life* (Harvard University Press 1989) 155–56.

[110] Chapter 1.

[111] We can answer the question by reference to deliberative hallmarks such as *inclusive, cooperative, open-minded, flexible, reflective, civil, well-informed, holistic, other-regarding,* and *reason-giving* decision-making: Levy and Orr, *The Law of Deliberative Democracy* (n 75) ch 2.

kind of analysis focuses in upon a given deliberative democratic process, such as a DPR, to ask whether that process has a positive influence on deliberation. We have just noted what the DPR may be up against: the prevailing anti-deliberative social conditions with which the DPR must contend. And as we said in Chapter 1, prospective deliberators will often gauge whether attempting to deliberate is a rational choice in the circumstances. This, we said, raises a prisoner's dilemma: until others appear ready to deliberate, it may be futile, even dangerous, to attempt to deliberate oneself. The prevailing anti-deliberative characteristics of a conflict society can thus depress popular belief in the plausibility of deliberation, and in turn depress deliberation itself—including deliberation in a DPR.

A critical mass of individuals willing to deliberate may be needed before deliberation can progress towards a constitutional settlement. As Mansbridge and her co-authors write, 'citizens are more likely to cooperate voluntarily, requiring only minimal coercion, when they see their polity living up in practice to their ideals'.[112] Absent any recent evidence of deliberation, a DPR should aim to persuade voters that deliberation may still be realistic. As we have described it, the DPR is a relatively controlled setting within which participants may deliberate—and may have greater confidence that others will do the same. Although intergroup deliberation may initially appear implausible, a DPR may make it appear more likely. The promise of a brief and carefully designed deliberative exercise such as a DPR—with its public-value ballot, managed information, and so forth—may, for a time, relax some conflict-society voters' reservations about deliberating.

IV. Conclusion

The forms of deliberative voting that we have described are doubtless hard to achieve. There is always reason to worry about people's capacities to engage in complex cognitive processes amid the referendum campaign and vote. Yet our first answer to this is once again that even incremental improvements—easing us away from the standard, largely non-deliberative approaches to past peace referendums—could increase, also by degrees, the prospects of achieving a constitutional settlement.

The institutional methods discussed in this chapter are, we have stressed, minimalist: they aim to create carefully controlled circumstances within which

[112] Mansbridge and others, 'The Place of Self-Interest' (n 43) 84.

a referendum may, just briefly, support deliberation. Hence the DPR is not intended in the first instance to eliminate social division. A wider meeting of minds and mending of cultural differences is far more elusive than the DPR's fleeting forms of agreement based on public values. For some conflicts, a brief deliberative moment within institutional constraints such as those of a DPR is all that is feasible. However, as we will see in the next chapter, only this minimal agreement may be necessary for a constitutional settlement to survive over the long term—given the wide perceptions of constitutional legitimacy that a DPR may generate.

4

Settlement Endurance

I. Introduction

In Chapter 2 we presented the case for thinking that a deliberative peace referendum (DPR) can have an important role to play in *settlement achievement*. The obvious objection at that point, however, could have been that the case was merely a theoretical one. In Chapter 3 we responded by demonstrating what a DPR might look like. Yet this still leaves us open to a further objection: that even if the DPR could help to deliver a settlement, we know that settlements collapse all the time. The utility of a fleeting settlement would be limited: foiled peacemaking efforts may only deepen public cynicism and entrench conflict. What, then, of *settlement endurance*?

This question is our focus here. We do not think that the DPR is a panacea, yet neither do we think that its benefits are limited to the first stage, settlement achievement. To assume this is to fail to notice what the DPR is all about. We aim here to show that the DPR is constitutional in kind and, consequently, has the potential to contribute to settlement endurance. In other words, we will show why the theory of the DPR is more far-reaching than it initially seems. It is not merely a theory of the referendum, but a theory about peace processes more generally (albeit one that takes the referendum as its central concept or concern). Across Chapters 2 to 4, the sum of our arguments will be that, after first scaffolding a tenuous settlement between parties in conflict, a referendum may help to cement durable constitutional settlement norms. The DPR may make the solidification of peace settlements into constitutional commitments more likely.

As previously mentioned, our work here addresses a conspicuous gap in deliberative conflict studies.[1] Is a one-off deliberative democratic event limited to prompting a transient meeting of minds, or can it help to ground a relatively lasting constitutional settlement resistant to repeal or large-scale breach? One reason why we focus on constitutional theory in addition to

[1] Chapter 1.

Deliberative Peace Referendums. Ron Levy, Ian O'Flynn, Hoi L Kong, Oxford University Press (2021). © Ron Levy, Ian O'Flynn, and Hoi L Kong. DOI: 10.1093/oso/9780198867036.003.0004

deliberative democratic theory is that the constitutional character of many settlements is relevant to questions of endurance. Norms perceived as constitutionally legitimate may endure longer, as we will see.

Peace settlements often touch on traditionally constitutional matters such as territorial boundaries, governance arrangements, and basic rights. But it is clearly not the case that all attempted peace settlements effectively gain (enduring) constitutional legitimacy. Among procedural accounts of how constitutionally legitimate norms arise, popular legitimation has a prominent place. A process that expresses popular sovereignty is often understood as contributing towards the creation of constitutionally legitimate norms. Yet the seemingly simple point that expressions of popular sovereignty can promote constitutional legitimacy hides a great deal of complexity. For instance, should the expressions occur in a referendum—and, if so, what kind of referendum? Are there other effective sources of constitutional legitimation, beyond popular sovereignty? And how does the conflict settlement context affect (and complicate) our answers to these questions?

Before we answer such questions, note a few clarifications of our approach. One is that we will rely on both empirical sociological description and on normative reasoning. Constitutional endurance is a measure of the productive life of a constitutional norm: of how long it persists in practice without being widely breached, substantially reformed, or wholly repealed. This is chiefly an empirical matter, and it turns on other empirical matters such as how people actually view a putative constitutional norm. Yet we will also need to rely on normative theory to identify and make sense of the reasons why people hold these views, or why it may be right or appropriate for them to do so.

A second clarification is that even though we focus on constitutions, we are ultimately agnostic as to whether the 'constitutional' label attaches to every conflict settlement. We suspect that it may not. For instance, semantic uncertainty about what is 'constitutional' can arise where settlements include international treaties: should international or constitutional law concepts prevail?[2] In other examples, even if settlements have some hallmarks of constitutions, it simply might never occur to the parties to view the settlements as constitutional. Some of what we will label 'constitutional' might also be called 'constitution-like'. But for simplicity we will just use the former term.

[2] Christine Bell, 'Lex Pacificatoria Colombiana: Colombia's Peace Accord in Comparative Perspective' (2016) 110 American Journal of International Law 165, 169–70.

Third, we will often use 'constitutional reform' to describe the process leading to a constitutional settlement. We will generally avoid more specific descriptions like 'constitutional amendment' or 'constitutional creation' (also known as 'constitution-making').[3] Most of our discussions will encompass constitutional settlements involving either amendment or creation, and with the generic terminology of 'reform' we intend to capture both.

Finally, we want to know chiefly how to design constitutional referendums, not constitutions themselves. Our main concern is therefore the *process* of constitutional reform. But some of our discussion will show this to be a porous distinction.[4] The processes that we need will sometimes be dictated by the constitutional content that we are seeking.

We will begin, in Section II, by providing background on key constitutional concepts. This will include a description of the form and content that a constitutional norm must have in a stable constitutional system—precisely the kind of system we are after. The *exclusivity* of a constitutional norm will be our principal focus. This feature reflects a constitutional norm's capacity to transcend or override other norms, and thus to quell contestation (a particularly relevant consideration in a conflict society) and become an enduring constitutional fixture.

We will then consider the ways in which a DPR process can mark out certain norms as exclusive and enduring constitutional settlements. Such accounts should be dictated, first, by the form and content of the constitutional norms we are after. In Section III, we will show how a DPR process may help to establish norms that are constitutionally *exclusive* by focusing on public values to expose a single and dominant intercommunal agreement.

Yet in addition, accounts of successful constitutional settlement may look at the sociological legitimacy of a process per se. In Section IV, we will discuss how a DPR can persuasively advertise that a norm should be perceived as constitutional by relying on the DPR's *deliberative popular legitimation*. As part of our discussion here, we will develop what we call the *realization thesis*: that while any peace referendum carries some potential to legitimate and entrench a constitutional settlement, that potential remains relatively weak unless and until the referendum includes institutional supports for deliberation.

[3] See Richard Albert, *Constitutional Amendments: Making, Breaking, and Changing Constitutions* (OUP 2019) 71–73.

[4] For a discussion, see Joshua Cohen, 'Pluralism and Proceduralism' (1994) 69(3) Chicago-Kent Law Review 589.

II. Endurance through a Constitutional Lens

Our preferred description of constitutions builds on Jon Elster's typology,[5] with its three criteria:

(i) Endurance: Elster describes constitutional norms as 'distinguished [by] stringent amendment procedures';[6] that is, they are formally entrenched and meant to be difficult to change. But norms that are 'constitutional' can also be entrenched in a less strict sense. Constitutional norms can be either formally codified within central constitutional documents or located elsewhere in legislation, case law, or custom. Wherever and however they appear, on most conceptions constitutional norms are expected to endure. Reforming constitutional norms is generally more onerous than changing ordinary laws or policies.[7] If this were not the case, constitutional norms could neither guide law-making nor give certainty or direction to political systems.[8]

(ii) Fundamentality: Constitutional norms are also fundamental: they enjoy ultimate priority over other rules and actions.[9] Unlike other norms, constitutional norms are undelegated and therefore sit at the apex of a hierarchy of authority. Constitutional norms establish and govern the main institutions of government, the relationships among those institutions, and the main contours of the relationships between those institutions and a defined people. Some constitutional norms also set out rules to govern conflicts among, or changes to, other constitutional norms.[10] Notably for our purposes, too, constitutional norms can powerfully shape social interactions,[11] and can enunciate a society's foundational values and collective goals.[12]

[5] Jon Elster, 'Forces and Mechanisms in the Constitution-Making Process' (1995) 45(2) Duke Law Journal 364.
[6] ibid 366–67.
[7] See, eg, Ivor Jennings, *The Law and the Constitution* (5th edn, University of London Press 1961) 136.
[8] Ulrich Preuss, 'The Politics of Constitution Making: Transforming Politics into Constitutions' (1991) 13(2) Law and Policy 107.
[9] Elster (n 5) 366–67; HLA Hart, *The Concept of Law* (3rd edn, OUP 2012) 80–81.
[10] John Gardner, 'Can There Be a Written Constitution?' (2011) 1 Oxford Studies in Philosophy of Law 162.
[11] John Rawls, *Political Liberalism* (Columbia University Press 1996) 246–47; John Rawls, 'The Idea of Public Reason Revisited' (1997) 64(3) University of Chicago Law Review 765, 781–82, 795. See also Alon Harel, *Why Law Matters* (OUP 2014) ch 5.
[12] Jeff King, 'Constitutions as Mission Statements' in Denis J Galligan and Mila Versteeg (eds), *Social and Political Foundations of Constitutions* (CUP 2013) 73–102.

A constitution's fundamentality helps to explain why the constitution is generally expected to endure. Constant revision would undermine the object of setting some norms aside as fundamental.[13] As already indicated, a society's broadest foundations need protection against capricious repeal. This has implications for our focus on constitutional settlements of conflict. An effective settlement would be one that overrides norms or actions that seek to negate the settlement once it is achieved. For instance, elites opposed to the settlement may ignore it or seek to revise it in ways that suit their own interests or purposes. They may also simply seek to 'spoil' or destroy it.[14] A norm that is constitutional in status should in principle be able to resist these kinds of challenges for more than a trivial length of time. Adopting 'stringent amendment procedures' means that formal alteration or erasure of fundamental constitutional norms does not readily occur. More generally, in the competition and clash of norms that characterize law in any society, constitutional norms are those that tend in practice to prevail against and outlast the others.

(iii) Sociological legitimacy. Elster's third criterion describes how some laws are collectively referred to as 'the constitution'.[15] More generally, there may be a widespread societal perception that some norms are constitutionally legitimate: that people view the norms as warranting constitutional status. In the constitutional literature, such notions of 'popular approval' and of 'the way in which public authority is justified' most commonly come under the label of 'sociological legitimacy'.[16] According to an account by Blokker,

> [a] constitutional sociology endorses the study of constitutions beyond a predominantly legalistic analysis (in which there is a largely internalistic perspective on constitutions) . . . and emphasizes the functional correspondence of constitutions to a variety of societal needs as well as studying the

[13] Kimmo Grönlund, 'Designing Mini-Publics for Constitutional Deliberative Democracy' in Min Reuchamps and Jane Suiter (eds), *Constitutional Deliberative Democracy in Europe* (ECPR Press 2016) 109.

[14] Chapter 1.

[15] Elster (n 5) 366–67. See similarly Hart (n 9) 97–120; Max Weber, *Wirtschaft und Gesellschaft* (Johannes Winckelmann ed, 5th edn, Tübingen 1972) 29.

[16] Joseph HH Weiler, *The Constitution of Europe* (CUP 1999) 80. See similarly Andrew Arato, *Civil Society, Constitution, and Legitimacy* (Rowman & Littlefield Publishers 2000). A cognate term is 'political legitimacy': John-Erik Fossum and Hans-Jörg Trenz, 'The EU's Fledgling Society: From Deafening Silence to Critical Voice in European Constitution-Making' (2006) 2(1) Journal of Civil Society 57, 59.

contextual and historical differences in the emergence of constitutions and constitutionalism.[17]

Notably, when we take societal perceptions on board, we ask measurable empirical questions about whether and when constitutional norms bind in practice. In later sections we will report on public opinion studies gauging sociological legitimacy and related terms such as trust. Descriptions of patterns of behaviour of large groups of individuals are sociological descriptions essential for understanding the successes—or otherwise—of constitutional settlements after peacemaking.[18]

Beyond Elster's three criteria, we also want to know more about what makes something specifically a constitutional *norm*, as later on we will focus on possible processes for forming such norms. A constitutional norm (or a set of such norms) must be *discrete* and *exclusive* as against all others. This is because a constitutional norm's overarching objective is to organize an ordered system[19]—to be a linchpin among the rules required to govern political and social relations stably and to minimize discord. Constitutional norms must therefore be relatively few and discrete; rather than bleed into one another as on a continuum, each needs to be relatively bounded. They must be capable of clearing the field around them of alternative kinds of legal or social action and, once established, to guide action solely along these cleared paths.[20]

Granted, such observations can also apply to other kinds of norms. To give an everyday example, two conductors at a busy traffic junction working independently of each other could hardly be effective. They could not function well if the boundaries separating their authorities were unclear. Nor could they if those boundaries (whether clear or unclear) substantially overlapped and had no established mechanism to resolve inconsistent behaviours.

But when we turn to constitutional norms these same worries become far more acute. Here norms must not only be discrete and exclusive within a narrow sphere of activity, but also as against all other norms in the jurisdiction. That constitutional norms are fundamental means that they establish where

[17] Paul Blokker, 'A Political-Sociological Analysis of Constitutional Pluralism in Europe' in Jiří Přibáň (ed), *Self-Constitution of European Society: Beyond EU Politics, Law and Governance* (Routledge 2016) 76.

[18] See, eg, Jürg Steiner and Maria C Jaramillo, 'How to Arrive at Peace in Deeply Divided Societies? Using Deliberation to Refine Consociational Theory' (2019) 15(3) Journal of Public Deliberation Art 9, expanding on Arend Lijphart, *The Politics of Accommodation: Pluralism and Democracy in the Netherlands* (University of California Press 1975).

[19] Lon Fuller, *The Morality of Law* (Yale University Press 1969) 210.

[20] Elisabeth Noelle-Neumann, 'The Spiral of Silence: A Theory of Public Opinion' (1974) 24(2) Journal of Communication 43 (describing such a process, but also criticizing it as coercive).

the hierarchy of norms lies (ie, how norms sit in relation to each other) and how conflict among norms ought to be approached or resolved. Generally, then, a society that effectively manages disagreements is unlikely to adopt more than one constitutional norm or system of norms.[21] In particular, only those norms that can plausibly claim to be the only ones that bind fundamentally are likely to develop enduring constitutional status. As John Carey puts the point, a

> primary job of constitutions is to resolve intractable coordination problems—for example, how political actors with diverse interests might contest for political authority on a regular basis without mutual destruction. Coordination equilibria require stable mutual expectations among actors.[22]

Of course, there is much that can prevent this. While constitutional norms are fundamental and exclusive vis-à-vis non-constitutional norms, constitutional norms do nevertheless often conflict with each other (eg, the freedom of speech may clash with rights of privacy). Many hard cases cannot be resolved in final ways but continue to be points of contestation.

In conflict societies the frequency and depth of contradictions among constitutional norms can be more pronounced. Here norm conflict may reflect not merely interpretive disagreement but outright fracture, in the sense of groups' lack of shared support for a single authoritative set of norms.[23] Deep social or political divisions may manifest as debates about which norms should be recognized as fundamentally and exclusively binding. For example, multiple groups may claim constitutional sovereignty within the same territorial space. The Northern Irish case is again emblematic. As we said in past chapters, a main problem that aggravated the conflict for decades and prevented its settlement was the parties' lack of recognition of each other's constitutional legitimacy. Two mutually exclusive constitutional projects (ie, British unionism and Irish nationalism) ran alongside each other, without a recognized way of bridging the normative expectations of each—nor therefore of managing the inevitable conflicts that arose on the ground as a consequence of maintaining both at once. The establishment of new norms amid conflict must somehow overcome this kind of pronounced tendency towards fracture.

[21] John M Carey, 'Does It Matter How a Constitution is Created?' in Zoltan Barany and Robert G Moser (eds), *Is Democracy Exportable?* (CUP 2009) 158.

[22] ibid 158, 160.

[23] David Easton, 'A Re-Assessment of the Concept of Political Support' (1975) 5(4) British Journal of Political Science 435, 444–47; Kent Greenawalt, 'The Rule of Recognition and the Constitution' (1987) 85(4) Michigan Law Review 621, 624.

Complicating matters even further, existing constitutional norms—even though they may be disparate and mutually contradictory—often create formidable barriers that must be cleared before new norms can take over. Except in rare cases (eg, where a society is newly established and is, constitutionally speaking, a blank slate), creating norms entails overcoming the 'inertia'[24] and 'status quo bias'[25] of existing norms. Often, people empowered by the existing fractured regime, such as government and insurgent leaders, resist constitutional changes. Other people, too, may fear that any constitutional reform will merely produce even more pronounced circumstances of social disorder.[26]

The challenges of establishing new constitutional norms in a conflict setting are thus formidable. Yet how have constitutional settlements sometimes still managed to push existing norms aside and become established themselves, and even to endure? In the next two sections we will focus on explanations that look, in turn, at the kinds of process that may yield norms with distinctively constitutional forms and content, and on the kinds that may confer sociological legitimacy per se.

III. Referendums and Constitutional Exclusivity

A successful process of constitutional reform can be one that exposes an agreement that has coalesced around just one norm or set of norms out of a number of contenders. At least since the French Second Empire, referendums have been used (sometimes successfully) to try to secure agreements leading to new constitutional norms, often over the heads of certain elites.[27] Peace referendums have occasionally been effective at corralling elites who would otherwise oppose or actively try to spoil a peacemaking effort, yet who would dare not ignore a clear popular agreement.[28] Loizides recalls Charles de Gaulle's referendum of 1961, which gave him a mandate to pursue Algerian independence and peace: de Gaulle 'received a massive [75] per cent "yes" vote and proceeded

[24] John Bell and David J Ibbetson, *European Legal Development: The Case of Tort* (CUP 2012) 48.

[25] Daniel Kahneman, Jack L Knetsch, and Richard H Thaler, 'Anomalies: The Endowment Effect, Loss Aversion, and Status Quo Bias' (1991) 5(1) Journal of Economic Perspectives 193.

[26] ibid 194–99.

[27] See, eg, AV Dicey, *Introduction to the Study of the Law of the Constitution* (5th edn, Macmillan 1897) 406. Setälä's review of *non-conflict* Western European cases found that a 'majority of the parliamentarians have followed the results' of even ostensibly non-binding referendums: Maija Setälä, 'On the Problems of Responsibility and Accountability in Referendums' (2006) 45(4) European Journal of Political Research 699, 713.

[28] In a number of cases, referendums have instead—or at the same time—been used to buttress the personal rule of a given leader: Albert Weale, *The Will of the People: A Modern Myth* (Polity 2018) 107.

to implement his policies to negotiate with Algerians, sidelining army radicals and *pied-noir* resistance in the process'.[29] In another example, though the hardline Democratic Unionist Party had aggressively opposed the Belfast Agreement in Northern Ireland, after a referendum overwhelmingly affirmed the Agreement the party conformed to the new constitutional arrangements.[30]

A social agreement exposed in a referendum can ground the norm exclusivity that we are after. Even among groups in conflict, there may be general agreement on the need to replace the status quo with a constitutional settlement in order to secure peace. There may even be some broad terms of agreement about the substance of such a settlement. In either case, the agreement is exclusive if it entails the abandonment of alternative possible norms—that is, norms that oppose settlement, or that call for a settlement on substantially different terms.

As we said previously, such an agreement may be latent in a conflict society.[31] But majority preferences for settlement may not otherwise have been visible, nor widely believed, had the referendum not revealed them.[32] Even in those cases where only a few voters actually change their minds during the referendum campaign, the referendum may still bring exclusivity to a social debate about peacemaking by clarifying that agreement already exists. In the referendum held in 1992 among White South Africans—a referendum meant to give President de Klerk a mandate to pursue settlement and end Apartheid—the eventual 'landslide victory' had not been anticipated.[33] One source of doubt stemmed from the need to get potentially intransigent rural Afrikaners on board. The eventual result surprised de Klerk's 'own party officials who had predicted a 55% "yes" majority, at best, well below the 68.7% he received'.[34] A consequence of the referendum was the greater public visibility that it provided to the existing, and overwhelming, majority sentiment in favour of constitutional reform and peacemaking. Against the assumptions of

[29] Neophytos Loizides, 'Negotiated Settlements and Peace Referendums' (2014) 53(2) European Journal of Political Research 234, 243. Referendums also later took place in France and Algeria to endorse the Évian Accords, with results, respectively, of 90.1% and 99.7% in favour.

[30] The DUP contested an election in 1998 under the new arrangements: Paul Mitchell, Brendan O'Leary, and Geoffrey Evans, 'Northern Ireland: Flanking Extremists Bite the Moderates and Emerge in Their Clothes' (2001) 54(4) Parliamentary Affairs 725, 725–26.

[31] Chapters 2 and 3.

[32] Majority voting can also be used to test whether what appears to be a deliberative consensus really is a consensus (eg, some people may simply not have spoken up): Alfred Moore and Kieran O'Doherty, 'Deliberative Voting: Clarifying Consent in a Consensus Process' (2014) 22(3) Journal of Political Philosophy 302, 306–07. See also Hanspeter Kriesi and Alexander H Trechsel, *The Politics of Switzerland: Continuity and Change in a Consensus Democracy* (CUP 2008) 62–63.

[33] Loizides (n 29) 239.

[34] ibid.

many, conciliatory sentiments had flourished even after (or perhaps because of) an extensive experience of conflict.

Ideally, the agreement exposed in a referendum should not be much in doubt. It may be useful for a referendum to have modest requirements for a supermajority or a 'timed double-majority',[35] to prevent reforms going ahead based on bare and possibly transient majority support. As noted in the last chapter, the ideal model would also require majority support within *each* of the main groups in conflict, or 'concurrent consent'. We are seeking agreement among members of each group in conflict, and not just among people who are part of a numerically dominant group.

Conflict is often accompanied in media and popular discourses by a prevailing cynicism about peacemaking's prospects. This can cause us to overestimate how widespread and intractable the conflict really is. Elites and non-elites alike may doubt the appetite of others besides themselves for a settlement. General popular sentiment may be read through the polarized lenses of overheated media and political commentaries, and of vocal absolutists online.[36] A relatively small number of people (elites and non-elites) often dominate public discussion and set the rhetorical tenor of politics with trolling, group-targeting, and other heated forms of speech.[37] In the outrage cycle of contemporary media, mutual opponents express not only disagreement with each other, but escalating claims of moral failing, deceit, and betrayal.[38] In this context, widespread doubts about the social capacity for agreement are understandable, and even inevitable.

Those who doubt the appetite of others for peacemaking, however, may still favour it themselves. Even in what appear to be the most intractable of cases, such as the Israeli-Palestinian conflict, we find a majority of people open to peacemaking.[39] A referendum may spotlight those often more conciliatory, usually unexpressed views of the greater part of a population. Results such as voters' 71.1 per cent and 94.4 per cent endorsement of the Belfast Agreement in Northern Ireland and Ireland, respectively, ultimately revealed certain prominent and bellicose leaders to be outliers. This is a familiar phenomenon outside of conflict too. Votes calling for legally recognized same-sex marriage in

[35] See Chapter 6.

[36] See, eg, Camilla Orjuela, 'Distant Warriors, Distant Peace Workers? Multiple Diaspora Roles in Sri Lanka's Violent Conflict' (2008) 8(4) Global Networks 436, 443–44.

[37] Matthew Levendusky, 'Partisan Media Exposure and Attitudes Toward the Opposition' (2013) 30(4) Political Communication 565, 567, 577.

[38] See Sarah Sobieraj and Jeffrey M Berry, 'From Incivility to Outrage: Political Discourse in Blogs, Talk Radio, and Cable News' (2011) 28(1) Political Communication 19, 19–20.

[39] Palestinian Center for Policy and Survey Research and Tami Steinmetz Center for Peace Research, Tel Aviv University, 'The Palestinian-Israeli Pulse: A Joint Poll' (June–July 2017).

Ireland and Australia, in 2016 and 2017, respectively, were surprising to many (even though opinion polls had long shown high levels of public agreement).[40] Pockets of fierce homophobic rhetoric in the campaigns helped to sour debate and generate doubt; yet final votes of over 60 per cent in both countries made for prominent, perhaps indelible statements of popular support.[41]

But exposure of agreement may still not be particularly likely when we throw voters into a referendum without adequate institutional support for deliberation. In order to establish constitutional norms with the potential to endure, we may need those norms to lay out the kind of content that allows people to find that the differences between them are not fundamental. Public-value deliberation is relatively suited to such a partial reconciliation of norms. Here we rely on our accounts of public reason in earlier chapters, which we will not reproduce in full. But recall briefly why we said that framing deliberation in public-value terms can facilitate agreement. It is a minimalist approach that does not suppose that constitutional norms must be based on comprehensive unity of outlook or identification between groups. It does not seek to resolve all value tensions and divides. The approach seeks only to enshrine a set of fundamental governing public values—values that can be reasonably agreed to by everyone, whatever their more comprehensive doctrines or beliefs.

From the design of the ballot to the official information and deliberations provided for in the campaign, any referendum frames debate. A key role for a DPR should be to use the opportunity this affords to structure debate to make agreement more likely. A DPR should thus seek to concentrate deliberation around public values in order to facilitate agreement. It may expose agreement at that level, even when people may be otherwise unable (as yet) to agree on the specifics of the content of constitutional settlement. Agreed public values could include equality, mutual respect, liberty, and the like. In addition, more process-oriented public values can establish how, in principle, ongoing disagreements—the inevitable remnants of conflict—ought to be approached. For instance, these values could include commitments to voting rather than violence, and to achieving democratic consensus between dominant groups and other groups (eg, the property and minority rights protections in the South African settlement).[42]

[40] Barbara Baird, 'Twenty-First Century LGBTI Activism in Australia: The Limits of Equality' (2018) 49(4) Australian Historical Studies 475. On Ireland, see Johan A Elkink and others, 'Understanding the 2015 Marriage Referendum in Ireland: Context, Campaign, and Conservative Ireland' (2017) 32(3) Irish Political Studies 361, 367–78.

[41] In Australia, after several years of stalled efforts in Parliament, legalization finally occurred just seventeen days after the ostensibly non-binding public vote: Baird (n 40).

[42] Loizides (n 29) 239.

Importantly, then, by focusing on public values the parties may come to an exclusive agreement—at a fundamental level no less, as Rawls in particular hoped—in spite of still prevalent normative conflict of other kinds. As we saw in Chapter 2, in a given conflict there may be just a few areas of agreement, if indeed there are any. But finding agreement is in any case most plausible at the level of public values.[43] And as we saw in Chapter 3, by prioritizing public values a DPR can encourage conceptual ascent. A well-designed and executed DPR may thus reframe deliberation to alight on those few places where agreement is most likely to exist. Among a DPR's most important benefits, then, is exposure of a single, fundamental, and public-value based agreement between groups—an agreement that may possess the exclusivity that we are after.

Of course, as we said, at one level even public values still conflict with each other. A priori, we cannot say with certainty where the balance between such values should lie in concrete cases. Since no public value clearly takes precedence over all others, in one sense constitutional exclusivity is still elusive. Yet generally this is only so in the *application* of the values—that is, when we interpret public values and propose how they should work out in concrete cases. As we said in previous chapters, however, such reasoning involves conceptual descent, which a DPR seeks to minimize.

Our expectation is therefore that, if it is carefully designed and executed, a DPR can recast debate in public-value terms and expose an existing, exclusive agreement between groups. Admittedly, other democratic options might sometimes do the same: majoritarian democracy generally relies on the conceit that the considered choices of the majority are adopted by the whole collective, and this, in theory, may also be a source of exclusive agreement.[44] A majority vote within a legislature or constitutional convention (a conclave of, usually, political elites) may, then, perhaps establish a putative constitutional norm's exclusivity just as well. But it is important to recall, as we argued at length in Chapter 2, that popular agreement is often more feasible than elite agreement—especially at the level of public values, and especially amid conflict.

Moreover, and ironically, one of the features often derided in a referendum—its simplicity—may actually benefit the clarity of popular expressions in support of settlement. A referendum either poses binary 'yes'/ 'no' questions or adopts a marginally more complex ranked-choice approach.

[43] Christine Blakeley, 'Conflict and Deliberation' in Stephen Elstub and Peter Mclaverty (eds), *Deliberative Democracy: Issues and Cases* (Edinburgh University Press 2014) 29.
[44] Moore and O'Doherty (n 32) 304–05.

In either case, one of the salutary consequences of running a referendum is, as Dicey argued, the referendum's relatively straightforward expressions of popular sentiment.[45] The decisions of legislative or convention bodies, and of any popular elections that constituted those bodies, are by contrast 'over-determined'.[46] (Elections, especially, often bundle together a voter's discrete views about diverse policy issues, as well as of the merits of those running for office.) Ambiguity and under-theorization in legislation is, in part for these reasons, inevitable.[47] But according to Dicey, a referendum avoids some interpretive confusion by fixing on—and authoritatively expressing a voting public's agreement about—a discrete policy matter. He perhaps overstates the point; after all, voters may have myriad reasons for supporting a given outcome.[48] But a referendum at least confines the policy outcomes that it endorses to a relatively small set. And a DPR, in particular, may provide tallies of public-value rankings that point to reasons for those outcomes that voters broadly share.

To be sure, it is also possible that any peace referendum, and not just a DPR, may facilitate the exposure of agreement. Many of the examples on which we have relied in fact did not see referendums use most, if any, of the DPR design principles outlined in Chapter 3. Thus even standard referendums may be effective at exposing agreement. However, as we have stressed, improving referendum design according to DPR principles may make public-value deliberation and thus exposure of agreement substantially more likely.

Still, we must consider whether merely exposing an exclusive agreement is sufficient. Does bringing an agreement to light suffice to displace existing constitutional norms, and to install new norms, based on that agreement, in their place? We will suggest next that it may not be: that what may also be required to secure a constitutional settlement is some further impetus or act—one, especially, that can confer constitutional legitimacy in a sociological sense.

[45] AV Dicey, 'Ought the Referendum to be Introduced into England?' (1890) 57 Contemporary Review 489, 495.

[46] Ron Levy and Graeme Orr, *The Law of Deliberative Democracy* (Routledge 2016) 92.

[47] Harry W Jones, 'Statutory Doubts and Legislative Intention' (1940) 40(6) Columbia Law Review 957, 959–63.

[48] eg, they may focus on 'the popularity or unpopularity of a particular party or leader': Lawrence LeDuc, 'Referendums and Deliberative Democracy' (2015) 38 Electoral Studies 139, 141.

IV. Referendums and Sociological Legitimation

A. Sources of Legitimation

Beyond merely exposing an agreement, the DPR may also legitimate the particular agreement that it exposes. Even in circumstances where intercommunal distrust and violence are established, a DPR may sometimes be able to apply a reset. Normative arguments and empirical clues below will suggest that a DPR may be a relatively sociologically legitimate process able to mark a particular constitutional norm out as worthy of adoption as a foundational commitment. As we will describe shortly, this effect may stem from the DPR's reliance on deliberative popular legitimation. We will also look at several other sources of sociological legitimation that a constitutional reform process might invoke.

As a preliminary observation, note that evidence of a pattern of conduct may assist in the formation of a constitutional norm. Evidence that the conduct has been fundamental over a long period may engender a perception that the conduct reflects a constitutionally legitimate rule. There may also be a recursive relation here: if evidence of fundamentality and endurance helps to solidify the sociological recognition of a norm's constitutional legitimacy, this in turn may reinforce the view that a norm, being constitutional, should be fundamental and enduring—and so on.[49]

But such circularity poses a problem. How might new constitutional norms develop in the first place, even against the inertia and headwinds of contrary norms? We look here to potential *non-normative* and *normative sources* of legitimation, inquiring into whether either kind may help to lock new norms into place. (We use 'normative' in this context not as a norm's adjectival form, but as an independent moral or philosophical rationale for authority.) Our conclusion will be that normative content may give stronger backing to the sociological legitimacy and the enduring establishment of a constitutional settlement.

(1) Non-normative sources

Non-normative sources can have roles in constitutional legitimation. However, these sources leave little room for individual and group agency, and particularly for the normative choices of individuals or groups. Instead the sources focus merely on whether there is evidence of past practice consistent with the norm, or whether a perceived obligation to comply attaches to the norm.

[49] On the self-recursive function of norms generally, see Cass R Sunstein, 'Social Norms and Social Roles' (1996) 96(4) Columbia Law Review 903, 912.

(i) Coercion: One putative non-normative source of legitimation recognizes that norms may gain momentum in the first place through the imposition of some external force.[50] Constitutional norms have indeed become established where a conquering or colonizing power enacted the norms—typically backed by military might—against people who neither consented to the norms nor could reasonably have been expected to. Many of the state boundaries that emerged after the twentieth century's major wars still persist, for instance, even though the boundaries were initially the arbitrary consequences of negotiations among victorious states or state-like entities.[51] Given the path-dependency of constitutional norms, coercion may be one plausible way of starting to build a norm up—even perhaps a norm of constitutional settlement. Coercion may begin a cycle of legitimation by forcing the development of a record of past conduct consistent with the norm.

But though coercion may bring settlement of a sort, the settlement may be thin and unstable. Granted, we have seen some important, though constrained, uses of coercion in DPRs to get a process of deliberation started.[52] In addition, some coercive enforcement of the terms of settlement may be useful after the fact (eg, deploying international peacekeeping forces). But we caution against settlements that are coercive at the core. Rather than defuse tension, coercion can fuel backlash and discontent, and may renew the prospects of violence. There are some important exceptions here. For example, the victors led the drafting of what ended up being durable constitutions for some of the defeated powers after the Second World War.[53] However, coercive constitutional drafting has commonly been unsuccessful at commanding adherence (eg, Bosnia in 1994 and Iraq in 2004 and 2005).[54] High levels of coercion are incompatible with positions that we have defended in this book, such as those favouring a volitional agreement through which parties reach an accommodation of their basic values after some deliberation.

(ii) Formality: A more complex possibility for non-normative constitutional legitimation is to rely on formality alone. Indeed, when we aim to enact new constitutional provisions, we may think first of using established constitutional

[50] Weber (n 15) 29, 122.

[51] Eugene L Rogan, *The Arabs: A History* (1st edn, Basic Books 2009) 8.

[52] Chapter 3.

[53] Albert, *Constitutional Amendments* (n 3) 12. After the Second World War, new Cold War allegiances encouraged cooperation between Japan and the West: Thomas K Robb and David J Gill, *Divided Allies: Strategic Cooperation against the Communist Threat in the Asia-Pacific During the Early Cold War* (Cornell University Press 2019) 70–78.

[54] Sumantra Bose, *Bosnia After Dayton: Nationalist Partition and International Intervention* (Hurst 2002) 42–60; Andrew Arato, *Constitution Making Under Occupation: The Politics of Imposed Revolution in Iraq* (Columbia University Press 2009) 1–2, 135–39.

amending procedures: rules 'codified in the constitution for public identification'.[55] Most such procedures are onerous and present hurdles to the enactment of the norm, such as requirements for legislative supermajorities, special timing conditions, and of course referendums.[56] Once formally enacted via these avenues, new constitutional provisions may take over a field, even absent evidence of past practice consistent with the norm.[57]

We may subdivide such formal legitimation into two kinds. The first is legitimation by *pedigree*.[58] A new constitutional norm may enjoy a perception of being constitutionally legitimate by virtue of its enactment under established amending formulas that are themselves understood as legitimate. Thus sociological legitimacy can be passed down from earlier norms to later ones.[59] Notably, a number of jurisdictions include referendums among the procedures required, de jure or de facto, for constitutional reform.[60]

On a second understanding, formality can be an *expressive* process that constructs or conveys a mystique of authority. This function is also occasionally an important tool for the development of constitutional norms—importantly, even if it is ad hoc (ie, it is not embedded in any settled de jure or de facto amending formulas). This expressive process can identify which particular constitutional principles or elements should be socially recognized as fundamental and enduring. In the extreme case, a founding event or myth can even construct certain constitutional elements as part of the 'underlying natural order'[61] (eg, a story that helps build an image of the monarch as the eternal embodiment of the nation).[62] More prosaically, expressive formality

[55] Albert, *Constitutional Amendments* (n 3) 44.

[56] On timing conditions, see, eg, Richard Albert, 'Temporal Limitations in Constitutional Amendment' (2016) 21 Review of Constitutional Studies 37.

[57] See similarly Miguel P Maduro, 'The Importance of Being Called a Constitution: Constitutional Authority and the Authority of Constitutionalism' (2005) 3 International Journal of Constitutional Law 332, 354.

[58] Weber (n 15) 130.

[59] Albert, *Constitutional Amendments* (n 3) 11. As Kelsen famously observed, a problem of infinite regress arises as we must still account for the legitimacy of the original constitution existing before any amendments: Hans Kelsen, *General Theory of Law and State* (2nd edn, Anders Wedberg tr, Harvard University Press 1961) 3.

[60] See, eg, *Commonwealth of Australia Constitution Act 1900* (Imp) 63 & 64 Vict, c 12, s 9, s 128; *Federal Constitution of the Swiss Confederation of 18th April 1999* (Switzerland); *Constitution of the Italian Republic 1947* (official tr, Constitutional Court of Italy) art 138; *Constitution of Ireland 1937* (official bilingual version, Department of the Taoiseach, 1 November 2018) art 47; *Constitution of Japan 1947* (official English tr, National Diet Library, 2003–04) art 96; *Constitution of Sweden: The Instrument of Government 1974* (Sveriges Riksdag) ch 8, arts 17–18. On de facto requirements see, eg, Canada: Peter H Russell, *Constitutional Odyssey: Can Canadians Become a Sovereign People?* (2nd edn, University of Toronto Press 1993) 219; and France: Zachary Elkins and others, *The Endurance of National Constitutions* (CUP 2009) 46.

[61] For a critical view see, eg, Robert M Unger, *Social Theory: Its Situation and Its Task* (CUP 1987).

[62] See Walter Bagehot, *The English Constitution* (2nd edn, Doubleday & Co 1872) 61–74; Cris Shore and David V Williams, 'Deliberative or Performative?' in Ron Levy and others (eds), *The Cambridge Handbook of Deliberative Constitutionalism* (CUP 2018) 342–44, 350.

can refer to any process that signals the sociological legitimacy of norms by managing the symbols of constitutional creation. For example, even if their use is not required by law or convention, referendums can serve as tools for legitimation. As Carey conjectures, to 'the extent that the mere occurrence of a referendum clearly signals the adoption of a constitution, one might expect referenda to foster coordination around the new set of rules'.[63]

This illustrates an important ambiguity or fluidity in the concept of formality. Even an ad hoc referendum may amount to a formal hurdle to constitutional change—a step that must be cleared as part of a process of amendment. Since formality usually denotes adherence to custom and established orthodoxy, the notion of 'ad hoc formality' may seem a contradiction in terms. Yet, even if wholly new and intended as a one-off formality, the onerousness of a process may signal that it is constitutionally significant—methodologically separate from ordinary lawmaking, and intended to yield norms with constitutional legitimacy. The referendum is typically a rare and prominent civic event. It is also costly to run and hard to organize. Putting a matter directly to the people for their consent may express the matter's outsized, constitutional significance. Ad hoc reform procedures can thus act out a public ritual of constitutional change: a ceremony of sufficient gravity to be perceived as altering or creating fundamental norms.

But our language here must be tentative. While formality (of either subtype) can be a useful part of constitutional legitimation and endurance, on its own it can be insufficient. Amid conflict, especially, the scenarios of formal constitutional reform above may be less realistic. 'Formality' is always a matter of degree: even notionally codified constitutional amending procedures must be supported by customs of compliance.[64] But amid conflict, especially, there is often a mismatch between a codified constitutional text and its real-world effects.[65] Customs of compliance will tend to be lacking where the sociological legitimacy of laws, institutions, or political leaders is either low or uneven. Amid conflict, institutions and leaders may more often be corrupt, and the

[63] Carey (n 21) 176. cf the European Commission for Democracy through Law (Venice Commission), *Report on Constitutional Amendment* (11–12 December 2009) CDL-AD (2010) 001, 6.

[64] Groups ignore codified procedures from time to time when doing so seems propitious. Constitutional foundings under revolutionary circumstances have especially tended to cause a break in the chain of formal change (eg, the US Constitution's post-conflict founding contrary to the Articles of Confederation): Peter C Oliver, *The Constitution of Independence: The Development of Constitutional Theory in Australia, Canada, and New Zealand* (OUP 2005) 292; Bruce Ackerman, *We the People, Volume 1: Foundations* (Belknap Press of Harvard University Press 1991) 168, 175.

[65] On such mismatches, see, eg, Albert, *Constitutional Amendments* (n 3) 51; David S Law and Mila Versteeg, 'Sham Constitutions' (2013) 101 California Law Review 863, 899.

laws they enact may more often serve just a particular subpopulation; hence the sociological legitimacy of a formal process of reform may be particularly elusive or uneven.

Amid conflict, there is ultimately little guarantee that a process that is meant to legitimize a new constitutional norm—merely by providing formal backing to it—will do so effectively. A key element of this problem is that formality (again, of either type) is an unusually nebulous legitimacy source. It focuses on constitutional endurance and on erecting hurdles to reform. Yet it does not provide a specific rationale to justify the endurance. There is only the bare and generic rationale of imposing a stable order through the establishment of a new constitutional norm—a rationale that is common to constitutional norms in general. The formality does not in itself indicate why one norm, and not another, should assume its place within a network of norms. Given the precariousness of formal constitutional reform amid conflict, formality—at least on its own—can be insufficient.

To establish a new constitutional norm it may be best if we can identify a specific normative logic of legitimation behind the norm.[66] For instance, where referendums are held as part of a constitutional reform process, they are not (usually) just empty formalities, but may manifest popular sovereignty or consent. In this way, referendums may sometimes help to overcome the inertia of existing norms. Our perspective here matches that of David Beetham, who applies a chiefly sociological lens to ask which norms actually command adherence, but who also recognizes that these social perceptions stem in part from beliefs about normative content—that is, from specific reasons why a given norm should bind.[67]

Beetham criticizes Max Weber's normatively empty sociological account, which leaves little room for a consideration of why people feel that a particular authority was justified. Weber relies on formal pedigree, or on a 'juridical answer [regarding] the source of the rules or laws in question'; however, a 'second kind of answer—a normative or philosophical one—looks to . . . principles about the rightful source of authority for political power'.[68] As Beetham observes:

[66] Readers may notice similarities here to customary constitutional and international law formation: Jennings (n 7) 136; Hugh Thirlway, *The Sources of International Law* (2nd edn, OUP 2019) 62–63.

[67] David Beetham, 'Max Weber and the Legitimacy of the Modern State' (1991) 13(1) Analyse & Kritik 34, 39–40. For empirical support see, eg, Tom R Tyler and Jonathan Jackson, 'Popular Legitimacy and the Exercise of Legal Authority: Motivating Compliance, Cooperation, and Engagement' (2014) 20(1) Psychology, Public Policy, and Law 78.

[68] Beetham (n 67) 40.

> It is the failure to provide any account at all of the normative (as opposed to the juridical) legitimation of the law that invalidates Weber's account of political legitimacy. . . . Weber's account omits elements that are necessary to a social-scientific analysis of legitimacy, since they relate to dimensions of what people actually believe and to principles that are actually embodied in constitutional rules.[69]

Like Beetham, we adopt a view of constitutional legitimation that identifies how, as an empirical matter, normative rationales can help to drive the creation of new constitutional norms.[70] These normative rationales are elementary principles on which constitutional legitimacy can find its foundation.

(2) Normative sources

Let us therefore look at several normative sources of constitutional sociological legitimation. We may generally discount two of these, *(i) divinity* and *(ii) elite authority*, for peacemaking purposes. Some constitutional reform processes expressly invoke spiritual traditions and values.[71] And some reforms rely on procedures that centre on experts, legislatures, and even monarchs, and justify these choices based on elites' presumed superior deliberation.[72] Yet while invoking the non-public, comprehensive value of divine authority could in some circumstances assist peacemaking, at best this is uncertain: spiritual cleavages have at least as often been the causes of abject conflict.[73] As for elite authority, the main thrust of Chapter 2, again, was that elite processes are commonly less viable than non-elite deliberations for constitutional settlement.

Other normative sources of legitimation may fare better. One is *(iii) international legitimation*. For instance, the sovereignty of new states requires the express endorsement of the international community.[74] As a source of legitimacy,

[69] ibid.

[70] But cf other theories of legitimacy that downplay the sociological angle: see, eg, Rawls, *Political Liberalism* (n 11) 137. Most, however, take it on board at least in part: see, eg, Ronald Dworkin, *Law's Empire* (Belknap Press of Harvard University Press 1986) 255–63.

[71] See, eg, Baogang He, Laura Allison-Reumann, and Michael Breen, 'The Politics of Secular Federalism and the Federal Governance of Religious Diversity in Asia' (2018) 46(4) Federal Law Review 575.

[72] See, eg, Joseph Schumpeter, *Capitalism, Socialism and Democracy* (3rd edn, Harper & Row 1950) ch XXII. Legislative sovereignty can also be derived from popular sovereignty: see, eg, AV Dicey: 'The Referendum' (1894) 23 National Review 65, 70.

[73] Matthias Basedau, Birte Pfeiffer, and Johannes Vüllers, 'Bad Religion? Religion, Collective Action, and the Onset of Armed Conflict in Developing Countries' (2016) 60(2) Journal of Conflict Resolution 226; Matthew Isaacs, 'Sacred Violence or Strategic Faith? Disentangling the Relationship between Religion and Violence in Armed Conflict' (2016) 53(2) Journal of Peace Research 211; Isak Svensson, 'Fighting with Faith: Religion and Conflict Resolution in Civil Wars' (2007) 51(6) Journal of Conflict Resolution 930.

[74] See Chapter 6.

such recognition may actually be derivative of other sources, such as formality (new states must clear elaborate obstacles),[75] elitism (ambassadors, UN delegates, and the like engage in closed-door negotiations) or even popular sovereignty (statehood requires the consent of the wider community of states). But international legitimation also has a distinctive form: it has a 'relational' aspect, in that one state's claims to sovereignty entail a give-and-take with other states in the international community (eg, a state that secedes takes a part of the sovereignty of another state with it).

Finally, contemporary theories of governance generally have a place for *(iv) popular legitimation*.[76] Popular sovereignty is a widely cited normative source of legitimacy, and arguably even a 'global normative entitlement'.[77] We might expect that in some revolutionary conflicts aiming for political systems other than liberal democracy (eg, Marxism or Maoism), popular legitimation would have less influence. And indeed there may be variation from place to place. But even the authority in authoritarian states is frequently, at least in the national imaginary, derived from the people's sovereignty (eg, in so-called 'People's Republics' and some varieties of populist governance).[78] There are myriad cases of authoritarian governments co-opting the language and symbols of popular sovereignty, even holding referendums, to shore up their regimes.[79] For as Kenneth Boulding reminds us, the 'powerful are always under some obligation to represent the mass, even under dictatorial regimes'.[80]

Some early and influential modern articulations of the notion that constitutions and public power should ultimately be grounded on the people's sovereignty arose during the American and French revolutions.[81] For instance,

[75] See similarly Martin Loughlin, *The Idea of Public Law* (OUP 2003) 90.

[76] See, eg, *United Nations Declaration of Human Rights* art 21; Beetham (n 67) 39.

[77] Thomas M Franck, 'The Emerging Right to Democratic Governance' (1992) 86(1) American Journal of International Law 46.

[78] See, eg, Benjamin Moffitt, 'Contemporary Populism and "The People" in the Asia-Pacific Region' in Carlos De la Torre (ed), *The Promise and Perils of Populism: Global Perspectives* (University Press of Kentucky 2014) 296.

[79] Carl Schmitt claimed that 'a dictator, "as a single trusted representative", could use plebiscites to "decide in the name of the people"': *The Crisis of Parliamentary Democracy* (Ellen Kennedy tr, MIT Press 1988) 34, quoted in Matt Qvortrup, *The Referendum and Other Essays on Constitutional Politics* (Bloomsbury Publishing 2019) 37. Qvortrup traces some of the paradoxes here, including that a manipulated plebiscite in a dictatorship draws on popular consensus even as it compels such consensus: at 41. Of course, all this 'in reality . . . may be only a façade': Albert, *Constitutional Amendments* (n 3) 50. See also Jorge González-Jácome, 'Authoritarianism and the Narrative Power of Constitutionalism in Venezuela' in Helena A García and Günter Frankenberg (eds), *Authoritarian Constitutionalism: Comparative Analysis and Critique* (Edward Elgar 2019) 150–52; Anita Breuer, 'Policymaking by Referendum in Presidential Systems: Evidence from the Bolivian and Colombian Cases' (2008) 50(4) Latin American Politics and Society 59, 60.

[80] Kenneth E Boulding, 'National Images and International Systems' (1959) 3(2) Journal of Conflict Resolution 120, 121.

[81] James Madison, 'The Federalist No. 49' in Clinton Rossiter (ed), *The Federalist Papers* (New American Library 1961) 313.

Emmanuel-Joseph Sieyès described the constituent power,[82] an idea that continues to influence continental European and, more recently, Anglo-American constitutional commentary.[83] A key precept for Sieyès was that state and constitutional authority derive from a largely inviolable will of the united people or nation. This constituent power in turn creates constituted powers—including constitutional laws and elite institutions—to help administer the state. Drawing on social contract theory, at least as he saw it,[84] Sieyès reasoned that the constituent power was premised on the continuing existence of the people, as a whole rather than individually, in a state of nature. This people should remain unfettered when collectively expressing its will. In Chapter 5, we will consider again this notion of democratic *unity*, which many (including ourselves) dismiss as artificial. We will show why we prefer an alternative, more realistic and flexible, view: the *democratic constitutionalist* perspective.

Yet for now our question is what popular sovereignty, on either notion, concretely entails for the process of constitutional reform. Most of all, is a referendum required for popular legitimacy?[85] Some revolutionary leaders in France assumed so when they called a popular vote to endorse the new Jacobin constitution in 1793. The use of referendums and plebiscites continued thereafter, including in the Imperial era. Yet others—Sieyès included—disapproved and assumed that a deliberative and representative assembly could express popular preferences better than direct popular voting ever could.[86] Ordinary citizens were thought to lack the necessary knowledge of legal and governmental affairs.[87] Direct popular rule also ran the risk that, absent the moderating influence of elites, lay citizens would sort into divisive voting blocs based on lines of region, religion, class, etc. Elite leadership might therefore better translate popular sentiments into coherent and concrete forms of positive law.

Even as early revolutionaries pioneered theories of popular constitutional authorship, then, some sought to curb the theories' practical expression. In

[82] Emmanuel J Sieyès, *Qu'est-ce que le Tiers-État?* (Edme Champion ed, Presses Universitaires de France 1982).

[83] Loughlin (n 75); Joel Colón-Ríos, 'The Legitimacy of the Juridical: Constituent Power, Democracy, and the Limits of Constitutional Reform' (2010) 48 Osgoode Hall Law Journal 199; Stephen Tierney, 'Sovereignty and Crimea: How Referendum Democracy Complicates Constituent Power in Multinational Societies' (2015) 16(3) German Law Journal 523.

[84] cf Locke, whose emphasis is on individual rights (especially property rights): John Locke, *Two Treatises of Government* (Peter Laslett ed, CUP 1988).

[85] Stephen Tierney, *Constitutional Referendums: The Theory and Practice of Republican Deliberation* (OUP 2012) 55.

[86] Emmanuel J Sieyès, *Vues sur les moyens d'execution dont les representans de la France pourront disposer en 1789*, 31–37; Sieyès, *Qu'est-ce que le Tiers-Etat?* (n 82) 72.

[87] A similar worry is evident in Jean-Jacques Rousseau, 'Du contrat social' in *Oeuvres completes* (GDH Cole tr, Bibliotheque de la Pleiade, 1964) bk 1, 31, 33.

the United States, except in certain radical corners,[88] a referendum was not assumed to be a requirement for an act of constitutional creation. The act was instead seen as best realized by voting within elite conventions or representative legislatures. Many later observers similarly derided methods of direct democracy as unschooled and minimally deliberative.[89] In this light, the idea of popular legitimacy falls short as a rationale for constitutional referendums. It does not unequivocally recommend referendums because it leaves questions unanswered about which model of democracy best manifests popular sovereignty.

Empirical studies often bring us to a similar impasse. For instance, Zachary Elkins and his co-authors found that when democracy features in the process of formation of constitutional norms, this seems to promote norm endurance.[90] Similarly, Carey's comparative study of constitutional endurance in sixty-six countries found that constitutions were half as likely to change soon after enactment if they originated from 'constitutional moments involving the most inclusive elected assemblies'.[91] Yet these results simply recap the problem we have identified: given the presumed deliberative faults of non-elite deliberation, does democratic decision-making via elite bodies establish popular consent better than the people's own expressions could? Or are referendums preferable? And, more especially, does this depend on the types of referendums that we have in mind? After all, within the genus 'referendum' there are many species.

Elkins and his co-authors sensibly remind us that the origins and design of a constitution are not the only factors behind constitutional endurance. But 'with respect to both human and constitutional mortality, it is more imperative to understand those conditions we can do something about than those we cannot'.[92] We agree. While a host of 'environmental' factors (eg, 'wars, economic crises, and the like') also of course impact on constitutional endurance, most of these are beyond the capacity of institutional designers to influence—at least directly.[93] Where there is significant and immediate give is at the point of design of the process or content of constitutional reform. We turn next,

[88] James S Fishkin, *When the People Speak: Deliberative Democracy and Public Consultation* (OUP 2009) 18 (discussing revolutionary Rhode Island).

[89] See, eg, Sir Henry Sumner Maine, *Popular Government: Four Essays* (New York H Holt 1886); Benjamin Moffitt and Simon Tormey, 'Rethinking Populism: Politics, Mediatisation and Political Style' (2014) 62(2) Political Studies 381, 392.

[90] Elkins and others, *The Endurance of National Constitutions* (n 60) ch 4 identifying 'democratic inclusiveness' (of both a constitution and its originating process), 'flexibility' and 'specificity' as affecting endurance.

[91] Carey (n 21) 172; See also Ian O'Flynn and Nicole Curato, 'Deliberative Democratization: A Framework for Systemic Analysis' (2015) 36(3) Policy Studies 298.

[92] Elkins and others (n 60) 3.

[93] ibid.

uniquely, to consider normative arguments and empirical data regarding the potential of DPRs as instruments of deliberative popular legitimation.

B. DPRs and Deliberative Popular Legitimation

(1) The realization thesis

In this last main section of the present chapter we develop what we call the *realization thesis*. On the one hand, referendums can widen the scope of democracy in a constitutional reform process, and this in principle may result in more legitimate and lasting reforms. Referendum democracy is indeed often perceived as an ideal, undiluted expression of popular sovereignty.[94] On the other hand, in practice the ideal is often set aside due to referendums' habitual deliberative faults. Yet since they are purposefully designed to be *deliberative referendums*, DPRs may address longstanding doubts about referendum deliberation—doubts that, as we saw, arose at the outset of the modern democratic era and never really abated. The crux of the realization thesis, then, is that when referendums include institutional supports for deliberation, the referendums may at long last be genuinely legitimating.

Our arguments here are admittedly speculative. They are based on normative reasoning and on suggestive empirical data. We cannot empirically examine our preferred DPR model directly; some partial exceptions aside, that model (detailed in Chapter 3) has yet to run. Next best are empirical clues about the features of a putative constitutional reform process that may influence sociological legitimation. We will rely mostly on evidence about the *trust* that various elite and non-elite groups have in specific values, actors, or institutions of constitutional reform. Trust is a less abstruse and multivalent term than legitimacy, and more widely cognizable. In both academic and general parlance, trust denotes a willingness to transfer to someone or something else the responsibility for what are often vital decisions, and an expectation that the power will be exercised in salutary ways.[95] Hence trust is 'a bet about the future contingent actions of others'.[96] As Tom Tyler has demonstrated in assorted contexts, the more people trust an official decision-making process, the more likely it is that the results of the process will be seen as legitimate, and that

[94] Richard A Posner, *Law, Pragmatism, and Democracy* (Harvard University Press 2005) 167; cf the recent interest in 'democratic innovations': see, eg, Graham Smith, *Democratic Innovations: Designing Institutions for Citizen Participation* (CUP 2009); Stephen Elstub and Oliver Escobar (eds), *The Handbook of Democratic Innovation and Governance* (Edward Elgar 2019).

[95] Karen Jones, 'Trust as an Affective Attitude' (1996) 107(1) Ethics 4, 5.

[96] Piotr Sztompka, *Trust: A Sociological Theory* (CUP 1999) 25.

many or most people will be content to defer to the result.[97] For constitutional settlement in particular, this may be advantageous if people come to see the issues around a conflict as closed and are disinclined to reopen them.

We will rely on data from both conflict and non-conflict societies. While deliberative-democratic faults are generally more severe in conflict societies, in Chapter 1 we noted that most faults are not unique to such societies. And as we stressed in Chapter 2, deliberation sometimes occurs in practice amid referendum-based peacemaking. Additionally, and importantly, in Chapter 3 we characterized DPRs as discrete settings within which particularly robust deliberation may occur for a brief time. Now, if we assume this latter assumption is accurate, then we want to ask how such a deliberative moment may affect trust and legitimacy in a constitutional settlement.

As in past chapters, our approach here is both institution-specific and comparative. We are interested in where the *balance of trust* lies as between alternative constitutional reform approaches, and especially between DPRs and entirely elite-led constitutional settlement procedures. Any drawbacks or criticisms of a given democratic model may be accurate as far as they go, but simplistic as long as they ignore institutional design's hard trade-offs.[98] Hence we must also account for the faults of the best available alternative.

Perhaps the best defence of elite-led decision-making is that which invokes the metaphor of a deliberative division of labour: ordinary people entrust power to governmental elites, but these elites must use that power only to filter—to rationalize and apply—the people's democratic choices.[99] This view assumes a relation of trust between people and their leaders or official decision-makers. Such trust is always precarious;[100] sometimes it may not even be warranted.[101] Still, at least for day-to-day matters, the balance of trust generally favours elites in light of their greater expertise in the arcana of law- and policy-making.

But the balance of trust markedly shifts for matters of a constitutional nature. We previously saw that constitutional reform is often value-based and

[97] Tom R Tyler, *Why People Obey the Law* (Princeton University Press 2006) 172. See also Tom R Tyler and Jonathan Jackson, 'Future Challenges in the Study of Legitimacy and Criminal Justice' in Justice Tankebe and Alison Liebling (eds), *Legitimacy and Criminal Justice: An International Exploration* (OUP 2013) 83.

[98] Robert A Dahl, *Democracy and its Critics* (Yale University Press 1989) 84.

[99] Chapter 1.

[100] E Allan Lind, 'Transparency, Trust and Public Value' in John Wanna and Sam Vincent (eds), *Opening Government: Transparency and Engagement in the Information Age* (ANU Press 2018) 87, 88.

[101] David L Ponet and Ethan J Leib, 'Fiduciary Law's Lessons for Deliberative Democracy' (2011) 91 Boston University Law Review 1249, 1256.

appropriately the preserve of non-elites.[102] In addition, when we empower elites not only to filter the values and preferences of their constituents, but to choose constitutional norms in the first instance, then the 'bet about the future contingent actions' of elites becomes riskier. Most concerningly, elites may recalibrate constitutional norms to give an enduring structural advantage to their own preferred political factions.[103] These observations become even more relevant in conflict, where elites are only more apt to rewrite political ground rules and cling to power. [104] Thus we may expect tepid (or at least uneven) trust in a wholly elite-led constitutional settlement process.

Even so, for constitutional matters the balance of trust still does not favour referendums unequivocally. Putting non-elites substantively in charge of constitutional reform via referendums raises its own distinct set of risks (eg, under-informed, capricious, exclusionary, or unfair voting). But when we take deliberative institutions into account, the balance may at last shift more firmly towards non-elites. The institutional supports in deliberative referendums may be perceived as substitutes for elite-mediated deliberation. If they are well-designed and executed, deliberative referendums may allay some of the classic worries associated with referendums. This brings us back to the realization thesis: that once we smooth off some of their harsher edges, referendums can come into their own as trusted tools of constitutional reform.

Indeed, while broad-brush studies find that even standard referendums are often well-regarded democratic tools (in both conflict and non-conflict societies),[105] when we drill deeper into such support we find that it is strongest when certain conditions for deliberation are met:

(i) *Matters of value:* Trust in constitutional referendums depends in part on the matters addressed. There is clear evidence that voters trust themselves to make decisions via referendums on matters directly concerning normative values (eg, abortion or euthanasia), and far less about elaborate political-institutional choices (eg, federal allocations of legislative responsibility).[106] These results in fact seem justified in light of what we said

[102] Chapter 2.

[103] Sanford Levinson, 'The Political Implications of Amending Clauses' (1996) 13 Constitutional Commentary 107, 114–17.

[104] See, eg, Sarwar Abdullah and others, 'Clientelism: Factionalism in the Allocation of Public Resources in Iraq after 2003' (2018) 54(4) Middle Eastern Studies 665. See also Chapter 2.

[105] Richard Wike and others, 'Democracy Widely Supported, Little Backing for Rule by Strong Leader or Military' *Pew Research Centre: Global Attitudes & Trends* (Report, 16 October 2017) 4.

[106] Paul Kildea, AJ Brown, and Jacob Deem, 'When Should the People Decide? Public Support for Direct Democracy in Australia' (2020) 73(4) Parliamentary Affairs (forthcoming).

about non-elites' relative capacities, in comparison with certain elites, for deliberating about values.[107]

(ii) *Majority-Minority Inclusion:* A main objective of deliberative democracy is to improve on bare majoritarianism to achieve something closer to consensus between majority and minority groups.[108] Indeed, more than majority rule per se, majority rule tempered by a fair and impartial process has been found to be trust-enhancing for constitutional reform.[109] Fairness may refer to a proportionate regard for the views of people affected by a reform. And impartiality generally means that a process is open to any reasonable decision without excessive partisanship or bias. Both of these deliberative hallmarks refer to the appropriate inclusion of groups and their perspectives. In any society there is a risk that political factions will 'capture the channels' of ostensibly democratic law-making for their own ends.[110] This may mean that a democratic process arbitrarily excludes certain groups, resulting in bias and unfairness. Thus Tyler and Jonathan Jackson find democratic minorities tend to buy into not just any democratic decision, but one in which minority groups are genuinely and robustly heard.[111] Similarly, according to Elkins and his co-authors, democratic inclusion encourages members of even 'losing interest groups' to feel as though they have a stake in the constitution.[112]

Deliberative referendums' efforts to broaden democracy by including minority group voices may have, therefore, special salience for legitimacy. DPRs may better include, or include more equally, minority groups both by virtue of the deliberation that happens within them, and more simply due to the rule of concurrent consent (where it is applied). In either case, DPRs may be particularly useful amid conflict, given that in conflict societies governing institutions are only more likely to be perceived as tools of clientelism and corruption, or as mouthpieces for a dominant social

[107] Chapter 2.

[108] See, eg, Jürgen Habermas, *Between Facts and Norms: Contributions to a Discourse Theory of Law and Democracy* (Willian Rehg tr, MIT Press 1996) 107; Rawls, 'The Idea of Public Reason' (n 11) 770 (on fairness); Joshua Cohen, 'Deliberative and Democratic Legitimacy' in James Bohman and William Rehg (eds), *Deliberative Democracy: Essay on Reason and Politics* (MIT Press 1997) 67, 72 (on inclusion).

[109] Ron Levy, 'Breaking the Constitutional Deadlock: Lessons from Deliberative Experiments in Constitutional Change' (2010) 34 Melbourne University Law Review 805, 834.

[110] Michael J Klarman, 'Majoritarian Judicial Review: The Entrenchment Problem' (1996) 85 Georgetown Law Journal 491, 498.

[111] Tyler and Jackson, 'Popular Legitimacy' (n 67). See also Jonathan Jackson and others, 'Why Do People Comply with the Law? Legitimacy and the Influence of Legal Institutions' (2012) 52(6) British Journal of Criminology 1051. See also, eg, John Beatty and Alfred Moore, 'Should We Aim for Consensus?' (2010) 7(3) Episteme 198, 209.

[112] Elkins and others (n 60) 81.

subpopulation that has captured government.[113] Trust in governing institutions may therefore be low to the extent that the institutions are understood as aligned with just one social sub-group, but higher when institutions such as DPRs succeed at widening the scope of democratic engagement.

(iii) *Well-informed process:* A well-informed process may enhance trust, especially among elites of various types. Balanced and accurate information is important for deliberation.[114] But information is also a basic determinant of normative legitimacy amid constitutional reform. Democratic consent is a mere fiction if it is under-informed and minimally considered.[115] As in less weighty contexts (eg, the signing of a commercial contract), amid constitutional reform an individual should first understand any relevant arguments and background before agreeing to the reform.[116]

Results specifically taking the institutional design of referendums into account also find that referendums can attract greater trust if they include support for deliberation. For instance, poll respondents better trust either hypothetical or real constitutional referendums when the referendums are led by deliberative mini-publics (in comparison with status quo models such as parliamentary leadership of referendums).[117] This appears to be an example of the realization thesis: trust increases when a referendum minimizes elite leadership but, in order to compensate for what may be lost, increases deliberative support for non-elite voters.

(2) Nuancing the realization thesis

The objective of any referendum run in good faith is to shift the locus of power from elites to non-elites. As we would expect, not all elites are content to cede power to referendums, especially if mini-publics (and not elites) control the referendums' design and running. Despite the generally favourable findings on trust above, when we ask who is doing the trusting the answers become

[113] Abdullah (n 104).

[114] Chapter 3.

[115] Ron Levy, '"Deliberative Voting": Realising Constitutional Referendum Democracy' [2013] Public Law 555, 563–64.

[116] ibid 564–66.

[117] Levy, 'Breaking the Constitutional Deadlock' (n 109) 836–37; Fred Cutler and others, 'Deliberation, Information, and Trust: The British Columbia Citizens' Assembly as Agenda Setter' in Mark E Warren and Hilary Pearse (eds), *Designing Deliberative Democracy: The British Columbia Citizens' Assembly* (CUP 2008) 166.

somewhat, or even markedly, uneven. This raises the possibility of holdouts—and, potentially, spoilers—unswayed by the DPR or its apparent legitimacy. Indeed, we must nuance the realization thesis to take on board several more detailed renderings of a DPR's possible effects:

(i) Majority versus minority trust: Deliberative democratic theory predicts that attitudes towards deliberation should be more positive among minority groups, whose members have more to gain from a deliberatively fair rather than purely majoritarian process.[118] We assumed above that, if a DPR can avoid some of the uneven influence that various groups have within a political system, then the DPR may attract higher trust. However, it is also possible that the DPR will attract uneven levels of trust if members of more dominant groups have less incentive to deliberate, less trouble supporting an abusive government and less inclination to upset their own favourable conditions. Consistent with these expectations, certain broad classes of elites, such as those who are the most educated and urban, and those who support political parties with a hold on power, trust deliberative mini-public-led referendums less than do certain other categories of people.[119]

Nevertheless, it is notable that the trust of majority group members in deliberative mini-public-led referendums still may tend to exceed their trust in elite-led referendums (even if by a smaller margin than we see with other groups).[120] Majority-group members may recognize that when a process fails to gauge the views of minorities, the referendum can constitute an illegitimate steamrolling of minority interests. Majorities may thus reject a minority-insensitive outcome on principled grounds. More pragmatically, they may fail to see the value of running a referendum that clearly privileges their own interests, when the purpose of the referendum had been to quell conflict. As we said in the last chapter, a referendum may not run at all until a mutually hurting stalemate has been reached.[121] In a similar vein, we can assume that many majority members may hesitate to endorse an obviously poorly conceived referendum—one that,

[118] Amy Gutmann and Dennis Thompson, *Democracy and Disagreement* (Harvard University Press 1996) 133. For empirical analysis, see Seraina Pedrini, André Bächtiger, and Marco M Steenbergen, 'Deliberative Inclusion of Minorities: Patterns of Reciprocity Among Linguistic Groups in Switzerland' (2013) 5(3) European Political Science Review 483.

[119] Ron Levy, 'Deliberative Constitutional Change in a Polarised Federation' in Paul Kildea, Andrew Lynch, and George Williams (eds), *Tomorrow's Federation: Reforming Australian Government* (Federation Press 2012) 364–66; cf Seraina Pedrini, André Bächtiger, and Marco R Steenbergen, 'Deliberative Inclusion of Minorities: Patterns of Reciprocity Among Linguistic Groups in Switzerland' (2013) 5(3) European Political Science Review 483.

[120] Ron Levy, 'Deliberative Constitutional Change' (n 119) 364–66.

[121] Ira W Zartman, 'The Timing of Peace Initiatives: Hurting Stalemates and Ripe Moments' (2001) 1(1) The Global Review of Ethnopolitics 8.

operating without minority safeguards, is liable only to prolong or intensify conflict.

There will of course be exceptions. Majority members may view their group as powerful (eg, militarily dominant) enough to proceed with a standard referendum that does not account for the views of the minority. The majority party may try to use the referendum to give some semblance of popular legitimacy and formality to what may actually be a constitutional *fait accompli*. And the minority group may in fact be unable to mount any effective opposition (military or otherwise). Yet, having said this, in recent years only a few referendums have appeared to be designed only to lend a false front of legitimacy to coercively imposed reforms (eg, the Crimean and Transnistrian votes on territorial annexation, both of which also lacked standard democratic safeguards).[122]

(ii) Dual legitimacy: As we first said in Chapter 1, even though many people may be ready to engage in deliberation, others may prioritize other kinds or values of decision-making. One cause of uneven commitments to deliberation, then, is that only some people value deliberation or assume it to be plausible and legitimating, and only under some conditions, while others assume deliberation to be unrealistic.[123] Indeed, the polling data on trust suggest that many people (albeit just a minority of respondents) trust a majoritarian process more than one that is fair and impartial, or well-informed.[124] Some groups may be less enculturated than others to liberal-democratic principles consonant with deliberative democracy (eg, expressive freedoms, mutual toleration, and equality). Cultural and legal distinctions between groups may contribute to particularly sharp differences in the levels of commitment to deliberation.[125] Moreover, among certain types of elites, a well-informed process is the most important determinant of trust in constitutional reform.[126]

Nevertheless, a DPR may still attract relatively wide trust due to what we call *dual legitimacy*: the development of trust in a constitutional reform for more than one reason. Since a DPR has both majoritarian and deliberative features, it may appeal both to those people who favour majoritarianism and to those who favour deliberation. DPRs are still referendums after all: they are mainly majoritarian institutions, even though they also support deliberation. DPRs

[122] Tierney, 'Sovereignty and Crimea' (n 83) 534–35.

[123] Chapter 1.

[124] Levy, 'Breaking the Constitutional Deadlock' (n 109) 834.

[125] See, eg, Jensen Sass and John Dryzek, 'Deliberative Cultures' (2014) 42(1) Political Theory 3; Baogang He and Mark Warren, 'Authoritarian Deliberation: The Deliberative Turn in Chinese Political Development' (2011) 9(2) Perspectives on Politics 269. See also Chapter 7.

[126] Levy, 'Deliberative Constitutional Change' (n 119) 364–66; Ron Levy, 'The "Elite Problem" in Deliberative Constitutionalism' in Ron Levy and others (eds), *The Cambridge Handbook of Deliberative Constitutionalism* (CUP 2018) 363.

may generate relatively widespread trust among those who trust purely majoritarian processes, among those who trust deliberative processes, and among those who trust both kinds (or see them as a unity). As well, given the elite preference for well-informed decision-making, the provision of accurate and complete information should be one of the main areas of focus for referendum designers (as it was in Chapter 3).

(iii) Governmental elites and popular legitimation: Variations in trust are most acute among governmental elites. In both non-conflict and conflict societies, these elites seem largely to disfavour participatory models such as mini-publics, even when the models are described to them as deliberatively democratic.[127] And even when matters are mostly value-based, parliamentarians and senior civil servants tend to see them as technical and properly resolved within their own offices, and thus to avoid heeding popular value choices.[128] We saw above that a deliberative division of labour assumes a relationship of trust between elites and non-elites, but that decision-making about constitutional matters brings this relationship into doubt. Now we see that such doubt may be justified. Many governmental elites do not view the constitutional nature of reforms as calling for humility and deference to constituents. To the contrary, among these elites such matters are often viewed as too important to be left to ordinary people. Given what we said in Chapter 2 about how often elites falter when they attempt value-based deliberation, that assumption is obviously questionable—not least in situations of conflict. But the assumption nevertheless arises.

These are challenges for a DPR, which stakes its ability to legitimate a constitutional settlement partly on the wide appeal of its deliberative procedures. We have already suggested that DPR design should focus partly on deliberative features of special interest to elites. However, this may be at best a partial solution.

Our more important answer to this challenge is to look at whether governmental elites who doubt the legitimacy of a DPR may nevertheless still heed its results if (as predicted) the DPR attracts widespread trust among voters. Popular trust in a process may cause elites to hesitate to oppose a settlement. As we saw, elites who had been vocal hold-outs eventually conformed to peace mandates or settlements in certain cases (eg, in Algeria, South Africa, and Northern Ireland). Governmental leaders may find a broadly based agreement

[127] Levy, 'The "Elite Problem"' (n 126) 364–65; John Garry, *Deliberative Democracy in Northern Ireland* (Northern Ireland Knowledge Exchange Seminar Series 2015–16) 4–5.

[128] Levy, 'The "Elite Problem"' (n 126) 363–65.

to be difficult to resist or deny. It may be hard to motivate armed resistance on behalf of an aggrieved people when that people, or a majority of them, voting by referendum has publicly disavowed the grievances or committed to resolving them without violence. After a *deliberative* referendum, the message that voters convey to elite and other hold-outs may be even harder to set aside. A judicious and informed public choice—one that has been robustly deliberated—may sharpen the message and add to its authority (eg, elite rhetoric claiming that voters misunderstood the issues may ring hollow).

In addition, and returning to language used earlier in this chapter, when a DPR both exposes an agreement and backs that agreement up with a significant act of sociological legitimation, the DPR may help to select one, and only one, norm as foundational and binding within a field. It may also help to suppress spoiling conduct. Exposing and legitimating a clear and considered result (if there is one) may render the discourse around peacemaking less chaotic and febrile, and more resistant to outliers. Would-be spoilers may fail at one of their principal aims: to cast doubt on the existence of widespread social agreement. A trusted DPR is, moreover, likely to be credited with *accurately* exposing an exclusive social agreement in favour of settlement.

Conceivably, alternative methods of popular legitimation could have the same effect. For instance, mass rallies aim to express a popular view and force (or oppose) progress on a policy such as peacemaking. The 100,000-plus person rally at which Prime Minister Rabin of Israel was assassinated had been billed as showcasing Israelis' overwhelming support for the peace talks then taking place. (In the event, it succeeded both at showing such support and demonstrating peacemaking's vulnerability to spoilers.[129]) A mass demonstration may indeed provide an approximate gauge of the intensities of popular sentiments and preferences. Yet it does so without any claim to accuracy, based as it is on self-selected samples. Rallies in favour of peacemaking must also contend with rallies against, and with factors that arbitrarily affect turnout (eg, planning, permits, intimidatory violence, and even weather).

An opinion poll could also expose agreement, and with less cost or effort than a referendum. But opinion polls, too, do not have the same legitimizing effects on constitutional reform, and on their own are seldom sufficient to mobilize parliamentary or other elite support. One reason is that polls may be

[129] Gadi Wolfsfeld, *Media and the Path to Peace* (CUP 2004) 86–92.

suspected of including manipulated questions or strategically sampled populations.[130] And in conflict societies, it may be even more difficult to gain a clear picture of popular sentiment if weak infrastructure prevents comprehensive door-to-door or phone-based polling.[131]

Yet a more basic concern returns us to the issue of formality. Opinion polls have at best limited formality, as either pedigree or expression. The stakes are higher in a referendum: in principle at least, elites must heed a clear result. Especially if conducted as a DPR, the referendum is no mere snapshot of unconsidered opinion;[132] it may reflect choices by people who expect their votes to count towards an actual decision. And, as Gutmann and Thompson observe, when deliberation backs up a decision, the decision has greater expressive value.[133] Even if people do not change their minds after deliberation, it matters that their views have been tested and confirmed—not just for epistemic reasons but for the sense of legitimacy that attaches to views that have been put through the deliberative process and survived. A DPR may not only reveal a pre-existing agreement, but may also test and confirm that agreement as worthy of enduring. Far more than a mere opinion poll, a DPR may formalize the agreement and enshrine it as a socially salient moment capable of displacing more jaundiced assumptions of the conflict's intractability.

If it endorses a fully fleshed out and concluded settlement proposal, then, a DPR may legitimate the settlement and safeguard, at least to a greater degree, against spoiler behaviour and general backsliding later on. Such legitimation in late stages may compel elites and others, who may be likely to heed considered democratic choices expressed in the DPR, to respect a settlement and see it as closed. Alternatively, if the DPR runs as a mandate referendum, then the effect of legitimation may be both to lend greater legitimacy to the final settlement and, in earlier stages, to negotiations towards that final settlement.

[130] Graeme Orr and Ron Levy, 'Regulating Opinion Polling: A Deliberative Democratic Perspective' (2016) 39(1) University of New South Wales Law Journal 318, 322–26.

[131] Of course referendums also may also be manipulated. In Chapter 3 we discussed neutral oversight to ensure integrity. See also Stephen Tierney, 'Using Electoral Law to Construct a Deliberative Referendum: Moving Beyond the Democratic Paradox' (2013) 12(4) Election Law Journal 508, 516.

[132] Setälä (n 27) 710, 714. cf deliberative polls, which can generate and gauge thoroughly considered opinions: Christian List and others, 'Deliberation, Single-Peakedness, and the Possibility of Meaningful Democracy: Evidence from Deliberative Polls' (2013) 75(1) Journal of Politics 80.

[133] Amy Gutmann and Dennis Thompson, *Why Deliberative Democracy?* (Princeton University Press 2004) 23.

V. Conclusion

Our core question in this chapter has been whether a DPR can generate constitutional settlement endurance. A key condition for that, in turn, was that a constitutional reform process should be capable of laying down norms that are discrete and exclusive in their fields. Another requirement was that the process should be able to legitimate a constitutional reform. In both respects, we have described DPRs as promising tools.

Across the last three chapters, then, we have argued that deliberation between parties to a conflict may help to achieve a settlement and thereafter solidify the settlement in a constitutional form. In particular, a DPR may help to translate the referendum's fleeting settlement agreement into a set of norms that, having constitutional status, plausibly may last over the long term. Constitutional norms that are enduring and binding as against all segments of societies—including elites—may form as a result of the expression of popular sovereignty, particularly when the expression is channelled through a deliberative referendum. Once a constitutional norm develops, this may affect whether elites are persuaded to go along with a mandate to negotiate for a peace settlement, or with the settlement once it is reached.

As usual, nothing we have said is meant to be read as solid and unvarying prediction. Instead, we have undertaken a comparative institutional inquiry. And we have acknowledged that the claims we have made will often fall short in practice. For instance, there is never a guarantee against spoilers. (This kind of caveat is obvious, but worth repeating given its importance.) Yet, while more effective referendum design carries no guarantees, poor design may all but guarantee poor peacemaking outcomes. Our conclusion, then, is that peace referendums refashioned as DPRs are *more likely* to lend constitutional legitimacy and endurance to settlements. Still, many obstacles remain to be addressed. In the next chapters we will turn to specific variations on the generic DPR model—variations that may be required to meet the model's aims in assorted contexts of conflict.

PART III

VARIATIONS

5

Group-Sovereignty Conflict

I. Introduction

In this part of the book we explore how deliberative peace referendums (DPRs) can be applied to assorted conflict types. For some conflicts, we recommend the generic DPR model outlined in Chapter 3. Other conflict types, however, necessitate variations in design. Of course we cannot be exhaustive; there are simply too many types of conflict to cover in a single volume. We leave many kinds to be covered, by ourselves or by others, in future work. But even though we do not lay claim here to a comprehensive account, we think that the conflict varieties to be seen are among the most important. They are either especially prevalent in practice or especially challenging to the generic DPR model.

We are not primarily concerned in this part with case studies in the form of extended examinations of particular historical conflicts. Instead, our purpose is essentially taxonomic: to identify which types of conflict may require which types of DPR designs. Omitting full case studies is unavoidable as no one has yet run a DPR in anywhere near the full sense of the term. That said, there are often examples of peace referendums with some deliberative institutional features. And we will of course want to use examples to illustrate particular conflict types. Intermittently examining real-world examples will allow us to think about both the kinds of difficulties that DPRs might encounter and the institutional variations that might be needed in response.

Chapter 6 will address secession conflicts, and Chapter 7 indigenous-settler conflicts. Both types are instances of conflict based on competing claims to group sovereignty.[1] Thus we will begin, in the present chapter, by examining theoretical and design considerations arising in group-sovereignty conflicts

[1] Other group-sovereignty conflict sub-types include border conflict (ie, contests between sovereign states over the precise locations of their mutual frontier, where the contested territory does not itself delineate a distinct group); conquest (ie, annexation or occupation following invasion); and ethnic cleansing (ie, group-sovereignty claims manifesting as exclusion or extermination of others from a territory). A conflict can instantiate more than one subtype.

Deliberative Peace Referendums. Ron Levy, Ian O'Flynn, Hoi L Kong, Oxford University Press (2021). © Ron Levy, Ian O'Flynn, and Hoi L Kong. DOI: 10.1093/oso/9780198867036.003.0005

more generally. Our use of 'conflict' throughout this book has always entailed a focus on groups; we defined conflict in relation to widespread violence between defined groups.[2] Yet many conflicts turn upon clashing claims of group *sovereignty*, and this concept has a specific meaning. In legal and political terms it entails a recognition that a group is free-standing: its power is not dependent on any other power. A sovereign group is also formally co-equal in status to other sovereign groups in the same system (eg, the international system of states).

Any group that claims sovereignty generally also claims a discrete identity for itself. For that reason, as well as others, group-sovereignty conflicts can be especially fraught. According to Dryzek, deliberative democratic 'reflection' and 'the possibility that minds can be changed' are 'unlikely if one's position is tied to one's identity'.[3] The relative obduracy of identity-based values can be a particular problem for DPRs, which as we have seen rely on public-value deliberation. When trying to reach constitutional settlements with members of other groups, group members may find it hard to see why public values ought to take priority.[4]

Yet, while group identities can impose a drag on deliberation, we cannot set groups aside. Expecting group allegiances and identities to go quiet or wither away would be wildly unrealistic. DPR design should therefore seek to accommodate groups. In particular, it should take group boundaries—the cultural, religious, linguistic, or other features that distinguish one group from another—as given and work with or around them. For example, a DPR can adopt concurrent consent voting rules. As noted in previous chapters, concurrent consent means that an affirmative vote requires majorities within more than one group to give consent, independently, to propositions on the ballot. If a majority within any one of the groups fails to support a proposition, the proposition fails.

Since this effectively gives powers of mutual-veto to some groups,[5] in one sense it raises extra hurdles to peacemaking. Yet we devote much of this chapter to recognizing what can still be done to aid public-value deliberation and promote peacemaking even when a referendum gives groups a formal

[2] Chapter 1.

[3] John S Dryzek, 'Deliberative Democracy in Divided Societies: Alternatives to Agonism and Analgesia' (2005) 33(2) Political Theory 218, 229.

[4] John Rawls, *Political Liberalism* (Colombia University Press 1996) 160, 386–87.

[5] Brendan O'Leary, 'The Nature of the Agreement' (1998) 22(4) Fordham International Law Journal 1628, 1638–39.

role.[6] Recall that public-value deliberation asks people to frame their arguments in terms of widely shared values and other such considerations that any person could reasonably be expected to endorse. From this common ground, the hope is that distinct groups can reach agreement on what Rawls terms constitutional essentials and matters of basic justice. Public-value deliberation itself does not wish away groups and their non-public values (including their comprehensive doctrines). On the contrary, Rawls introduces the notion of an overlapping consensus to explain how people may modify their non-public values so that these values overlap in positively supporting the same constitutional norms.[7]

Rawls hopes that conflicts between public and non-public values will gradually disappear, resulting in more stable constitutional arrangements over time. But he does not provide an actual institutional account of how this might happen. We began to do so in earlier chapters (although our preferred process, centred on the DPR, was not gradual). We now seek to deepen this analysis. We will consider whether and in what ways groups can deliberate despite the disunity between them. There may yet be space to deliberate over the public values that groups can share between them, including the value of sovereignty itself.

The chapter will proceed as follows. In Section II, we will provide background on the roles of groups, including the places that have been ascribed to them in deliberative and constitutional theory. Here we will also defend our conclusion that the boundaries of groups must be left essentially as is in a DPR. And we will explore, in broad terms, the possibility that conflicting groups may deliberate despite their disunity. At least for the duration of a referendum, it may be possible to diminish the extent to which group members see their groups as locked in zero-sum competitions for status with other groups.

In Section III, we will then be in a position to outline certain DPR features that may make such intergroup deliberation more feasible. Public-value deliberation, in particular, is again our focus. Such deliberation is not always possible amid conflict, and it is never easy; we will describe a number of formidable hurdles. Yet, the ability to make sovereignty claims without (or with relatively muted) prejudice towards the claims of other groups is sometimes a condition-precedent for the achievement and endurance of a constitutional settlement.

[6] On veto players, see, eg, George Tsebelis, 'Decision Making in Political Systems: Veto Players in Presidentialism, Parliamentarism, Multicameralism and Multipartyism' (1999) 25(3) British Journal of Political Science 289.

[7] Rawls, *Political Liberalism* (n 3) 160; Chapter 2.

II. Deliberating Despite Disunity

A. Conflict and Group Rigidity

This section deals with the question of what a sovereign group is and, in general, how sovereign-group conflict bears on the prospects for deliberation. Conflicts between sovereign groups can occur either within states or across international borders. But even though group-sovereignty conflicts can occur intra-state, conflicts *wholly* of that kind are, in a certain sense, rare. Conflicts could in theory arise where group members fight for new federal or quasi-federal autonomy inside of an internationally recognized state of which the group is already a part. Yet it is hard to find examples of conflicts that *start off* with the maximalist tactics of armed warfare being used to push merely for sub-state autonomy. Sometimes, on the other hand, groups in conflict do eventually compromise and settle on legal autonomies short of full international statehood. Hence, practically speaking, most group-sovereignty conflicts have an international dimension: they tend to involve either existing international states, or groups pursuing international statehood.

While many conflicts directly concern group claims to sovereignty, not all do. For instance, we can distinguish *group-sovereignty* conflicts from *political-systemic* conflicts. Group-sovereignty conflicts are ultimately based on group members' felt need to secure legal and political recognition of their group's distinct identity. But conflicts over political systems are generally distributional, as some combatants (eg, Marxist, liberal) seek to alter a society's relative allocations of rights and interests.[8] Having said this, these two broad conflict types actually tend to appear in combination: political-systemic revolutionary movements frequently have parallel group-sovereignty aims (eg, in Darfur, the Darfurian Justice and Equality Movement sought to improve social and legal conditions for the Darfurian minority, but also arguably had secessionist objectives).[9]

What do we know, then, about the nature of asserted interests in group sovereignty? One possibility is a *unitary* theory of sovereignty—a relatively maximalist, exclusionary account that views a people as indivisible and necessarily

[8] On the recognition-distribution distinction, see again Chapter 1.

[9] The secessionist intentions of another rebel group, the SLA (Sudan Liberation Movement), were more explicit: Ulrich Mans, 'Sudan: the New War in Darfur' (2004) 103(411) African Affairs 291. Even the Cold War can be seen not as a contest of ideologies so much as a contest between powers vying for sovereignty over, eg, the Eurasian landmass: Andrew J Bacevich, 'The Revisionist Imperative: Rethinking Twentieth Century Wars' (2012) 76(2) Journal of Military History 333, 338. The American Revolution was also of course a War of Independence.

dominant within a territory. In the last chapter we briefly introduced Sièyes's social contractarian conception of popular legitimacy, which understands a discrete people, rooted in a state of nature, as having unfetterable authority. Even if most philosophers (and even at times Sièyes himself) do not sign on to this view in all of its particulars, some of the more muscular notions of nationalism—in Sièyes's time and our own—are consonant with the unitary view.[10] Yet unitary notions can appear artificial, naïve, even dangerous. Carl Schmitt, for one, drew a connection between the constituent power and theories of unrestrained nationalism, which allowed him to provide intellectual support for militant German nationalism before the Second World War.[11] Unitary assumptions notably challenge contemporary rule of law ideas by providing that a people's constituent power has priority over the constituted authority, including over constitutions themselves.[12]

Many argue that a wholly united group rarely eventuates anyway.[13] This latter concern is especially live in states experiencing conflict, where political unity is elusive across the deep divisions that may have given rise to the conflict. Theories of legitimacy based on constituent power tend to be statist: 'strictly related to the Westphalian triptych of territory, people, and jurisdiction' of the state.[14] From this perspective, conflict societies—whether they include just one state or several—present challenges to the legitimacy of a constitutional settlement. As Joel Colón-Ríos writes, the 'very meaning of the concept of constituent power requires that the constitutional forms be jointly created' by members of a group.[15] Thus it can be difficult to see how constitutional legitimacy can ever be realized within a disunited state, or between two or more states deeply divided against each other.

[10] Kenneth E Boulding, 'National Images and International Systems' (1959) 3(2) Journal of Conflict Resolution 120, 123.

[11] See, eg, Carl Schmitt, 'The Führer Protects the Law: On Adolf Hitler's Reichstag Address, 13th July 1934' (reprinted in Carl Schmitt, *Positionen und Begriffe im Kampf mit Weimar, 1923–1939* (Clara T Picker and John P McCormick trs, Berlin 1994) 32). On Schmitt's unitary theory see Carl Schmitt, *Constitutional Theory* (Jeffery Seitzer tr, Duke University Press 2008) 131.

[12] But cf Richard Stacey, 'Popular Sovereignty and Revolutionary Constitution-Making' in David Dyzenhaus and Malcolm Thorburn (eds), *Philosophical Foundations of Constitutional Law* (OUP 2016) 161.

[13] Jürgen Habermas, *The Inclusion of the Other* (Ciaran Cronin and Pablo De Greiff trs, MIT Press 1998) 159; Serdar Tekin, *Founding Acts: Constitutional Origins in a Democratic Age* (University of Pennsylvania Press 2016) 2; Neil MacCormick, *Questioning Sovereignty: Law, State and Nation in the European Commonwealth* (OUP 1999) 133.

[14] Paul Blokker, 'A Political-Sociological Analysis of Constitutional Pluralism in Europe' in Jiří Přibáň (ed), *Self-Constitution of European Society: Beyond EU Politics, Law and Governance* (Routledge 2016) citing Dieter Grimm, 'The Achievement of Constitutionalism and its Prospects in a Changed World' in Petra Dobner and Martin Loughlin (eds), *The Twilight of Constitutionalism* (OUP 2010) 21.

[15] Joel Colón-Ríos, 'The Legitimacy of the Juridical: Constituent Power, Democracy, and the Limits of Constitutional Reform' (2010) 48 Osgoode Hall Law Journal 199, 210.

The *democratic constitutionalist* principle of government by consent,[16] which in its several variations has also been a cornerstone of social contract thinking,[17] presents an alternative that is more flexible and amenable to peacemaking. This principle stems from an understanding of what the political equality of democracy entails. The main proposition is that no persons should be excluded arbitrarily from a decision-making process that potentially binds them, nor from influencing its outcome for or against.[18] This applies with particular force to the making of constitutional laws given their typically outsized effects. Constitutional reform should rest on wide-ranging popular consent; anything less would raise serious questions about the political equality of democracy.

The consequences of adopting the democratic constitutionalist perspective include, first, that it allows a constitutional settlement whereby 'diverse and disagreeing groups can live'.[19] Thus a constitutional settlement becomes an 'agreement among . . . peoples' that is premised on a 'direct relationship between [the] law and those peoples'.[20] There is no requirement, as there might be under unitary theories, that a single constitution be tied to a single people.[21] Consent is what matters most, and a constitution can conceivably reflect the consent of more than just one group.[22]

Indeed, there is no necessary role for groups at all. A second implication of democratic constitutionalism is that the theory allows the individual to be the agent of constitutional consent. There is no requirement that a group or set of groups authorize a constitution. Democratic constitutionalism instead contemplates individuals joining and leaving coalitions to form the temporary democratic majorities (or supermajorities) needed to legitimate constitutional reforms. Even a society put together from diverse and divided members can

[16] Blokker (n 13).

[17] See, eg, John Locke, *Two Treatises of Government* (Peter Laslett ed, 2nd edn, CUP, 1988) 110–16.

[18] Thomas Christiano, *The Rule of the Many: Fundamental Issues in Democratic Theory* (Westview Press 1996) 53–56; Ronald Dworkin, *Taking Rights Seriously* (Harvard University Press 1978).

[19] Vivien Hart, *Democratic Constitution Making*, vol 31 (United States Institute of Peace 2003).

[20] Miguel P Maduro, 'The Importance of Being Called a Constitution: Constitutional Authority and the Authority of Constitutionalism' (2005) 3 International Journal of Constitutional Law 332, 337. See also Arend Lijphart, *The Politics of Accommodation: Pluralism and Democracy in the Netherlands* (University of California Press 1975) 2–3, 103.

[21] A similar assumption is central to consociational theory, which stresses equality between 'consociated *peoples* and *groups*', and does 'not presume that there is one demos': Christopher McCrudden and Brendan O'Leary, 'Courts and Consociations, or How Human Rights Courts May De-stabilize Power-sharing Settlements' (2013) 24(2) European Journal of International Law 477, 483 (emphasis in original) .

[22] As we first noted in Chapter 1, the norms that we simplify here as 'constitutional' may also have the character of international law. Sovereignty can at once manifest in the terms of a sovereign state's constitution (eg, in norms enabling treaty-making and other foreign relations powers) and in international law.

collectively give consent to the constitution; there is no reason why that society need conceive of itself as unitary.

Unlike unitary conceptions, which proceed from an a priori assumption of the sovereignty of the group, democratic constitutionalism generally understands groups as valuable only insofar as individuals ascribe value to them. And many individuals indeed place great stock in democratic choices about group aggregations. In Avishai Margalit and Joseph Raz's well-known account, the value of what they call 'encompassing groups' reduces to the interest of the individual in belonging to a group that helps to construct individual self-identity,[23] as well as contributing to the 'character of their social and economic environment, their fortunes, the course of their development and the fortunes of their members'.[24] These descriptions are consistent with, and help to flesh out, the democratic constitutionalist perspective. While we may have doubts about unitary group theories, the democratic constitutionalist perspective presents a more workable alternative that can still recognize a role for groups in the popular legitimation of constitutional reforms. Individual members may view their group as an organized and coherent unit brought together by (among other possibilities) a sense of shared history, culture, land, religion, language, ethnicity, or nationality identity.[25] As such, individuals can have a shared or collective interest in seeing the group flourish.[26]

In turn, legal sovereignty can be a way to manifest these group identities—one of a range of options that group members have in order to realize their group's distinctiveness and status.[27] Sovereignty-based movements, prevalent in the politics of non-conflict and conflict societies alike, seek to establish (or retain or extend) groups as masters in their own houses ('maîtres chez nous'). Such rhetoric has long infused state-building movements. To give just one example, in the late nineteenth century, the Zionist leader Theodore Herzl dreamed of 'sovereignty . . . over a portion of the globe large enough to satisfy

[23] Avishai Margalit and Joseph Raz, 'National Self-Determination' (1990) 87(9) The Journal of Philosophy 439, 444–46, 450; see also Joseph Raz, *The Morality of Freedom* (Clarendon Press 2009) 208. For empirical support see Shalom H Schwartz, 'Universals in the Content and Structure of Values: Theoretical Advances and Empirical Tests in 20 Countries' (1992) 25(1) Advances in Experimental Social Psychology 1.

[24] Margalit and Raz (n 22) 440.

[25] ibid 443–44; Jürg Steiner and Maria C Jaramillo, 'How to Arrive at Peace in Deeply Divided Societies? Using Deliberation to Refine Consociational Theory' (2019) 15(3) Journal of Public Deliberation Art 9, 6.

[26] On the corporate versus collective distinction, see Peter Jones, 'Group Rights and Group Oppression' (1999) 7(4) *Journal of Political Philosophy* 353; Dwight Newman, *Community and Collective Rights: A Theoretical Framework for Rights held by Groups* (Hart Publishing 2011).

[27] Kwame A Appiah, *The Ethics of Identity* (Princeton University Press 2005) 70; Charles Taylor, *Multiculturalism* (Amy Gutmann ed, Princeton University Press 1994) 5.

the rightful requirements of a nation'.[28] Not uncommonly, dreams of sovereignty contemplate the group's dominion over its own internal affairs, from the lofty to the mundane. For instance, in Herzl's vision a Jewish state would run its own system of criminal justice with Jewish secular laws, Jewish police, and even Jewish offenders.[29] Such aspirations—albeit with different colour and detail—are familiar features wherever identity groups have imagined their readiness to run states on a basis of equality with other international states.

Even without formal recognition of their sovereignty, many groups are cohesive enough to have (or indeed because they have) internal norms that effectively govern their members on matters of culture, religion, language, etc.[30] But legal recognition of sovereignty is an act that confirms the co-equality of the group vis-à-vis other groups,[31] and potentially stabilizes the group's territorial borders, membership, and scope of self-governance. To paraphrase Margalit and Raz, the current international state system is such that, in the main, political power rests with sovereign states. It is understandable, therefore, that different groups should wish to begin to exercise their sovereignty each within states of their own (see Chapters 6 and 7).[32] Equally, within existing international states, there is often a concern to keep—or to strengthen—a given group's sovereign control over a territory, as against the sovereignty claims of other groups (eg, in Afghanistan, Bosnia, the Democratic Republic of the Congo, Iraq, Lebanon, Syria, and Yemen). Hence group sovereignty is often a prime concern of individuals. Legal sovereignty may demonstrate members' feelings that the group has enough significance and distinctiveness to be, or to remain, its own state, with everything this entails

Yet if, according to the democratic constitutionalist perspective, the normative value of groups lies in the choices that individuals make to unite or stay united, then this seems to leave open the possibility that the boundaries of the groups that have or seek sovereignty can themselves be questioned and deliberated. Indeed, according to constructivists, identities are socially constructed and therefore fluid and open to questioning, reaffirmation, and revision.[33]

[28] Theodor Herzl, *The Jewish State* (Sylvie d'Avigdor tr, R Searl 1946) 92. cf Dmitry Shumsky, *Beyond the Nation-State: The Zionist Political Imagination from Pinsker to Ben-Gurion* (Yale University Press 2018).

[29] Herzl (n 27) 148.

[30] Margalit and Raz (n 22) 443–44, 446.

[31] Zachary Elkins, Tom Ginsburg, and James Melton, *The Endurance of National Constitutions* (CUP 2009) 41–42.

[32] Margalit and Raz (n 22) 440–41.

[33] Kanchan Chandra, 'What is Ethnic Identity and Does It Matter?' (2006) 9(1) Annual Review of Political Science 397; Kanchan Chandra, 'Cumulative Findings in the Study of Ethnic Politics' (2001) 12(1) APSA-CP 7; cf Donald L Horowitz, 'Electoral Systems: A Primer for Decision Makers' (2003) 14(4) Journal of Democracy 115, 115.

Group identity is thus sensitive to circumstances, including to our relationships with others.[34] For instance, the term 'Serb' refers not to a single group entity but to a range of associations and institutions (eg, the Orthodox Church, political parties, women's groups, sporting associations, etc). These different institutions offer a range of definitions of what being 'Serbian' means, and act in a range of ways to pursue those definitions, often in competition with one another. Group identity is not a property or a set of essential attributes that, for instance, all Serbs must inevitably possess, but a relationship that Serbs establish and re-establish among themselves and between themselves and others over the course of time.

Group or segmental identities may thus be open to reconsideration; in principle, change is always possible. Just as some rhetoric can delegitimize the other (which may be a step towards dehumanizing members of the group or targeting them with violence), the opposite rhetoric can perhaps serve to highlight unities and bring one group into the fold of another. One could, for instance, point to shared identities and to how neither of the groups in question would have existed in quite the same way without the formative influence of the other. Skilful rhetoricians might show longstanding common cause and identity between the groups (eg, how Mizrahi Jews are, or were, sometimes known as Arab Jews).[35]

In a similar vein, recall Addis's contention that 'identities are partly bound up with discourse, and what has been imagined through stories and discourses can partly be reimagined through discourse as well'.[36] One variant of this claim notices how the values that define identity are 'pre-rational' or 'primordial': they are principally felt, rather than derived directly from reasoned argument.[37] In turn it is possible that *because* these values lack a basis in 'rational' forms of argument that the values are mutable in the course of deliberation.[38] Sometimes minds can even be changed by mutual exposure to emotive appeals that highlight the interests and identities—including the stories 'of loss and hurt'—of others.[39]

[34] Michael R James, 'The Political Ontology of Race' (2012) 44(1) Polity 106.

[35] Yehouda Shenhav and Hannan Hever, '"Arab Jews" after Structuralism: Zionist Discourse and the (De) Formation of an Ethnic Identity' (2012) 18(1) Social Identities 101.

[36] Adeno Addis, 'Deliberative Democracy in Severely Fractured Societies' (2009) 16(1) Indiana Journal of Global Legal Studies 59; see again Chapter 2.

[37] Donald L Horowitz, 'The Primordialists' in Daniele Conversi (ed), *Ethnonationalism in the Contemporary World: Walker Connor and the Study of Nationalism* (Routledge 2003) 72–82. See also Michael Walzer, 'Deliberation, and What Else?' in Stephen Macedo (ed), *Deliberative Politics: Essays on Democracy and Disagreement* (OUP 1999) 58; David Hume, *A Treatise of Human Nature* (David F Norton and Mary J Norton eds, OUP 2000) 266.

[38] See Jane Mansbridge and others, 'The Place of Self-Interest and the Role of Power in Deliberative Democracy' (2010) 18(1) Journal of Political Philosophy 64, 69, 79, fnn 15, 40.

[39] Stephen Tierney, *Constitutional Referendums: The Theory and Practice of Republican Deliberation* (OUP 2012) 254.

Yet the goal of being able to shift identities is overly optimistic amid conflict. Even in non-conflict areas a rhetoric of unity of identity may have little effect.[40] The fractures that generate conflict often run so deeply, and are premised partly on identitarian differences thought so fundamental, that a merger of identities may be inconceivable. It is especially difficult to ask people who have resorted to the use of arms to accept the academic's questioning of the inexorableness or salience of the group's boundaries. Many feel powerful identitarian group ties—often manifested in what Horowitz terms 'ethnic parties and ethnic voting'.[41] Many will connect their anxieties over security and their particular interests and aspirations to groups that are solidly established (even if their boundaries are ambiguous).

Although the democratic constitutionalist principle is, then, initially focused on the individual, groups usually end up having primary importance amid conflict. Even constructivists recognize that, under some circumstances, deep social and political division can mean that group identities become extremely durable: once crystallized, they can be very hard to reconstruct.[42] External observers often fail to see how inevitable the dividing lines of group identity can feel to those on the ground. For instance, why Protestants and Catholics in Northern Ireland ever fought can seem obscure to those on the outside who, peering in, see both groups as Irish after all.[43] Yet seemingly small differences can be intimately felt and can pervasively coordinate political life;[44] and often, to those on the inside, the distinctions do not seem so small.

Group boundaries especially resist change under pressure. Identities sometimes crystallize due to the group targeting and systemic discrimination that we described earlier in this book.[45] Reacting to legal disabilities and other exclusionary policies, some members may try to depart the group (eg, many nineteenth-century European Jews assimilated to Christian cultural practices,

[40] Henry E Hale, 'Explaining Ethnicity' (2004) 37(4) Comparative Political Studies 458, 460. See also Christopher H Achen and Larry M Bartels, *Democracy for Realists: Why Elections Do Not Produce Responsive Government* (Princeton University Press 2016) 2, fn 2.

[41] Donald L Horowitz, 'Ethnic Power Sharing: Three Big Problems' (2014) 25(2) Journal of Democracy 5. See similarly Brendan O'Leary, 'Debating Consociational Politics: Normative and Explanatory Arguments' in Sid Noel (ed), *From Power Sharing to Democracy: Post-Conflict Institutions in Ethnically Divided Societies* (McGill-Queen's University Press 2005) 10.

[42] See Hale (n 39) 460.

[43] It is often (and, up to a point, rightly) said that 'Protestant' and 'Catholic' are simply markers for British unionism and Irish nationalism, respectively: see, eg, John McGarry and Brendan O'Leary, *Explaining Northern Ireland: Broken Images* (Blackwell 1995).

[44] Michael Billig and Henri Tajfel, 'Social Categorization and Similarity in Intergroup Behaviour' (1973) 3(1) European Journal of Social Psychology 27.

[45] Chapter 1.

or formally converted, to overcome exclusions in areas such as politics and the arts).[46] But many others double down on their group affinities and recommit to protecting the group's security and survival.[47] Some have no choice in the matter: few can transcend their identities, much less engage in deliberation about those identities, when invidious laws relying on essentializing ethnic and other classifications lock the identities in place.

As a normative matter, too, we should not assume intergroup unity to be the correct or best response to conflict. Whether it is in a given case should be a matter for a voting public to decide, and not one answerable through the dispassionate application of expertise. If a referendum does not employ concurrent consent, but instead sees voters of all groups vote as an undifferentiated whole, then the referendum may simply privilege larger groups capable of mustering outright majorities.[48] This failure to take separate groups into account could put an early end to meaningful deliberation. And it could prejudge precisely the matter up for deliberation and decision: for instance, in secession cases, whether to split up or stay together. Hence it is not merely unrealistic, but also often undesirable, to try to mitigate communal conflict by reconceiving specific groups as not so different from each other after all.

B. Group 'Pride Without Prejudice'

We do not think that formal group accommodation precludes constitutional settlement. Under the theory of democratic constitutionalism, recall, constitutional norms can bind more than one distinct sovereign group. Indeed, this is no mere theoretical conceit. In practice, sovereign (or putatively sovereign) groups in conflict sometimes establish binding constitutional norms between them. Yet, on what substantive basis can they do so? We will outline a set of broad answers to this question here, in order that we may gear our discussions of DPR institutional design to them in later sections.

Public-value deliberation directly addresses not the boundaries of group identity, but certain basic and generalized democratic principles. Recall that the ideal of public reason requires people to defend their political proposals

[46] Michael R Marrus, 'European Jewry and the Politics of Assimilation: Assessment and Reassessment' (1977) (49(1) The Journal of Modern History 89, 105–06.

[47] Dryzek (n 2) 229.

[48] Joanne McEvoy, 'Letting "the People(s)" Decide: Peace Referendums and Power-Sharing Settlements' (2018) 25(5) Democratization 864, 868. A less effective alternative—addressed below—is that of supermajority voting.

by showing how they are supported by values that others can endorse as consistent with their freedom and equality. What this entails is a switch in roles: we decide constitutional questions not in our capacity as private persons but in our capacity as members of a public.[49] For instance, a public value of group sovereignty would acknowledge that many groups are entitled to sovereign self-determination. Thus it would recognize the significance of sovereignty per se, regardless of which groups aspire to sovereignty from time to time. While the value of a specific claim of sovereignty may resonate only with members of the group making the claim, on a more generalized understanding sovereignty is a value to which members of other groups can also relate.

Goodin and Elster each observe that a deliberative process can attempt to expose and wear down claims that are wholly self-interested and appear hypocritical.[50] We occasionally see such attempts in discussions of sovereignty. For instance, when some people of a province have sought sovereignty and secession (eg, Québec from Canada), others have occasionally argued that the activists for sovereignty must also accept the sovereignty of other discrete groups (eg, Indigenous peoples from Québec).[51] Those who value their own sovereignty should, in principle, be able to appreciate why others value theirs, and why sovereignty has general appeal.

Far from requiring groups to abandon their particular commitments, public-value deliberation instead requires them to adopt a broader or more encompassing point of view. David Miller puts the point like this:

> [E]ven if initially my aim is to support the claims of a particular group to which I belong or which I represent, I cannot in a general discussion simply say "I claim that group *A*—farmers, say, or policemen—should get more money". I have to give reasons for the claim. These might be that the group in question has special needs, or that it is in the common interest to improve the living standards of the group. By giving these reasons, however, I am committing myself to a general principle, which by implication applies to any other similarly placed group. Thus I am forced to take a wider view, and either defend the claim I am making when applied not only to my group but to groups

[49] Ian O'Flynn, 'Deliberating About the Public Interest' (2010) 16(3) Res Publica 299. Another view is that this entails 'abstraction from one's own point of view': James Bohman, *Public Deliberation: Pluralism, Complexity, and Democracy* (MIT Press 1996) 81 (describing and critiquing this notion).

[50] Robert Goodin, *Motivating Political Morality* (Blackwell 1992) 132–33; Jon Elster, 'Deliberation and Constitution-Making' in Jon Elster (ed), *Deliberative Democracy* (CUP 1998) 97–122.

[51] Reg Whitaker, 'Sovereignties Old and New: Canada, Quebec, and Aboriginal Peoples' (1999) 58(1) Studies in Political Economy 69.

> *B*, *C* and *D*, which are like *A* in the relevant respects, or else to back down and moderate the claim to something I am prepared to accept in these other cases too.[52]

Rawls offers a similar analysis. As we saw, he insists that deliberation about constitutional essentials and matters of basic justice should be couched in terms of public values.[53] Yet he allows that, on a 'wide view' of public reason, participants in deliberation may appeal to their own non-public values provided that appropriate public reasons are also introduced in due course. For example, a Christian group might introduce a Gospel story (eg, the parable of the Good Samaritan as told by Jesus in the Gospel of Luke) in support of their claims or proposals. Yet at some point in the deliberations they must also be able to show that the same claims or proposals could be equally well justified in public-value terms.[54] The idea that group differences must be expunged for deliberation to be productive is not only quixotic in a practical sense, then, but also misses an essential point about public-value deliberation: it is the fact that some differences are ineliminable that leads theorists such as Rawls to focus their attentions on what we already share.

Many other commentators have argued that the judicious design of institutions can shift the self-perceptions of identity groups in relatively benign directions—for instance, from 'antagonism' to 'agonism',[55] or towards a 'spirit of accommodation' between separate, constitutionally recognized groups.[56] Donald Rothchild distinguishes among three different types of intergroup perception: *essentialist* (each group views the other as an implacable existential threat), *pragmatic* (conflict remains acute, but compromise is possible at the margins), and *reciprocative* (groups 'seek to transform the structure of relations to achieve mutual interest').[57] When properly supported or institutionalized, public-value deliberation may assist a shift from one type of perspective to another.

[52] David Miller, 'Deliberative Democracy and Social Choice' (1992) 40(Supp 1) Political Studies 54, 55.

[53] Chapter 2.

[54] Rawls, *Political Liberalism* (n 3) li–lii; John Rawls, 'The Idea of Public Reason Revisited' (1997) 64(3) University of Chicago Law Review 765, 783–87; cf David A Reidy, 'Rawls's Wide View of Public Reason: Not Wide Enough' (2000) 6(1) Res Publica 49.

[55] Chantal Mouffe, 'Deliberative Democracy or Agonistic Pluralism?' (1999) 66(3) Social Research 745, 755.

[56] Lijphart, *The Politics of Accommodation* (n 19) 104.

[57] Donald Rothchild, 'Hegemonial Exchange: An Alternative Model for Managing Conflict in Middle Africa' in Dennis L Thompson and Dov Ronen (eds), *Ethnicity, Politics and Development* (Lynne Rienner 1986) 87–93 (quoted in Timothy D Sisk, *Power Sharing and International Mediation in Ethnic Conflicts* (USIP 1996) 14).

For example, while some constitutional cultures conceive of state sovereignty as absolute or essential—as granting one group an undivided power to govern within the bounds of a territory—another vision of groups and sovereignties embraces 'multiple or overlapping loyalties'.[58] Maintaining that latter vision may require adopting certain public values even more fundamental than generalized sovereignty. Jürg Steiner and Maria Clara Jaramillo suggest that 'if members of deeply divided groups begin to listen to each other with respect and take seriously the arguments of others, then mutual trust will develop. This, in turn, may increase the willingness to engage in common projects'.[59] That is, the groups may realize a common constitutional project that entails equal toleration, trust, and perhaps also mutual recognition, even if this falls well short of mutual group identification. We would see a weakening of group claims to normative primacy or dominance over perceived rivals. The essential step in the process would involve mutual deliberation, achieved through the free expression of views, mutual justification, respectful exchanges, and a commitment to probing the foundations of any reasons given.[60]

What specifically occupies us in the rest of this chapter is what, if anything, a peace referendum can contribute in this regard. We must again acknowledge the size of the challenge. In previous chapters we warned about the anti-deliberative effects of low information and misinformation, enclave deliberation, polarization and intra-group outbidding, group targeting, uneven deliberation, and violence. Granted, groups are not always bad for deliberation. Associations such as ethnic political parties can aid inclusion by providing a signal boost to the interests of minority groups.[61] And such groups may help to crystallize contested matters into just a small number of issues, helping to make deliberation more manageable.[62] Yet we also see deep pathologies. Group-sovereignty claimants' normative reasons are often entirely self-serving—based on the contingency of one's place, culture, or religion of origin.[63] Some reasons are non-public (eg, comprehensive doctrines based in divine revelation). Others are superficially public, but selective: groups may seize on just the narrow slice of public justifications that support their own sovereignty (eg,

[58] Whitaker (n 50) 72. See similarly James Tully, *Strange Multiplicity: Constitutionalism in an Age of Diversity* (CUP 1995) ch 6.

[59] Steiner and Jaramillo (n 24) 3.

[60] ibid 4.

[61] Mansbridge and others (n 37) 77–78; Joshua Cohen, 'Deliberation and Democratic Legitimacy' in Alan P Hamlin and Philip N Pettit (eds), *The Good Polity: Normative Analysis of the State* (Basil Blackwell 1989) 31.

[62] Bernard Manin, *The Principles of Representative Government* (CUP 1997) ch 6; Robert E Goodin, *Innovating Democracy: Democratic Theory and Practice After the Deliberative Turn* (OUP 2008) 258.

[63] Billig and Tajfel (n 43).

claims based on histories of habitation or persecution). One consequence is precisely the phenomenon that we are working against here: mutually exclusionary sovereignty claims. To support such claims, participants on each side of a conflict, and armchair warriors online,[64] often recognize moral virtue in just one group, and moral fault wholly in another.[65]

Yet, as we previously said, any referendum—and any other democratic institution—influences the deliberation that occurs within it.[66] Can recasting a peace referendum as a DPR help to reveal or construct common ground at the level of public values, even while formally recognizing distinct and divided groups? Can the DPR reshape deliberation between those groups, at least for the duration of a referendum campaign and vote—that is, just long enough to achieve a constitutional settlement?

III. DPR Design for Group-Sovereignty Conflicts

A. Public-Value Deliberation

In Chapter 3 we proposed a ballot that initially presents voters with a list of public values. We also said that public information and pre-voting tutorials should be framed in the language of public values. For group-sovereignty conflicts, what this means is that DPR deliberation should, to the extent possible, be concerned not with the boundaries of groups, but with the nature of the groups that those boundaries demarcate. Thus a DPR should focus on public values that leave group boundaries as is, but that seek to soften voters' exclusionary (and hence, in Rawls's terms, comprehensive) positions for the duration of the referendum. Yet, as we will see, when it comes to group sovereignty it is no small challenge to maintain the distinction between deliberating about public values on the one hand, and deliberating about boundaries or other technicalities on the other. We will need to tweak DPR designs to address this challenge.

While no DPR featuring outright public-value balloting has run as yet, there has been at least one rough historical analogue. Recall the principles of consent and parity of esteem that were central to the peace process leading to the Belfast

[64] See, eg, Camilla Orjuela, 'Distant Warriors, Distant Peace Workers? Multiple Diaspora Roles in Sri Lanka's Violent Conflict' (2008) 8(4) Global Networks 436, 443–44.

[65] Ralph K White, 'Empathizing With the Rulers of the USSR' (1983) 4(1) Political Psychology 121, 133–34.

[66] Chapter 3.

Agreement. The opening 'Declaration of Support' of the Agreement—which referendum voters eventually endorsed—used language such as 'reconciliation', 'tolerance', 'mutual trust', 'human rights', 'partnership', 'equality', 'mutual respect', and 'exclusively democratic and peaceful means'.[67] The referendum also had a *de facto* concurrent consent rule, since it was 'not likely the [political] parties and the two governments would have supported a countermajoritarian procedure'; had majorities of Catholic and Protestant voters not each supported the Agreement, 'the prospects for the [Agreement] would have been in serious jeopardy'.[68]

The Agreement enshrined the principle of parity of esteem (basically, a form of mutual group respect or recognition). It also came with extensive human rights and equality measures (eg, the creation of a Human Rights Commission and an Equality Commission, and the promise of a Bill of Rights). The process of creating an enduring constitutional settlement did not require the combining of cultures; during the referendum campaign, the two sides made few concessions to each other based on identity, and neither consented to become either less Irish or less British (though the Agreement did make it possible to be both British and Irish). There were some modest levels of mutual identification across Northern Ireland's two sharply defined groups, after conversations surrounding the peace process and referendum; however, identity groups remained largely separate.[69] The Agreement that was put to voters contemplated the legitimacy of both groups: 'a binational polity in which both nationalists/republicans and unionists/loyalists can govern the polity together'.[70] This evidently did not diminish communal pride or the senses of belonging to distinct communities, but it did encourage a reconceptualization of these qualities as less exclusionary—as not necessarily prejudicing the status claims of other groups.[71]

[67] '*Belfast Agreement*', Britain-Northern Ireland-Government of Ireland, signed 10 April 1998, No 50 (2000) Cm 4705 (entered into force 2 December 1999) Preamble paras 1–6.

[68] McEvoy (n 47) 871. 96% of Catholics and 55% of Protestants voted for the Agreement. Indeed, by contrast, while a 1973 referendum of Northern Irish voters yielded 98% support for continued union, only 1% of Catholics attended the polls that year while the rest boycotted the proceedings and stayed home; far from legitimation of the constitutional system, the result was further deep entrenchment of intercommunal divisions: Bleddyn Davies, 'The EU Referendum: Who Were the British People?' (2016) 27(3) King's Law Journal 323, 325–26.

[69] See also Ian O'Flynn, 'Why Justice Can't Have It All: In Reply to O'Neill' (2004) 4(4) Ethnicities 545, 554.

[70] McEvoy (n 47) 871. In stressing the importance of deliberation, we do not mean to play down the importance of other, equally important variables (historical, sociological, moral, etc). For example, of great importance to the Northern Ireland peace process was the election in 1997 of a Labour government committed to devolution right across the UK. In particular, the creation of local legislatures in Scotland and Wales made local government in Northern Ireland seem less of an anomaly.

[71] Note the distinction between norm *exclusivity* (Chapter 4) and norms that are in substance *exclusionary* with respect to certain groups. See this again in Chapter 7.

We should not seek to extend the lessons from a single case too far. But the case can be read as a 'proof of concept'—as a pilot or prototype for a referendum model that places public values front and centre. Of course, much can go wrong in future cases of this type. We contend that DPR design should do significantly more to promote public-value deliberation. The design of peace referendums should build on the indirect Northern Irish model, in which a set of declaratory public values merely provided background to the vote. DPRs should require voters to engage with public values directly and in a sustained fashion, especially via balloting and tutorial models such as those that we recommended in Chapter 3. Voters may otherwise remain unaware of the values or, even if aware, may lack opportunities to be informed and deliberate about them.

Yet even a DPR that adopts our full suite of recommendations faces, in the context of group-sovereignty conflict, a high risk of conceptual descent. As we said in previous chapters, conceptual descent refers to deliberation that slips into a non-public (eg, applied) key. Group-sovereignty conflict may generate particular difficulties in this regard, stemming from the conceptual ambiguity of group sovereignty itself. An unusually slippery distinction divides group sovereignty as a *value* from group sovereignty as a *legal category*. As we saw, sovereignty is central to the self-conception or to the aspirations of many groups. As we also saw, many groups seek to express their collective maturity and their status vis-à-vis other groups by holding on to, extending, or gaining specifically *legal* sovereignty.[72] Law confers a host of legal privileges, statuses, and responsibilities on groups that it recognizes as sovereign.[73]

Group sovereignty therefore has a double aspect: it is both a value and a legal category that applies the value. Invoking group sovereignty as a value raises relatively immediate questions about what that value implies in law—questions that may be unusually difficult to set aside. The values portion of the DPR ballot can include a proposition such as 'All distinct groups should enjoy a right of peaceful pursuit of sovereignty'. But the ballot perhaps should not invoke sovereignty in this way as doing so risks prejudging which applied substantive directions constitutional reform should take. This is a problem because, as we have stressed, the non-elites who make up the vast bulk of referendum voters may possess little expertise or facility for deliberation in applied modes.[74]

[72] Margalit and Raz (n 22) 440–41.
[73] Thomas D Grant, *The Recognition of States: Law and Practice in Debate and Evolution* (Greenwood Publishing Group 1999).
[74] Chapter 2.

To be sure, when a value such as sovereignty appears on a ballot, it can have an ambiguous definition and be compatible with several constitutional reform options. For example, sovereignty might be expressed, legally, as a group's outright independence, as greater sub-state autonomy, or as a hybrid of independence and continuing loose association with another state. But in practice, the concrete legal meanings of sovereignty (or similar values) are likely to be relatively clear to most observers. Sovereignty may derive its meaning from its context. To give an example, in a secessionist context, group sovereignty is likely to be taken as signifying secession leading to international statehood. In both Québec secession referendums (1980 and 1995), the term 'sovereign'/ 'sovereignty' included on the ballot was (possibly by design) ambiguous as to whether it referred to outright international statehood.[75] But in the course of the referendum campaigns, agreed connotations of key terms emerged: voters, politicians, and the media largely saw the ballot as implying international statehood.[76]

Thus in a DPR called to address a secessionist conflict, if group sovereignty were included in the list of public-values on the ballot, then perhaps only voters who favoured secession would rank this value highly. Group sovereignty could ultimately, therefore, be read not as a value proposition, but as a concrete option for substantive constitutional reform. Similar considerations apply to values such as 'independence', 'self-determination', and 'autonomy'. Each is, at once, both a value and a legal category. Each implies a concrete and even detailed set of legal implications. And, in the course of a referendum campaign, a broad consensus (informed, again, by the context of the conflict) may emerge regarding the value's substantive constitutional consequences.

As a result, while earlier in this book we expressed general confidence that referendums can avoid conceptual descent, deliberation directly about the values of *group sovereignty* may lead more often to legalistic readings. We therefore suggest that the DPR ballot should leave sovereignty off of the public-value ballot. However, that ballot may still play an important role in identifying common ground between groups defined by their distinct (existing or asserted) sovereignties. The ultimate objective of the DPR in a group-sovereignty conflict should be to ensure that multiple group sovereignties can be accepted at once as legitimate. What this may mean in

[75] For discussion of this ambiguity see François Rocher and André Lecours, 'The Correct Expression of Popular Will: Does the Wording of a Referendum Question Matter?' in Laurence Morel and Matt Qvortrup (eds), *The Routledge Handbook to Referendums and Direct Democracy* (Routledge 2017) 227.

[76] In 1995, only 23% of voters believed Québec would remain part of Canada after an affirmative vote: ibid.

precise constitutional terms is not yet a concern during public-value balloting. Decisions over whether to create, for instance, a new independent state, a consociational system, autonomy within a federal or devolved system, etc, will eventually need to be made at the negotiation stage. But in the interim the focus should be on encouraging voters to accept that a settlement will acknowledge multiple groups' *as legitimate*. This, as we foreshadowed above, is the first and often the highest hurdle to clear before any constitutional settlement can be reached.

Recall from Chapter 3 the social-psychological evidence that certain values can 'prime' poll respondents to be better able to agree, if those values are to some extent 'self-transcendent'. These values, when presented as part of preliminary information given to poll respondents, can suppress more 'self-enhancing' (ie, selfish) values such as 'power' and 'status'.[77] Conversely, priming respondents with nationalistic and identitarian values (eg, causing them to recall, first, their national affiliation) had none of the generalized, other-regarding priming effects of self-transcendent values. Indeed, as one might expect, a contrary effect resulted: respondents expressed less favourable attitudes towards cooperative, stability-enhancing policies (eg, environmental regulation).[78]

These empirical findings are broadly consistent with our expectations for a DPR's public-values ballot, in that the aim is to present voters with values that are incompatible with interpretations of sovereignty (or indeed of other values) that benefit only a voter's own positions. Even if we cannot include sovereignty itself on the public-values ballot, we can still encourage groups to accept each other in principle, in ways that presuppose non-exclusionary ideas of sovereignty. Rather than address sovereignty directly, then, we may see movement towards a constitutional settlement begin around questions of how to understand groups more generally. A public-value ballot that encourages movement away from exclusionary (or essentialist) ideas about groups may give impetus, indirectly and implicitly, to the notion that distinct group sovereignties can exist at once in the same spaces.

Plenty of values can express or presuppose the idea that multiple groups can be sovereign at once. The last section above suggested a few such values.

[77] Gregory R Maio and others, 'Changing, Priming, and Acting on Values: Effects Via Motivational Relations in a Circular Model' (2009) 97(4) Journal of Personality and Social Psychology 699, 700.

[78] Kennon M Sheldon, Charles P Nichols, and Tim Kasser, 'Americans Recommend Smaller Ecological Footprints when Reminded of Intrinsic American Values of Self-Expression, Family, and Generosity' (2011) 3(2) Ecopsychology 97, 101. These authors classify identity as 'extrinsic', and generosity or similar values as 'intrinsic'.

(i) Toleration: Rothchild's notion of pragmatism in intergroup relations is roughly equivalent to 'toleration' or, as it was described in the Belfast Agreement's preambular Declaration of Support, 'tolerance'.[79] As Peter Jones notes:

> [f]undamentally, we tolerate when we object to something but nevertheless refrain from impeding it. Religious faiths, for example, are conflicting as well as different in that they present rival bodies of belief. . . . We tolerate when we refrain from impeding that to which we object; if we do not object, we have no occasion to tolerate.[80]

Toleration entails an acceptance of others, despite disapproval of them. Some might assume that this is the most that we can usually hope for from people entangled in conflict.

(ii) Reciprocative values: Yet other, less grudging value options could be 'reconciliation', 'partnership', 'mutual respect', and 'mutual recognition' (each of which also appeared in the Declaration of Support),[81] as well as 'equality', 'dignity', or 'equal dignity'. This is only a partial list; a mini-public or other neutral body charged with writing a public-value ballot may choose others. Whatever the precise formulations of such values, each goes beyond mere toleration and instead signifies a relatively robust judgement that another person or group is actually worthy of our respect. These values are reciprocative (again drawing on Rothchild's terms).[82]

Granted, in a DPR ballot, where voters themselves rank values, some voters may reject (eg, abstain from endorsing) or may devalue any options that would seem to require them to challenge their own presumed superior normative positions (including an essentialist, exclusionary view of sovereignty). Some (as we saw) will characterize other groups as morally abject and as not at all deserving of dignity, equal respect, or trust. On the other hand, it may be doubtful that large numbers of voters would wish to reject the sorts of public values that concern us here. A voter may feel compelled to vote in favour of reciprocative values precisely because a self-evaluation as being without fault requires it. It may be difficult for a voter to declaim the other group's abjectness only to reject high-minded values oneself.

[79] *Belfast Agreement* (n 66).
[80] Peter Jones, *Essays on Toleration* (ECPR Press 2018) 1–2.
[81] *Belfast Agreement* (n 66).
[82] See, eg, Charles Taylor, 'The Politics of Recognition' in Amy Gutmann (ed), *Multiculturalism: Examining the Politics of Recognition* (Princeton University Press 1994) 25–76.

(iii) Human rights: An additional option is to include human rights on the ballot. To use the Irish example again, the positive referendum result in 1998 saw a significant meeting of minds across seemingly fixed sectarian boundaries; 'human rights' and 'equality' were among the values expressly included in the Declaration of Support, as was a commitment to 'exclusively democratic and peaceful means'.[83] Rights values in future DPR ballots (and in publicly promulgated information) can include, for instance, freedom of association, free assembly, free expression, and again 'human rights' themselves. Human rights values are generally neither overly vague nor emptily symbolic, at least in comparison with concepts such as 'mutual respect'. The meanings of rights are likely to be widely understood and amenable to deliberation in public-value terms.

This is a potentially critical effect because merely affirming another kind of value (eg, toleration) may be read as merely a symbolic trope, and may even generate distrust if it means too little in tangible terms. Group members who seek formal recognition of their group's status may understandably express cynicism towards values that, even if endorsed in a referendum, are not accompanied by substantive guarantees such as rights.[84]

At the same time, however, rights are not just rights; they also stand for equal regard towards, and for the legitimacy of, multiple distinct groups and individuals. Though rights are relatively tangible and codify particular interests, there is also an overarching objective common to most of them: recognition of equal dignity and status.[85] As Habermas notes, human dignity has become (and arguably has long been) 'the moral "source" from which all of the basic rights derive their meaning.'[86] Rights are generally understood as bulwarks against arbitrary and unequal conduct. A legal presumption in many countries provides that, if rights are owed to anyone, then they are owed to all other similarly situated people, and on the same terms.[87]

[83] *Belfast Agreement* (n 66) Preamble paras 1–6. Note how 'equality' can be classed both as toleration value and right.

[84] See, eg, Expert Panel on the Constitutional Recognition of Indigenous Australians, *Recognising Aboriginal and Torres Strait Islander Peoples in the Constitution* (2012) 130.

[85] See, eg, Jürgen Habermas, 'The Concept of Human Dignity and the Realistic Utopia of Human Rights' in Claudio Corradetti (ed), *Philosophical Dimensions of Human Rights: Some Contemporary Views* (Springer 2012) 63.

[86] ibid 65.

[87] See, eg, David Dyzenhaus, 'Law as Justification: Etienne Mureinik's Conception of Legal Culture' (1998) 14(1) South African Journal on Human Rights 11, 34; Albie Sachs, *The Strange Alchemy of Life and Law* (OUP 2009) 33; David Dyzenhaus, 'Dignity in Administrative Law: Judicial Deference in a Culture of Justification' (2012) 17 Review of Constitutional Studies 87, 92–93.

But though we have said rights can secure and concretize vaguer values and make them more predictable, that is not to say that rights produce determinate outcomes; far from it, as we observed previously.[88] Explicit commitments to rights may nevertheless convey—with a degree of firmness and definition perhaps absent in other values—the equal dignity of each individual (or, with some rights, of each group) vis-à-vis others. The values underlying rights—values that can include toleration, dignity, equality, and mutual respect—are generally incompatible with exclusionary group-sovereignty claims. But what these values may mean can be made clearer by the inclusion of human rights as tangible examples. Exclusionary sovereignty claims can only be sustained by dismissing the dissenting claims of those people with values and interests different from those of a dominant group. The objective of human rights is precisely to allow these kinds of dissenters to press their claims. It may be too cognitively challenging to maintain both an exclusionary view of group sovereignty and to acknowledge rights and their implied self-transcendent universalism.

Of course, as soon as we begin speaking of rights as universal, we open ourselves to certain well-trod criticisms of 'human rights imperialism' and of rights as (arguably) Western creations.[89] Without wading into this debate, we must nevertheless acknowledge that in some places the debate itself could place a drag on the salutary effects that we are claiming for rights. On the other hand, it is also important to recall that distressful experiences in conflict have frequently served as vivid reminders of the salience of fundamental human rights and interests[90]—as potentially powerful, tangible counterweights to these theoretical reservations.

In sum, while conflicts over the boundaries of identity may be intractable, and the places of group identity largely irreducible, groups in conflict may nevertheless be able to agree on certain sets of public values. This becomes more plausible when the values in question are highly generalized values such as toleration, mutual recognition, non-violence, and equality, and perhaps even more when these values are housed within the relatively concrete forms that human rights can provide. In these ways we can perhaps find a measure of inter-group agreement even while bracketing indissoluble clashes over the boundaries of the groups' identities.

[88] Chapter 2.

[89] See, eg, Makau Wa Mutua, 'The Ideology of Human Rights' (1995) 36 Virginia Journal of International Law 589, 592.

[90] Habermas, 'The Concept of Human Dignity' (n 84) 64.

B. Boundary Problems

But if we are committed to taking the boundaries of groups as given, then which groups should the DPR accommodate? And how shall we define them? As an illustration of these 'boundary problems',[91] consider the multifaceted Israeli-Palestinian, or Israeli-Arab, conflict. Should just two distinct groups enjoy distinct rights of consent (eg, 'Jews' and 'Palestinians')? Or should some further, more diverse set of groups have these rights too (eg, Arab Israelis, Gazans, Arab West Bank residents, Christian Palestinians, Druze, and Jews)? Compounding these ambiguities are the uncertain definitions surrounding the conflict. How far does the conflict extend and whom does it 'affect'? Finally, are the relevant ethnic categories, like 'Arab' and 'Jew', as distinct as we commonly assume?[92] Should groups that are only partly distinct (eg, Gazan versus West Bank Palestinian Arabs, and Druze versus other Israelis) be counted independently, or together?

In general, at least three types of DPR-design boundary questions need to be addressed.

(i) *Combatant and non-combatant groups:* A DPR's main objective is to convince groups that have taken up arms to put them down again. This means that at a minimum the groups that are (or have been, or conceivably will be) combatants in the conflict should be asked to give their consent, each as a separate group. But should groups that are not significantly involved in a conflict also be asked to consent in a referendum?

One objective of any constitutional referendum is to ensure that all people affected by fundamental reforms can give or withhold their consent. Undue exclusion should be avoided, therefore, even where a group is not a combatant group but is otherwise deeply affected by a conflict or a constitutional settlement. Indeed, a policy that denies concurrent consent to groups that historically did not engage directly in conflict, yet are of the conflict area (eg, Druze), may perversely reward groups that do take up arms. And excluding the group from deliberations may be the original triggering event that seeds resentment and violence.

However, counting too many groups can make achieving a settlement more difficult. Groups at the centre of a conflict may even object

[91] Robert A Dahl, *After the Revolution? Authority in a Good Society* (Yale University Press 1990 [1970]) 60–61.

[92] Emily B Gottreich, 'Historicizing the Concept of Arab Jews in the Maghrib' (2008) 98(4) The Jewish Quarterly Review 433.

to including smaller groups from the conflict's periphery. Such inclusion may undermine the potency of holding a referendum as a formal act to address the specific set of grievances that initially spawned the conflict.[93] A group that seeks sovereignty may also perceive itself to be categorically distinct from other groups.

Faced with these conundrums, DPR designers may need to arrive at flexible solutions. For instance, the consent of only some groups may be deemed to be *required*, while that of other groups may only be given an *advisory* status. As well, instead of outright consensus, adopting a majority or supermajority requirement (eg, 4/7 or 5/7 groups must vote 'yes') can prevent the raising of too many veto points capable of blocking a settlement. Many constitutional amending formulas similarly reject complete consensus and still manage to give rise to socially accepted constitutional norms.[94] However, far less certain is whether this approach can be viable amid conflict where, as we previously said, the legitimacy of the amending process may not be accepted by all as a matter of course.[95] Achieving settlement without the consent of key combatant groups may only aggravate conflict and underscore the group's exclusion from the settlement. In this regard, much may depend on the group's margin of rejection. A substantial margin could indicate the group's clear rejection of the settlement, and flag the risks—especially to long-term endurance of a settlement—of proceeding with the settlement process.

(ii) *Diaspora and expatriate voters:* Laws concerning the voting franchise can treat diaspora or expatriate voters many different ways. ('Diaspora' approximately refers to people, and especially the descendants of people, who left or were forced to leave an ethnic homeland en masse.[96]) These laws may disallow non-resident voting; allow it for non-residents physically present in the territory at the time of the vote; allow non-resident citizens to vote, either indefinitely or for several years after their departure; or allow votes by people considered to be ethnic kin scattered in diaspora. In cases of conflict, these democratic boundary choices are, as with so much else, particularly vexed.

[93] McEvoy (n 47) 869.

[94] Joel Colón-Ríos (n 14) 212 (citing Canada's constitutional reforms adopted despite objections by Québec); cf Richard Albert, *Constitutional Amendments: Making, Breaking, and Changing Constitutions* (OUP 2019) 129, 224.

[95] Chapter 4.

[96] Jonathan Grossman, 'Toward a Definition of Diaspora' (2019) 42(8) Ethnic and Racial Studies 1263, 1271.

Adopting the concurrent consent approach can defuse some boundary problems around the inclusion of external voters (eg, expatriate/diaspora Israelis or Palestinians). Concurrent consent sees majorities within each main group counted separately, with each group as a collective having an equal say. Thus there is little risk of one community numerically overwhelming another when external voters are included. As well, in theory, diasporans may be better able to regard conflicts with an open mind. They may be relatively immune to the 'insider problem' that people long exposed to the ins and outs of a dispute can struggle to envisage alternatives to the status quo. External voters' comparative insights from abroad may even highlight how constitutional systems and group relations can be conceived differently.

But an overly inclusive franchise can also have deleterious effects—for instance, on deliberation and voting outcomes. Voters who remain abroad may not participate meaningfully in deliberations during the referendum campaign. Extensive deliberative engagement online (eg, via interactive tutorials preceding an electronic vote) can to some extent mitigate this problem.[97] Yet some external voters may particularly fail to see the conflict in balanced terms, especially if they are not subject to the hurt of a mutually hurting stalemate. Put another way, if those who live physically outside of the conflict do not see the conflict as directly affecting them, it may be harder for them to imagine their own reciprocal obligations vis-à-vis other voters. It is notable that in some cases (eg, Northern Ireland and Sri Lanka) large diaspora communities have funded violence and egged conflicts on with uncompromising rhetoric.[98] But in other cases (eg, Nagorno Karabakh and Israel/Palestine), the influence of diasporans on peacemaking has been decidedly more mixed.[99]

(iii) *Deciding boundary questions:* Thus far we have raised more questions than we have answered, since any answers must remain tentative. Rather than improbably seek to answer all boundary questions once and for all, we prefer to see boundary decisions issued case-by-case. Yet who should make these decisions?

We cannot straightforwardly turn boundary questions over to the people themselves in a preliminary boundary-setting referendum as this

[97] Chapter 3.
[98] Orjuela (n 63).
[99] Bahar Baser and Ashok Swain, 'Diasporas as Peacemakers: Third Party Mediation in Homeland Conflicts' (2008) 25(3) International Journal on World Peace 7, 15; Yossi Shain, 'The Role of Diasporas in Conflict Perpetuation or Resolution' (2002) 22(2) Sais Review 115.

> would raise a problem of regress: who should vote in the initial referendum?[100] Any boundary question must be answered in theoretical and historicized terms, and thus in relatively closed settings such as expert bodies. Nonetheless, get the answer 'wrong' in some way, and some voters may register their displeasure by ultimately voting against a settlement proposal. And no mere handful of elites should make these decisions, which could hand to them too much power to steer the course of referendum outcomes,[101] and may also undermine trust in the referendum.

Our preferred approach would therefore be to make use of deliberative mini-publics, which were key to the DPR model proposed in Chapter 3. We said much about how mini-publics are relatively trusted, inclusive, and deliberative bodies. Randomly selected members are exposed to extended, facilitated learning and deliberation phases, in which they hear both from subject area experts and from each other.[102] Another body, such as a neutral international body or third-party government, could in principle be employed instead. Yet this is a second-best option as it lacks widespread social inclusion and therefore may not engender trust.

To some extent the problem of regress also arises in those mini-publics that descriptively represent the broader society's discrete identity groups. In such cases, designers of mini-publics must decide which groups the mini-public will represent. However, once the mini-public gets underway, there is a reasonable likelihood that members will not merely reason from their own groups' interests. We noted above that group identification is usually a relatively rigid condition, especially amid conflict. Yet the more particular experience of mini-publics has shown that, within these bodies, group identification may be less determinative of deliberation outcomes. Mini-publics can remain both inclusive and, relatively speaking, open-minded.[103]

[100] On the infinite regress problem in boundary questions, see Frank I Michelman, 'Constitutional Authorship' in Larry Alexander (ed), *Constitutionalism: Philosophical Foundations* (CUP, 1998) 64–98.

[101] Davies (n 67) 332; Arend Lijphart, *Democracies: Patterns of Majoritarian and Consensus Government in Twenty-One Countries* (Yale University Press 1984) 204; cf Mads Qvortrup, 'Research Note: Are Referendums Controlled and Pro-hegemonic?' (2000) 48(4) Political Studies 821.

[102] Chapter 3.

[103] See, eg, Robert S Ratner, 'British Columbia's Citizens' Assembly: The Learning Phase' (2004) 27(2) Canadian Parliamentary Review 20; Ian O'Flynn and Gaurav Sood, 'What Would Dahl Say? An Appraisal of the Democratic Credentials of Deliberative Polls and Other Mini-Publics' in André Bächtiger, Kimmo Grönlund, and Maija Setälä (eds), *Deliberative Mini-Publics: Involving Citizens in the Democratic Process* (ECPR Press 2014) 41. M Lydia Khuri, 'Facilitating Arab-Jewish Intergroup Dialogue in the College Setting' (2004) 7(3) Race Ethnicity and Education 229, 244; Robert Luskin and others, 'Deliberating across Deep Divides' (2014) 62(1) Political Studies 116; Alex Norman, 'The Use of the Group and Group Work Techniques in Resolving Interethnic Conflict' (1992) 14(3/4) Social Work with Groups 175; Didier Caluwaerts and Kris Deschouwer, 'Building Bridges Across Political

A final concern, however, is whether the mini-public ought to see equal or proportionate representation of any groups that it includes (a concern we first raised in Chapter 3). Proportionate representation is standard in many mini-publics. The objective is not for members to represent their own groups' views unreflectively and rigidly, but rather to make sure that a wide range of perspectives gain inclusion into the proceedings. Exposed to these perspectives, mini-public members in practice often change their own views—or at least better understand the bases of, and also better respect, the views of others with whom they may still disagree. However, in cases of conflict, it may be preferable to split membership on the mini-public equally between or among groups, even if some groups are actually more numerous in the population.

This approach could backfire if ultimately it only signifies that all ideas are to be accorded equal value, irrespective of deliberation. It could also entrench identity-based decision-making. But these risks may be no more likely than under a rule of descriptive proportionality. And equal representation better expresses the ideal of an equal airing of all points of view, regardless of their social prevalence. The rule of equality may be especially appropriate for intergroup conflict, where the mini-public is created precisely to address group tensions. That is, in cases *about* group tensions, it would be incongruous if some groups were better represented in the mini-public and given outsized time and opportunity to present their points of view regarding these tensions.

IV. Conclusion: Themes and Variations

We have seen the relative intransigence of boundaries in group-sovereignty conflicts. And yet we have argued that, despite the drag that groups may impose on deliberation, deliberation still remains a real possibility. It may particularly be so at the level of public values, under the DPR model that we propose. We thus began to see some ways in which DPR design might improve the possibility of deliberation between groups in conflict that enjoy rights of concurrent consent. To be sure, having made this case for DPRs addressing group-sovereignty conflicts, we also saw a number of problems that potentially follow—including the risk of conceptual descent, as well as open questions about which groups to include and how to define them.

Divides: Experiments on Deliberative Democracy in Deeply Divided Belgium' (2014) 6(3) European Political Science Review 427; and discussion in Chapter 3.

In the next two chapters, we will move beyond these general points to consider more particular conflict types within the 'group-sovereignty' umbrella. This is a capacious term. Within it there are several further categories. But in the next two chapters we focus on two types in particular: secessionist conflicts (Chapter 6) and indigenous-settler conflicts (Chapter 7).

6

Group Secession

I. Introduction

In the last chapter we looked broadly at the issue of group sovereignty. As we saw, a group is sovereign when, in the relevant legal and political sense, it is independent of other groups and its standing as a group is equal to that of every other sovereign group. It may have duties or obligations towards other groups, but those obligations must be freely willed. As we also saw in the last chapter, public-value deliberation does not require groups, or individual group members, to deliberate about the boundaries of their group identities. Rather, it requires them to frame their arguments in terms of values and other general considerations that any democratic person could reasonably be expected to endorse, whatever their more particular comprehensive beliefs, values, or commitments. And it does so in the hope that agreement on constitutional norms—or, in Rawls's terms, constitutional essentials and matters of basic justice—can be reached from common ground. We have argued that the deliberative peace referendum (DPR) can serve as an important instrument or facilitator of this fundamental democratic goal.

That said, one would not expect this argument to play out in the same way, no matter what the context. Different types of conflict raise different types of challenge, and these differences are likely to have an important bearing on how the DPR is institutionally conceived and implemented. At the most general level, the nature of the conflict will bear on the question of who should be included in the vote or, otherwise put, on where the boundaries of the electorate should be drawn. In the last chapter, we argued that, in the case of group-sovereignty disputes, a new peace agreement should in principle secure the consent of all the major groups that are parties to the conflict. More precisely, it should secure their consent concurrently: the approval of a new peace agreement should be conditional on the approval of a majority within each of these groups, as expressed through a DPR. Insofar as this condition can be met, there is reason to think that concurrent consent can secure not just settlement agreement but also settlement endurance. However, concurrent consent is far

Deliberative Peace Referendums. Ron Levy, Ian O'Flynn, Hoi L Kong, Oxford University Press (2021). © Ron Levy, Ian O'Flynn, and Hoi L Kong. DOI: 10.1093/oso/9780198867036.003.0006

more problematic when it comes to the type of group-sovereignty conflict with which we are concerned in this chapter, namely secessionist conflict.

As it is normally defined, secession refers to the withdrawal of one political unit from another political unit—usually, a territorially concentrated group manifesting its sovereignty by withdrawing from a larger, existing state. The existing state may sometimes allow a secession referendum to take place—for example, the 2014 Scottish referendum on independence from the UK was legally authorized by the UK government. Yet while in that sense one might say that concurrent consent has been secured, the decisive choice remains with the seceding group; only Scottish voters were entitled vote in the Scottish independence referendum.[1]

In other cases, however, the existing state will seek to block the referendum, usually by declaring it unconstitutional or illegal, or even unjust. Recent examples include the 2017 Catalan independence referendum and the 2017 Kurdistan Region of Iraq (KRI) independence referendum.[2] In cases like these, the referendum tends to be deeply divisive: the existing state will claim that the referendum cannot go ahead without its consent, while the secessionists will claim that the state's consent is not required—that, as a sovereign group, the right to determine their future political status is entirely theirs. Under such conditions, concurrent consent may seem beside the point.

In this chapter, we will consider in detail the idea of group secession and its challenges for the DPR. To set the scene we will begin, in Section II, by looking more closely at the concept of secession itself. To draw out its distinctive features, we will start by contrasting secession with partition. We will then stress that while secession refers to the withdrawal of one political unit from a larger political unit or existing state, the degree to which the seceding unit acts unilaterally is likely to have an important bearing on the perceived legitimacy of its actions. To deepen this analysis, we will return to the distinction, first introduced in Chapter 4, between formal legitimacy as *pedigree* versus formal legitimacy as *expression*.

In Section III, we will consider the relationship between secession and the DPR. We will do so by examining the question of how secession might be justified. Broadly speaking, there are two main approaches. The first, *remedial right only* approach holds that secession should be allowed only as a remedy

[1] *Agreement between the United Kingdom Government and the Scottish Government on a referendum on independence for Scotland* (15 October 2012).

[2] Sean Mueller, 'Catalonia: The Perils of Majoritarianism' (2019) 30(2) Journal of Democracy 142; Dylan O'Driscoll and Bahar Baser, 'Independence Referendums and Nationalist Rhetoric: the Kurdistan Region of Iraq' (2019) 40(11) Third World Quarterly 2016.

for severe human rights abuses; the second, *primary right* approach holds that secession should be allowed only if that is what a majority of a territorially concentrated sovereign group so determines.[3] A DPR is one (though certainly not the only) way in which such a determination might be reached. Yet since remedial right only theorists level some serious criticisms at the primary right approach, those criticisms must be addressed before we can describe the institutional specifics of our case. If the primary right approach is found wanting—if secession cannot be justified on such grounds—then the case for seeking to manage secessionist conflicts through a DPR will also be found wanting. We will show, however, why this worry does not hold.

In Section IV, we will return to questions of institutional design of the DPR. We will do so by starting from the question of who should be included in the vote—the so-called 'boundary problem'—thus building on discussions in Chapter 5. As we will see, the boundary problem is especially problematic for secession referendums. While only the secessionist region should have the vote, secession also deeply affects people in the larger existing state, who therefore must still be represented in some way. We will suggest how mini-publics might be organized to deal with this dilemma. We will also discuss how the peculiar circumstances of a secession referendum should affect, among other DPR features, the structure of the ballot and the degree of international involvement.

II. Secession, Unilateralism, and Formality

As we indicated, one way of getting to grips with the concept of secession is by contrasting it with partition.[4] While the two terms are often used interchangeably, they are overlapping rather than coextensive. In secession, one part of an existing state intends to break away to form its own independent state. Thus, even when the existing state agrees to allow the secession to go ahead, the final decision rests with the members of the seceding group or region. In that sense, consent in a case of secession is *unilateral*. As we will see later on, there are

[3] On the remedial approach, see Allen Buchanan, 'Theories of Secession' (1997) 26(1) Philosophy & Public Affairs 31; see also Allen Buchanan, *Secession: The Morality of Political Divorce from Fort Sumter to Lithuania and Quebec* (Westview Press 1991). On the primary right approach, see, eg, Harry Beran, 'A Liberal Theory of Secession' (1984) 32(1) Political Studies 21; Avishai Margalit and Joseph Raz, 'National Self-determination' (1990) 87(9) Journal of Philosophy 439; Margaret Moore, 'The Moral Value of Collective Self-Determination and the Ethics of Secession' (2019) 50(4) Journal of Social Philosophy 620; Daniel Philpott, 'In Defense of Self-Determination' (1995) 105(2) Ethics 352; Christopher Wellman, *A Theory of Secession: The Case for Political Self-Determination* (CUP 2005).

[4] Brendan O'Leary, 'Analysing Partition: Definition, Classification and Explanation' (2007) 26(8) Political Geography 886, 887–88.

different views on the question of if and when secession is justified. But many legal and political philosophers agree that secession does not require the consent of the existing state—even if, in practice, it is better if the existing (and soon to be 'remnant') state does agree.[5]

In practice, secession and partition can be hard to disentangle. Yet the two are analytically distinct. Like secession, partition is the division of an existing state into two or more independent states. But unlike secession, partition is either *bilateral* or *imposed*. When bilateral, the two parts of an existing state decide to go their separate ways. The decision to dissolve the former Czechoslovakia—agreed by both the Slovak prime minister Vladimir Mečiar and the Czech Prime Minister Václav Klaus—is a case in point.[6] When imposed, however, the intentions of the different groups or regions are not directly in play (ie, the partition is not bilateral in any politically meaningful sense). Historically, partition has been imposed by colonial powers—for example, the British partition of India in 1947 and Palestine in 1948—and has often led to chronic problems, including persistent intergroup violence and poor interstate relations.

There are other ways in which the contrast between secession and partition might be drawn. For example, Brendan O'Leary points to the importance of geographic ties. As he argues, secession is usually driven by putative sovereign groups' seeking formal independence for (what they regard as) their historic territory—for example, Scottish nationalists seek to unwind time to before the Act of Union of 1707. By contrast, partition is often blind to the importance of territory or identity—for example, the Turkish army's partition of Cyprus in 1974 created an entirely new internal border, displacing as many as 200,000 people in the process.[7] We do not dispute these other distinctions. However, the unilateral/bilateral distinction in particular is especially germane to our concerns: as we will see over the course of this chapter, it carries the analytic power that we seek.

While some secessions are relatively peaceful, others are deeply conflictual, even violent. It is not always easy to say what makes the difference, but one

[5] Secession attempts in which the consent of the existing state is absent tend to fail. However, as we will see, a notable exception was the (legally suspect) 2014 Crimean Status Referendum: see, eg, Thomas D Grant, 'Annexation of Crimea' (2015) 109(1) American Journal of International Law 68; Stephen Tierney, 'Sovereignty and Crimea: How Referendum Democracy Complicates Constituent Power in Multinational Societies' (2015) 16(3) German Law Journal 523.

[6] Though it seems to have been an elite-led process, David Lake and Donald Rothchild attribute a 'mutually agreeable separation' to the two ethnic groups, Czechs and Slovaks: David Lake and Donald Rothchild, 'Spreading Fear: The Genesis of Transnational Ethnic Conflict' in David Lake and Donald Rothchild (eds), *The International Spread of Ethnic Conflict: Fear, Diffusion and Escalation* (Princeton University Press 1998) 11; cf O'Leary, 'Analysing Partition' (n 4) 982; Philpott (n 3) 380.

[7] Charis Psaltis and others, 'Internally Displaced Persons and the Cyprus Peace Process' (2020) 41(1) International Political Science Review 138, 140.

important point of comparison is the degree to which the secession was *legally permitted* in constitutional or international law. At one end of the spectrum of legality, one might point to the secession of Montenegro from Serbia in 2006, conducted under the terms of the 2003 Constitutional Charter of Serbia and Montenegro. While the result was viewed as a personal blow to the Serbian nationalist prime minister, Vojislav Kostunica, it was nevertheless accepted by the Serbian federal government in Belgrade.[8] It was also roundly welcomed by the European Union (EU), which had invested heavily in the process.[9] The fact that the referendum took place within a recognized constitutional framework and had EU support indicates that the secession complied with international norms.

At the other end of the spectrum of legality, one might point to the Crimean status referendum of 2014. As Stephen Tierney notes, this 'event was deeply controversial because it was organised against the backdrop of Russian intervention and the Ukrainian Government's (which had no involvement in the process) challenging of its legality'.[10] Like the Montenegrin referendum, the Crimean referendum was unilateral: only Crimeans had a vote on whether to secede with a view to re-joining Russia. But while the referendum had the support of the Russian state, that support most conspicuously took the form of Russian soldiers, with military insignia removed, on the ground. The Crimean referendum had no clear basis in domestic (ie, Ukrainian) law and even less in international law.[11] As Tierney points out, the 'Supreme Council of Crimea (Crimea's Parliament) proclaimed that it was acting "[w]ith regard to the charter of the United Nations and a whole range of other international documents"'.[12] It also pointed to what it saw as the precedent set by Kosovo.[13] Yet the relevance of these international norms to the specific case of Crimea has not been established by a body empowered to issue an authoritative statement about the case.[14] Under such conditions, with the legal authority of the referendum and the annexation doubtful, it is hardly surprising that the case proved—and continues to prove—so controversial.

[8] Nicholas Woods, 'Montenegro Votes to Secede from Serbia', *The New York Times* (news article, 21 May 2006).

[9] Judy Batt, 'Montenegro and Serbia after the Referendum', European Union Institute for Security Studies, *Alerts* (1 May 2006).

[10] Tierney (n 5) 523.

[11] ibid.

[12] ibid 528, citing Christian Marxsen, 'Crimea's Declaration of Independence', *EJIL:Talk!* (18 March 2014).

[13] Tierney (n 5) 528.

[14] The presence of Russia troops may also have undermined the legitimacy of Crimea's secession tout court.

To explain why (*bona fide*) legality may matter, recall our discussion of the concept of formality in Chapter 4. There we drew a distinction between formal legitimacy as *pedigree* versus formal legitimacy as *expression*. In the pedigree view, legitimacy stems from an act of lawmaking that relies on established legal norms and authority. Thus, when a government enacts a putative constitutional reform via pre-existing laws or authority (eg, constitutional amending formulas, or the general authority to legislate), that enactment potentially confers legitimacy on the outcomes of the reform process. Since the Montenegrin referendum relied on established legal norms and authority, apparently more than did the Crimean referendum, the outcome in the former case had the better claim to legal pedigree.

In cases of secessionist conflict, a formal imprimatur such as this may be particularly important if it can mitigate the degree—as well as the destabilizing effects—of a secession's unilateralism. The Montenegrin referendum was still essentially unilateral, as only Montenegrins had the vote. Yet the established norms invoked in this case can be taken as proxies for wider consent, and may even have given the process of secession certain 'bilateral dimensions'. Formal legal pedigree may, partly for this reason, help to determine whether a settlement in practice will manage to quell conflict.

Of course, we cannot take for granted that established norms enabling secession will actually exist or that they will be invoked. In many cases, as we began to see above, domestic or even international support for secession will simply not arise. Even so, as we said, formality can also be expressive and extra-legal. Recall from Chapter 4 that on our preferred, sociological view of constitutional legitimation, the expressive effects of a putative reform process indicate which norm, out of a field of contenders, should be adopted exclusively and assume a fundamental position within a hierarchy of norms. We also said that expressive legitimation is especially effective when it is no mere empty formality, but a process backed by some normative content.

Take, for example, the Catalan secession referendum of 2017. That referendum had no basis in Spanish constitutional law and hence no formal pedigree.[15] But did it have expressive legitimacy? On some accounts, the referendum, and the threat of independence that it entailed, were merely bargaining tools—not *bona fide* democratic exercises—that the Catalan government sought to employ to wring greater political and economic concessions out of

[15] Montserrat Guibernau, 'Secessionism in Catalonia: After Democracy' (2013) 12(4) Ethnopolitics 368, 379.

the central government in Madrid.[16] In that case, the answer would appear to be 'no'. But on other accounts, the referendum had its origins in a grass-roots movement that had long argued for a 'right to decide' and which had, in fact, begun to organize unofficial votes on independence starting in 2009.[17] In that case, the answer would appear to be 'it's complicated'.

Pro-independence Catalan elites, particularly those in the local governing parliamentary coalition, seem to have acted strategically. They 'wagered that if they could provoke a strong enough response from the Spanish government, then that would galvanise feelings of regional identity. Pro-independence voters would turn out, and everyone else would find a good reason to stay home'.[18] In that, they seem to have had some success; 90 per cent of voters cast ballots in favour of independence on the back of what the Catalonian government said was turnout of 41.6 per cent.[19] But success of this sort does not occur in a vacuum. Regional identity had been growing for some time. And while grass-roots unofficial votes may have no legal standing, they can still in some respects be effective. They may expose agreement in favour of independence (or, in the Catalan case, the right to decide on whether or not to be independent). But also significantly, the rarity, expense, and popular imprimatur of the unofficial referendum can indicate the outsized importance of the process and its outcomes. It can, that is, contribute to their formal legitimacy as expression.

It is no part of our purpose to celebrate or promote unofficial or extra-legal referendums per se, though neither is it any part of our purpose to decry them. Our concern throughout this book is with the role of referendums in aiding the transition from conflict to peace. Settling secessionist conflicts usually will require some form of domestic settlement and international recognition. It is, however, also plausible to assume that the manner in which a secession

[16] See, eg, Josep M Colomer, 'The Venturous Bid for the Independence of Catalonia' (2017) 45(5) Nationalities Papers 950. cf Jaume López and Marc Sanjaume-Calvet, 'The Political Use of de facto Referendums of Independence: The Case of Catalonia' [2020] Representation (forthcoming); cf Mueller (n 2) 149–51.

[17] Guibernau (n 15) 384; López and Sanjaume-Calvet (n 16) 5–7.

[18] Erik Jones, 'Catalonia and the Problem of Identity Politics' (2017) 59(6) Survival 41, 42. For a rational choice-inspired analysis of the conditions under which referendums on ethnic and national issues are most likely to occur, see Matt Qvortrup, *Referendums and Ethnic Conflict* (University of Pennsylvania Press 2014). As Qvortrup concludes, '[s]tatistically speaking, the best predictors of whether an independence referendum will be held are political competition and external military threat': at 67. O'Driscoll and Baser's analysis of the 2017 Kurdistan Region in Iraq independence referendum lends support to this conclusion: O'Driscoll and Baser, 'Referendums and Nationalist Rhetoric' (n 2).

[19] Actual turn out may have been as low as 27%: André Lecours, 'The Political Consequences of Independence Referenda in Liberal Democracies: Quebec, Scotland, and Catalonia' (2018) 50(2) Polity 243 fn23.

referendum is conducted—especially, though by no means only, when the secession lacks formal pedigree—will have a significant bearing on future relationships between the secessionist group, the existing state, and the wider international community. A secession referendum conceived, and so as far as possible conducted, as a DPR may have greater expressive legitimacy than another kind of referendum. Expressive legitimacy secured through a DPR may make a difference to what happens in the longer run. For instance, even if secession receives a negative response in a referendum, if the referendum is run fairly and deliberatively it may defuse some of the forces driving conflict and long-term instability. And, as we will see below, elements of the DPR can be designed to add (much like existing legal norms can) a degree of bilateral deliberation to what is, essentially, still a group's unilateral choice to secede.

With these thoughts in mind, in a moment we will turn to the design question of how exactly a DPR might look in the case of secession. Yet before we can do so, there is a prior question that needs to be addressed. Thus far we have simply assumed that referendums can have a role to play in authorizing a group's choice to secede or in re-authorizing the status quo—that a referendum may be integral to formal or expressive legitimacy in either case. However, that assumption is not straightforward. To see why, it is important to consider the legal and philosophical debate over whether and when secession is justified.

III. Are DPRs Appropriate to Address Secession?

When it comes to the justification of secession, political and legal theorists interested in the question tend to divide into two broad camps. On the one hand, *remedial right only* theorists argue that a group has a right to secede if and only if it has suffered certain injustices—principally, serious and persistent abuses of human rights—for which secession is the appropriate remedy of last resort.[20] On the other hand, *primary right* theories accept that a group can have a right to secede on remedial grounds, but they contend that the right to secede can also exist even when the group has not been subject to injustice. For some primary right theorists, groups may have a right to secede simply because

[20] Buchanan, 'Theories of Secession' (n 3) 34–35, 37. According to Buchanan, a more expansive remedial right only account would include among the injustices that can ground a unilateral right to secede not only (1) the violation of basic human rights but also (2) unjust annexation and (3) the state's persistent violation of intra-state autonomy arrangements: Allen Buchanan, *Justice, Legitimacy, and Self-Determination: Moral Foundations for International Law* (OUP 2003) 218.

their individual members share the relevant ascriptive characteristics.[21] Yet for other primary right theorists, groups may have a right to secede simply because that is what a majority of their membership decides (whether or not they share the same ascriptive characteristics).[22]

Of course, majority support can be tested indirectly—for example, through a vote in parliament. Yet according to some primary right theorists, the ideal method of decision is the referendum.[23] Secession, on this view, is regarded as a collective act of self-determination. In turn, self-determination is commonly understood in terms of two (analytically distinct) dimensions: *constitutive* and *ongoing*. As James Anaya explains:

> substantive self-determination consists of two normative strains: First, in what may be called its *constitutive* aspect, self-determination requires that the governing institutional order be substantially the creation of processes guided by the will of the people, or peoples, governed. Second, in what may be called its *ongoing* aspect, self-determination requires that the governing institutional order, independently of the processes leading to its creation or alteration, be one under which people may live and develop freely on a continuous basis.[24]

Constitutive self-determination refers to the normative or evaluative idea that each sovereign group should be free to decide on its own political status. That could involve 'opting for or rejecting independent statehood or inclusion in a state other than the one it is currently a part of'.[25] By contrast, ongoing self-determination refers to the idea that each sovereign group should have political control over significant areas of its own collective life—including its own collective deliberations—free from external domination. That could be within its own sovereign state or it could be within a federal region with certain constitutionally protected powers.[26]

Of the two, the constitutive dimension is especially relevant in cases of secession. In this spirit, for example, Margaret Moore argues that, when supporters of Catalonian independence expressed shock at the 'violent and repressive

[21] See, eg, Margalit and Raz (n 3); see also David Miller, 'Secession and the Principle of Nationality' (1997) 26 Canadian Journal of Philosophy 261 (supplementary volume 1).

[22] For an associative or consent-based theory of secession, see Beran (n 3).

[23] Philpott (n 3) 379; cf Moore (n 3) 624–30.

[24] James Anaya, *Indigenous Peoples in International Law* (OUP 1996) 81 (emphasis in original). cf Margalit and Raz (n 3) 439.

[25] Buchanan, *Justice, Legitimacy, and Self-Determination* (n 20) 332–33.

[26] cf Margalit and Raz (n 3) 239–440.

response' of the Spanish state, they were implicitly appealing to the constitutive aspect of self-determination—to their right 'to determine the character and boundaries of the political community itself' via a referendum.[27] But what exactly is the relationship between constitutive self-determination and the institution of the referendum? Why, on a primary right view, might one think that a referendum is required to settle the question of secession? Secession is not just an act of constitutive self-determination but a *collective* act of state creation. Collective acts of state creation can be indirect, and thus left to a parliament or constitutional convention. But since constitutional norms are fundamental (because they enjoy ultimate priority over other rules and actions), their reach and gravity is likely to be such that, as a matter of basic political principle, ordinary people should have their say over them directly. We first made these arguments in Chapters 4 and 5 when discussing popular sovereignty and democratic constitutionalism.[28]

Unfortunately, matters do not end there. On a primary right view, sovereign groups should have the right to determine their own political statuses. Accordingly, if a majority wishes to see the group secede, it should be allowed to do so. This wish can, and on some primary right accounts should, be tested and expressed in a referendum. However, remedial right only theorists argue that the primary right approach is misguided: they argue that secession cannot be grounded in either ascriptive characteristics or in the right to collective self-determination (and specifically in its constitutive dimension). This argument has been most forcefully pressed by Allen Buchanan.[29] Insofar as it holds, it undermines the claim that DPRs can have an important role to play in managing secessionist conflicts between sovereign groups. As we have presented it here, the DPR depends for its justification on the right to collective self-determination; but if the right to collective self-determination cannot ground a right to secede, then the case for the DPR in secessionist conflicts will also disappear.

Before we look at this argument in more detail, it is important to get some sense of Buchanan's own, preferred remedial right only conception. According

[27] Moore (n 3) 623.

[28] Not all secession movements seek the creation of a democratic state; they might, for instance, seek the creation of a theocratic state—though, as we saw in Chapter 4, even authoritarian states use popular sovereignty to lend key normative support for the constitutional order. But for those secession movements that do seek the creation of a democratic state, a contradiction arises if the effort to create such a state occurs without appreciable democratic participation: Ian O'Flynn and Ron Levy, 'Deliberative Constitutional Referendums in Deeply Divided Societies' (2020) 53(1) University of British Columbia Law Review 205, 214–15.

[29] Buchanan, 'Theories of Secession' (n 3); Buchanan, *Justice, Legitimacy, and Self-Determination* (n 20).

to Buchanan, as mentioned, the right to secede is not a primary right; it is instead 'derived from the violation of other, independently characterisable rights'.[30] Clearly, this approach sets the bar extremely high. But in so doing, it appears to privilege the wishes of the existing state over the wishes of the would-be secessionist region. In response, Buchanan argues that the remedial right only approach is much more likely than the primary right approach to meet a number of important tests, including what he terms the test of 'minimal realism' (ie, a significant prospect of eventually being adopted): remedial right only theories have a much better likelihood of being adopted since they pose much less of a threat to the existing international state-based order.[31]

That argument is vulnerable to the charge that it is excessively realist—that it is too much about protecting the special interests of pre-existing states.[32] However, as Buchanan points out, a state's interest in preserving the integrity of its borders also carries significant *moral* weight. More specifically, the principle of state integrity serves two important moral goals: it protects individual rights and expectations as well as the integrity of political participation.[33] To the extent that territorial integrity helps to support these goals, the charge that the remedial right only approach is excessively realist appears not to hold. Interestingly, Buchanan adds that,

> the ability of representative institutions to approximate the ideal of deliberative democracy . . . also depends, in part, upon stable control over a definite territory, and thereby the effective exercise of political authority over those within it. This stability is essential if it is to be reasonable for citizens to invest themselves in cultivating and practicing the demanding virtues of deliberative democracy.[34]

This claim is questionable: some deliberative theorists argue that deliberative democracy should not be thought of as confined to states since it can also be located in, for example, transnational social movements.[35] Yet from a deliberative perspective, there is still much to applaud in Buchanan's approach: while

[30] Buchanan, 'Theories of Secession' (n 3) 39–40. He also says it is a condition that 'there be credible guarantees that the new state will respect the human rights of all of its citizens and that it will cooperate in the project of securing other just terms of secession': ibid 37. But such 'just terms of secession' could probably not be determined in the absence of deliberation: Ian O'Flynn and Nicole Curato, 'Deliberative Democratization: A Framework for Systemic Analysis' (2015) 36(3) Policy Studies 298, 301.

[31] Buchanan, 'Theories of Secession' (n 3) 40, 45.

[32] cf Moore (n 3) 633, 640 fn 26.

[33] Buchanan, 'Theories of Secession' (n 3) 46–47.

[34] ibid 48–49.

[35] See, eg, John Dryzek, *Foundations and Frontiers of Deliberative Governance* (OUP 2010) 178–97.

it aims to be realistic, it ultimately rests on a commitment to the importance of public values. In particular, his emphasis on the protection of individual rights and expectations, as well as on the good or value of political participation, suggests that the remedial right only approach is compatible with public reason as Rawls defines it. Indeed, according to Buchanan, a feasible theory of secession should meet not only the condition of 'minimal realism', but should also be 'morally accessible to a broad international audience. It should not require acceptance of a particular religious ethic or of ethical principles that are not shared by a wide range of secular and religious viewpoints'.[36]

Therein, however, lies a fundamental problem for his argument. On a public reason view, it is perfectly permissible to appeal to the importance of individual civil and political rights. But it is equally permissible to cast one's arguments in terms of the right to collective self-determination.[37] That is because the right to collective self-determination is not reducible to any one particular way of life or to any particular comprehensive doctrine. Its application in any given case may be controversial, but it is still a right that any democratic person might reasonably be expected to endorse. Of course, the right is typically characterized as a group right rather than an individual right. But it can still be grounded in the interest individual members *share* in being able to determine their own political status (the approach that, in Chapter 5, we saw Margalit and Raz advocating).[38] Not all groups will want to claim this right. But for those that do, the claim is in principle consistent with a commitment to public reason.

Buchanan's argument is curious in that, while it rejects the primary right approach, it does so without having seriously engaged with the right to collective self-determination.[39] As Margaret Moore puts it, Buchanan 'simply ignores the issue of whether self-determination itself is a value when applying this to the analysis of the justifiability of secession'.[40] In her view (and ours), 'a right to self-determination is a morally legitimate right of groups . . . because such a right would protect individuals'.[41] On this view, groups of individuals can jointly hold rights (properly classed as 'group rights') that derive from their

[36] Buchanan, 'Theories of Secession' (n 3) 44. cf Moore, who claims that this latter condition 'is not particularly salient to the issue of secession': (n 3) 632. However, as we will show, we are of the opposite view.

[37] Moore (n 3) 633.

[38] See also Joseph Raz, *The Morality of Freedom* (Clarendon Press 1986) 207–09; Peter Jones, 'Group Rights and Group Oppression' (1999) 7(4) Journal of Political Philosophy 353.

[39] What makes this all the more curious is that the existing state will itself have an interest in its own self-determination: Miller, 'Secession and the Principle of Nationality' (n 21) 110. In fairness, Buchanan does discuss the principle in his 2004 book, but for the most part only in the context of *intra*-state autonomy arrangements: Buchanan, *Justice, Legitimacy, and Self-Determination* (n 20) 206–48.

[40] Moore (n 3) 632.

[41] ibid 633.

shared interests. Buchanan fails to consider whether group sovereignty can be valuable in itself, or whether it can be an intrinsic part of the well-being of its members. This, we think, undervalues the individual's right—which is central to democratic constitutionalism—to assert membership in a sovereign group.

Granted, the right to self-determination does not have a privileged status; it is but one right among many. But it is, nonetheless, an important public value, and when public values conflict, we must seek to resolve those conflicts through deliberation. We must weigh the reasons on all sides with a view to arriving at an agreed view or judgement on how those values should be ordered. Some of that weighing may be properly conducted at the theoretical level. Yet not a great deal can be finally decided at the level of abstract theory. Actual conditions on the ground are also likely to have an important bearing on our understanding and assessment of a right—on its meaning, scope, and application. This is not to minimize the importance of theoretical analysis. It is, rather, to suggest that theoretical and empirical questions are likely to be mutually implicating.[42] Among other things, secessionists must be able to show that common-pool resources will be dealt with fairly and, perhaps more importantly still, that minorities within the claimed territory will not be made worse off by independence.[43]

Clearly, these issues are enormously complex. Yet, the reason why we look at Buchanan's work is ultimately to set it aside in favour of on our own, alternative view: that, in principle, self-determination is a right that a group may vindicate through a referendum. As we will soon see, secession can be likened to divorce.[44] This metaphor is important because it highlights an irreducible role for human agency. One never loses the right to leave a marriage, and indeed to do so for any reason—or simply for the reason, which cannot be reviewed and second guessed, that one no longer wishes to be in it. We cannot alienate our autonomies on matters as fundamental as these. In cases of secession the same principle applies, and for the same reason. A community is, on the definition that we saw in Chapter 5, not an indivisible unit. Democratic constitutionalists understand the group as an association of willing people: a consequence of individual human choices, not an a priori metaphysical category. Buchanan is right to say that secession is an important option as a remedy for large-scale

[42] cf Andrew Mason, 'Just Constraints' (2004) 34(2) British Journal of Political Science 251.

[43] Miller, 'Secession and the Principle of Nationality' (n 21) 118–24; for an approach to secession that focuses on the question of distributive justice, see David Gauthier, 'Breaking Up: An Essay on Secession' (1994) 24(3) Canadian Journal of Philosophy 357.

[44] cf Miller, 'Secession and the Principle of Nationality' (n 21) 116.

human rights violations. But self-determination is a right too, which, perhaps ironically, a remedial rights approach fails to vindicate.

Having said all of this, while there is a great deal of talk about referendums in the secession literature, little or no attention has been paid to the question of how they should be designed. Moore, for one, defends the primary right approach but assumes that referendums are far too crude or reductive an instrument of constitutive self-determination.[45] A great deal of the present book, however, has been devoted to showing why concerns of this sort need not always hold. In the next section we will take up this question. As we remarked earlier, the nature of a conflict may require variations in the design of a DPR. We will discuss some of those variations below, a number of which respond to the vitally important boundary question of who should be included in the vote

IV. DPR Design for Secessionist Conflicts

The boundary problem as discussed in legal and political philosophy is the problem 'of deciding who should be included in the *demos* or constituency when democratic decisions are taken'.[46] In more prosaic terms, it is the problem of determining who should get to vote. In the last chapter we made the general case that the approval of a new peace agreement should be conditional on the approval of a majority within each major group that is a party to the conflict. That approval should be tested via concurrent consent in a DPR (or multiple, parallel DPRs). Yet in secessionist conflicts, the same logic does not straightforwardly apply. On a primary right view, the vote instantiates the right to constitutive self-determination. Since only the secessionist group claims this right, only the secessionist group should have the vote.[47] To include other sovereign groups or territories in the vote would in practice hand a veto to the larger parent state (eg, in the Bougainvillean independence referendum, this would have meant including voters in the rest of Papua New Guinea). From the perspective of the would-be secessionists, this would be akin to one spouse having the right of veto over divorce proceedings initiated by the other. It would, in other words, undermine the right of self-determination and the interests it seeks to protect.

[45] Moore (n 3) 626–28.
[46] David Miller, 'Democracy's Domain' (2009) 37(3) Philosophy & Public Affairs 201. See also Robert A Dahl, *After the Revolution? Authority in a Good Society* (Yale University Press 1990 [1970]) 60–61.
[47] cf Miller, 'Secession and the Principle of Nationality' (n 21) 110–11; Mueller (n 2) 154.

As we defined it earlier, secession is essentially a unilateral act. But a wholly unilateral process of secession would fail to make use of opportunities for deliberation between groups—including deliberation that may establish expressive legitimacy and help ground secession (or its rejection) upon a stable constitutional settlement. Thus our proposals below will provide means by which legitimate concerns are duly considered, such that, in principle at least, it would be reasonable for groups excluded from a vote to accept the referendum result even if they disagreed with it. Secessionist movements may garner what we call the *hypothetical* consent of groups that are excluded from voting in the referendum.

Sovereignty is relational: the pursuit of independence makes claims on other states, including on common-pool resources and the treatment of minorities. Even if they initially manage to form a separate state, a seceding group will continue to affect and be affected by the state from which it secedes (as well as by other groups within that state). Secession not only creates new sovereign states, but also significantly changes the shape of the states that remain. It relies on recognition by the wider international community,[48] as well as the creation of clear and mutually acceptable constitutional norms binding on both seceding and remnant states. Specifically, sovereignty creates new relationships or détentes between states by reallocating powers, assets, resources, debts, private businesses, and ethnically defined populations. Failing to address such substantive matters would mean that, even if a secession went forward, it would not rest on an agreed and stable constitutional settlement—the kind of settlement that, as we have said throughout this book, may be needed to avoid future discord and violence.

A settlement with at least some advance buy-in from all sides is therefore ideal. A contrary, and cautionary, case is the 2017 KRI independence referendum. This referendum had little formal pedigree: the Kurdish Regional Government (KRG) was suspended at the time. The decision to hold the referendum was made by presidential decree; constitutionally, however, the decree should have been issued by the KRG parliament and signed by the President.[49] The referendum's expressive force was also questionable: domestically at least,

[48] Sovereignty norms are hybrids of constitutional and international law. On the domestic constitutional side, they direct the powers and organization of the state. But they also reside in the international recognition of sovereignty by other states: J Samuel Barkin and Bruce Cronin, 'The State and the Nation: Changing Norms and the Rules of Sovereignty in International Relations' (1994) 48(1) International Organization 107. See also Joseph HH Weiler, 'The Reformation of European Constitutionalism' (1997) 35 Journal of Common Market Studies 97.

[49] Dylan O'Driscoll and Bahar Baser, 'Referendums as a Political Party Gamble: A Critical analysis of the Kurdish Referendum for Independence' [2019] International Political Science Review (forthcoming) 9.

the campaign for independence relied heavily on extreme rhetoric—instead of seeking to engage voters in deliberation (eg, about public values), pro-independence parties sought to stoke nationalist feelings.[50] There were also important boundary problems in that the referendum was conducted not just in the KRI but in the disputed, oil-rich territory of Kirkuk. Kirkuk's oil may have been crucial to the success of any future independent Kurdish state, but is equally crucial to the financial viability of the Iraqi state.[51] Just as importantly, the referendum had little if any regional or international support.[52]

There are signs that, in the longer run, the KRI referendum may actually improve relations between the KRG and the central government in Baghdad. On some accounts, the ensuing crisis precipitated something like a mutually hurting stalemate: both sides seem to have belatedly accepted that success for one cannot be achieved without success for the other.[53] But in the immediate aftermath, the referendum was widely seen as a massive setback for Kurdish aspirations.[54] The referendum was perhaps always likely to fail; powerful domestic, regional, and international actors were firmly fixed against the referendum. But the punitive measures that were subsequently imposed on the KRI, in response to the referendum, may have been less severe had the KRG made a greater appeal to international norms, and not just abroad but at home as well. Greater efforts to assuage legitimate Iraqi concerns about oil, water, and other common-pool resources could also have helped.

As we see here, remnant and other outside groups left wholly out of the process of constitutional change may have little motivation to cooperate with a wholly unilateral referendum outcome. But if remnant communities cannot be included in the referendum vote per se, are there alternatives that may still allow genuine inter-group deliberation to occur? In cases of secession, we propose not to abandon but to modify the generic concurrent consent model. This requires reconceiving what qualifies as consent—especially moving away from voting towards greater focus on deliberation. Institutional design may still allow robust deliberation to take place between

[50] O'Driscoll and Baser, 'Referendums and Nationalist Rhetoric' (n 2); cf Kamaran Palani and others, 'Strategies to Gain International Recognition: Iraqi Kurdistan's September 2017 Referendum for Independence' [2019] Ethnopolitics (forthcoming) 12–13.

[51] See, eg, 'After Iraqi Kurdistan's Thwarted Independence Bid', *International Crisis Group* (Middle East Report No 199, 27 March 2019).

[52] Morgan L Kaplan, 'Foreign Support, Miscalculation and Conflict Escalation: Iraqi Kurdish Self-Determination in Perspective' (2019) 18(1) Ethnopolitics 29.

[53] See, eg, Karwan Faidhi Dri, 'Iraqi Oil Minister Hopeful Erbil, Baghdad to Reach "Sustainable" Solution', *Rudaw* (news article, 28 June 2018). See also Raya Jalabi, 'New Kurdish PM says priority is stronger Baghdad ties, rather than independence', *Reuters* (news article, 10 July 2019).

[54] See, eg, Joost Hiltermann, 'The Kurds are Right Back Where They Started' [2017] The Atlantic 31.

sovereign groups in cases of secession. We suggest the following variations on the generic DPR:

(i) Mini-publics: Deliberative mini-publics are the subjects of copious scholarship in deliberative democracy precisely because they provide viable non-traditional democratic models, including models that range beyond—or even reject—the bare act of referendum voting. Arguably, deliberation about secession does not need to culminate, on all sides, in a referendum vote. Groups with robust access to deliberative democratic processes of consultation may still voice their concerns prior to settlement. Especially when the referendum does not have the agreement or acquiescence of the existing state, a mini-public on secession can potentially increase the referendum's expressive legitimacy. The mini-public's processes may demonstrate that the act of secession is no mere power play, but a genuine act of constitutive self-determination.

Mini-publics may help address the crucial boundary dilemma of how to consult outside groups short of providing them with a direct vote. Distrust and opposition to the process of secession can be expected to diminish if outside groups can present their views in a robust deliberative forum. Indeed, there will usually be competing voices within the secessionist group or territory too. As David Miller notes in relation to secession and national self-determination,

> nations are not individuals with a single will. They are likely to embrace a wide range of opinions about how national identity is best expressed—through union with a larger nation, through devolution, through an independent state, and so forth.[55]

In holding—and vigorously publicizing—a mini-public, a secessionist region can therefore demonstrate its democratic *bona fides* not just to its own sovereign people but to wider communities, including putatively sovereign subgroups inside the secessionist territory, and others in the existing state and wider world.

The mini-public should have members drawn from all of the communities involved in the conflict, and potentially others with a stake in the constitutional issues under discussion. This raises certain considerations discussed in Chapters 3 and 5. Recall, for instance, our proposal for a rule of equality in group representation. In the case of secessionist conflict, such equality may be appropriate only as between the secessionist group and the existing state. Other groups in the region, or those more peripherally involved in the conflict,

[55] Miller, 'Secession and the Principle of Nationality' (n 21) 116.

may be included as well; however, equal inclusion of those other groups may be unnecessary or undesirable, especially if it would detract from the main line of peacemaking deliberations between the key conflicting groups. As usual, these are matters best resolved contextually based on considerations of the case.

A sceptic might, of course, respond that including outside groups is little more than a fig leaf. It may give the appearance of meaningful, inclusive deliberation, but once the mini-public has concluded the secessionists are free to ignore the outside groups' contributions. Yet certain design features may mitigate against this possibility. One option, familiar from deliberative polls, is to televise or livestream the deliberations. As we said in Chapter 3, a mini-public can have an 'integrated'[56] or 'open'[57] design that includes, at certain stages, both small-scale deliberations and broad television or internet audiences. Those watching could then see how the course of the deliberations was shaped by the contributions from all sides.[58] Another option would be to highlight the contributions of the outside groups in a mini-public-vetted information booklet sent to voters.[59] Voters could have relatively direct access to these contributions, relatively free from the potential distorting effects of demagogic elites and other self-interested parties.

(ii) Public-value ballot: The peculiar nature of a secession referendum should also affect the design of the ballot (on which, again, only voters in the secessionist group or region should vote). As we said in Chapter 3, the first segment of the DPR ballot should focus on public values. And as we said in Chapter 5, some public values on the ballot can be expressed as rights. Yet as we also noted above, the right to self-determination does not have a privileged status. The right is both powerful and evocative, and (*pace* remedial right only theorists) is also the right on which secessionists typically rely.[60] However, it remains but one right among many. Other important rights and values will also be in play, even in a secessionist conflict. These may include free speech rights, rights of group equality, and guarantees against the use of arms.

[56] Ron Levy, 'Deliberative Voting: Realising Constitutional Referendum Democracy' (2013) Public Law 555, 572–74.

[57] Hélène Landemore, *Open Democracy: Reinventing Popular Rule for the 21st Century* (Princeton University Press 2020) 218–19.

[58] See, eg, James Fishkin, 'The Televised Deliberative Poll: An Experiment in Democracy' (1996) 546(1) Annals of the American Academy of Political and Social Science 132. For critical responses, see John Parkinson, 'Rickety Bridges: Using the Media in Deliberative Democracy' (2006) 36(1) British Journal of Political Science 175; Stefan Rummens, 'Legitimacy Without Visibility? On the Role of Mini-Publics in the Deliberative System' in Min Reuchamps and Janes Suiter (eds), *Constitutional Deliberative Democracy in Europe* (ECPR Press 2016).

[59] See, eg, Katherine Knobloch, Michael Barthel, and John Gastil, 'Emanating Effects: The Impact of the Oregon Citizens' Initiative Review on Voters' Political Efficacy' (2020) 68(2) Political Studies 426.

[60] Moore (n 3) 620.

The ballot could also seek to gauge attitudes and dispositions towards the existing state and, in particular, towards the state's vital needs and interests. This is especially important in terms of generating expressive legitimacy in strongly or wholly unilateral secessions, and provides a further way to avoid treating the inclusion of outside groups in the deliberative process as a mere fig leaf. As usual, applied specifics should be avoided (eg, precise questions about how oil revenues should be distributed or water management). Instead, voters should be asked about such matters as the importance of dealing fairly or justly with the existing (but soon perhaps to be former) state, with due regard to its legitimate concerns.

The ballot could also ask about international relations. In particular, it could ask about the importance of good relations with external states and the international community more generally. As Michael Freeman remarks, '[t]he right to self-determination is dynamite. It is so because its sets people power against the states system'.[61] Yet it need not do so. Some secessionists may advocate 'Us First!', but others may be keenly aware of the potential disruption that secession brings and, out of respect for other communities, the need to rebuild bridges. In other words, they may be aware of the need to balance the value of constitutive self-determination with other important goods and values. The ballot could, and arguably should, seek to gauge these kinds of considerations.

(iii) Negotiation mandates: As we said in Chapter 3, while the first segment of the DPR ballot should pose questions about public values, the second segment should then ask voters to endorse a negotiating mandate (assuming that the DPR runs as a mandate referendum) for elites to engage in negotiations. In a *concurrent consent* referendum, this would have meant that each group involved in a conflict empowers its representatives to meet, following the referendum, to resolve applied issues such as territorial boundary demarcations. But again, since secession referendums should be wholly unilateral, the referendum may only empower elite negotiators on behalf of the seceding group. Arguably, therefore, a problematic lack of symmetry arises, if the secessionist group can empower its own negotiators through a mandate referendum, but the existing state cannot. This may reduce the scope for the referendum to impel elites from all sides to the negotiating table.

However, in lieu of a referendum that includes everyone in the existing state, a partial solution is to rely on the mini-public approach developed above, albeit in this case to establish a negotiating mandate. In the mini-public, as noted, the

[61] Michael Freeman, 'Democracy and Dynamite: The Peoples' Right to Self-Determination' (1996) 44(4) Political Studies 746, 761.

views of those outside the secessionist group can receive a fair hearing—and, moreover, can matter. In principle, mini-public members drawn from diverse communities could, either jointly or severally, endorse mandates for negotiation towards a constitutional settlement.

It is of course possible that those outside the secessionist group will act strategically, for instance by 'spoiling' the mini-public, and seeking to block, disrupt, or derail the secession (eg, by criticizing the legitimacy of the mini-public from without, or filibustering it from within).[62] But as we have often stressed in this book, ordinary members of publics are not as prone to such recalcitrance as are their elite counterparts,[63] and even in conflict contexts such risks have not seemed to materialize in and about mini-publics.[64] Moreover, in secessionist conflicts, the mini-public may provide outside-group members with incentives for meaningful participation. The process may offer them the best opportunity to influence the outcome of a vote on secession by allowing them to present arguments in favour of remaining. It also may allow an opportunity to influence the content of any eventual settlement, in case the secession does occur. It may be wisest to try to shape the course and outcome of negotiations by participating in good faith, early on, in the mini-public's procedures (eg, helping to shape broad principles and values such as equity in debt and resource apportionment). Whether outsiders would actually participate if invited to do so is not possible to say. But the mini-public at least can offer the path of least resistance to gain a fair hearing for outside groups' interests.

As we noted in Chapter 3, sometimes there is also a case for including certain non-value options on the DPR ballot, beyond the mandate question. These could stipulate several possible reform options. We expressed doubts about this approach, given its potential to undermine the public-value deliberation on which, we think, the DPR should stake its success. But we also said that sometimes leaving concrete reform options off of the ballot is, for various reasons, impossible. If included in a secession referendum amid conflict, reform options should be phrased broadly to avoid asking voters to engage unduly in technical reasoning. For instance, presenting voters with specific federal or devolution models would stray well into the area of applied legal specifics. Better ballot options would be ones phrased in broad terms, calling for example for independent statehood, greater regional autonomy, or the status quo. As with mandate questions, it would generally not be appropriate for outside voters to vote

[62] cf Buchanan, 'Theories of Secession' (n 3) 43.
[63] Chapter 2.
[64] Chapter 5.

on these concrete constitutional reform options, which most directly affect the secessionist group; but, again, outside groups are affected and should make contributions on these matters via mini-public deliberations.

(iv) International backing: As noted, a key tension for DPRs amid secession conflict is that we cannot include outside groups as concurrently consenting voters, but neither should we exclude them wholly from deliberations. One option—alternative or additional to the mini-public option—is international involvement in the secession peace process. In the extreme case, the main outside interlocutor called on to deliberate with the secession group should be not the government of the existing state but the international community itself. This possibility matches what we said earlier in this chapter: that when international legal authorities invoke international legal norms, this can offer one way to legitimate decisions regarding secession—akin to a form of proxy or hypothetical consent.

Admittedly, in the case of secession, the international community is always an interested, supervening party; secession changes the nature of that community because it changes the relationships among its members. One might therefore worry about the extent to which the international community will deliberate impartially. Yet the degree to which this worry holds will likely vary from case to case. We pointed to the EU's role in supporting the referendum on Montenegro's secession from the Federation of Serbia and Montenegro. The EU has an obvious interest in peace, stability, and economic development in the Balkans. So, while the EU was not a neutral bystander, the nature of its interests was nevertheless conducive to deliberation (and, indeed, to public-value deliberation).

Where available, international involvement may be an important option for legitimation of the referendum process and outcome.[65] International deliberation may lead to international recognition. In addition, and importantly, international deliberation can be a practical alternative to engaging with uncooperative state representatives. The existing state may oppose secession, or even use means including violent repression to block deliberation towards secession, as in the cases of Kosovo, East Timor, or, more recently, Ambazonia.[66]

[65] In the KRI case discussed above, the international community seems to have resisted this role; it was, and remains, against secession. Similarly, the EU rejected in advance the idea of Catalan independence.

[66] While a great deal has been written on Kosovo and East Timor, Ambazonia—an anglophone breakaway region in Cameroon—is less well-known: see, eg, Reginald Chikere Keke, 'Southern Cameroons/Ambazonia Conflict: A Political Economy' (2020) 23(2) Theory and Event 329.

Where available, international community involvement is also an important expressive symbol of the idea that state autonomy is relational—that is, that a critical mass of existing independent states recognize a new putative state as sovereign. International referendum observers and administrators may include, for example, electoral commissioners on loan from other countries, military forces, and judicial observers. These participants should each be drawn from a trusted international or third-government institution. They may be able to rely on their own legitimacy and neutrality to prevent discord about the legitimacy of the referendum, as well as violence around the referendum. International oversight by UN and other international bodies (or by neutral third-party governments, where parties do not trust the UN) may in any event be useful to the fair running of the referendum and related processes.

As always, it is important not to claim too much. The international community can play an important, constructive role in secession conflicts. But the solution of an international interlocutor in secession deliberations can also be problematic. Indeed, it can be highly problematic, as we saw in the discussion of the Crimea status referendum above. It is at best a second-best solution to the problem of finding interlocutors with whom to deliberate:[67] it is generally preferable that those most directly affected by a constitutional reform, including secession, be robustly and directly represented. Yet the second-best solution is better than no deliberative solution at all. Fully unilateral moves towards secession ignore sovereignty's relational aspect and the need to engage outside groups in deliberation. Another problem—which is sometimes all too obvious—is that the international community may be divided itself, for example along lines of allegiance to leading powers such as the US, China, and Russia. This is one reason why disinterested third parties may sometimes be better choices than UN bodies, which must heed the views of UN member states and often operate strictly majoritarian rather than deliberative decision-making.

(v) Thresholds: Lastly, we must consider the thresholds that should be set for a referendum proposal to be considered passed. A simple 50 per cent plus one vote standard has the downside that in a close result (eg, Brexit's 51.9 per cent 'yes', and the bare 50.6 per cent majority 'no' in Quebec's 1995 secession referendum) the winning option may be in doubt. For instance, at close margins any voting irregularities, and the vagaries of turn-out (eg, fewer than half of eligible voters participating), can feed a view that the vote was insufficiently or

[67] On the political theory of the second best, see Robert E Goodin, 'Political Ideals and Political Practice' (1995) 25(1) British Journal of Political Science 37.

improperly legitimate. Perhaps it was not accurately indicative of the balance of public opinion or, if indicative, reflected only a fleeting popular preference, which is not itself sufficient to legitimate a long-term constitutional reform.

This is an especially acute concern in cases of secession. Here we often witness an outsized anxiety that *irreversible* secession will occur on the thinnest of democratic bases. As Qvortrup points out,

> secession is a process of far-reaching and irreversible consequences. Once undertaken, the process of a political divorce between two groups sharing the same territory is a one-way street.... [N]o counties that have split up, or from which one part has seceded, have become unified.[68]

After the secessionist group has excised itself from the larger constitutional community, the same constitutional reform process cannot simply be run in reverse a second time. Once claimed, the 'right to decide' cannot easily be returned. Some divided countries have reunited (eg, East and West Germany) or have talked about doing so (eg, North and South Korea). Yet the divisions in these cases came about through imposed partition rather than secession. Moreover, the groups involved shared obvious bonds of ethnicity, which is usually not the case in secessionist conflicts. More generally, then, after secession has yielded a new state, the state and the leaders it empowers are unlikely to consent to diminished sovereignty and power. For this reason, a bare 50 per cent majority may—and, just as importantly, may appear to—offer insufficient legitimacy to a mooted secession.

Some referendum designers respond to this kind of problem with supermajority requirements (eg, in the Montenegrin case, the threshold was set at 55 per cent). Supermajority rules for vote counting could even conceivably, in some cases, substitute for concurrent consent, if in effect they require majority support from multiple groups in the secessionist region. This could even serve as an engine of deliberation.[69] A related approach would be to require, as a prerequisite for constitutional change, that at least 50 per cent of all *eligible* voters vote 'yes';[70] in practice this would effectively be another kind of supermajority requirement.

However, supermajority methods raise difficulties that, in our view, make them unsuitable in many cases of conflict. Even at supermajority levels, an

[68] Qvortrup (n 18) 47.

[69] Joanne McEvoy, 'Letting "the People(s)" Decide: Peace Referendums and Power-Sharing Settlements' (2018) 25(5) Democratization 864, 869.

[70] Robert A Dahl, *On Political Equality* (Yale University Press 2006) 15.

affirmative vote may be attained without the consent of a dissentient group. Supermajority thresholds also of course make formal agreement harder to reach. And they are problematic if and when they deny a clear majority of voters their preferred options. The British Columbian electoral reform mini-public and referendum of 2004 provide an example: the referendum vote achieved 57.7 per cent support, but fell short of an unusually high, 60 per cent threshold.

Another option has been attempted in Canada with respect to Québec: federal legislation now requires a clear majority on a clear question in any future secession referendum.[71] However, this option could raise serious risks in conflict areas, given the ironic vagueness as to what counts as 'clear', and about who ought to decide the matter.

The most palatable approach, in our view, is one that we call a *timed double-majority*.[72] This approach would require a second referendum vote to be held within a specified time after the first vote (eg, one year), if and only if the first vote falls short of a clear majority (eg, the result is above 50 per cent but below 53 per cent). In addition, there should be a 'voter quorum' set, for example, at 50 per cent turnout among eligible voters.[73] This could guarantee that wide-reaching constitutional change cannot take place if fewer than a majority of eligible voters participate. Of course, a critic might say that even with a quorum requirement (as opposed to a supermajority requirement) the process favours the status quo. But if the second vote were to fall short of a clear majority, the two votes leaning in the same direction and separated in time would suggest that a population has deliberated about the issues—especially after the first vote makes clear to them that secession is a real possibility. Arguably, a pro-secession result based on two referendums would be not a mere chance outcome, but a reflection of voters' considered views.

V. Conclusion

We have sought in this chapter to identify a class of group-sovereignty conflicts broadly characterized by one group's efforts to secede from another. Secession is in many respects a nebulous concept, and there is great variation among cases. For instance, as we saw above, secession referendums are unilateral events but,

[71] *Clarity Act*, SC 2000, c 26.

[72] Also known as 'two-stage referendums': Spencer McKay, 'Building a Better Referendum: Linking Mini-Publics and Mass Publics in Popular Votes' (2019) 15(1) Journal of Public Deliberation 1.

[73] Zoltán T Pállinger and others (eds), *Direct Democracy in Europe: Developments and Prospects* (Springer 2007) 27.

crucially, the degree to which they are so varies from case to case. As well, some secession referendums may be entirely legal, even as others will be ruled illegal by the existing state and perhaps also by the international community.

Yet, despite such variation, we have argued as a general proposition that, whether secession succeeds or fails, certain institutional tools may go some way towards improving the odds of achieving and sustaining constitutional peace settlements—our ultimate concern throughout this book. As we indicated early in this chapter, it is no part of our intention to celebrate or decry secession. Instead, our aim has been to think about the nature of secession itself, to reflect on the conditions under which it might be justified, to tease out the relationship between secession and the institution of the referendum—and from there to think about the design challenges that can arise across different case types. The next chapter picks up where we leave off here, focusing especially on indigenous sovereignty and settler conflicts.

7
Indigenous-Settler Conflicts

I. Introduction

In this chapter we will bring the theoretical and institutional design arguments of this book to bear upon deliberative peace referendums (DPRs) in the context of indigenous-settler conflicts. We will see that these conflicts give rise to specific challenges to our preferred model of DPR and that some of these challenges flow from distinctive harms of 'domination and dispossession'[1] that colonialism visits upon indigenous peoples and their sovereign societies.

Before we enter into a discussion of these issues, however, we must set some parameters of the discussion. By 'indigenous' we intend to refer to groups that have the following UN-defined characteristics: '[s]elf-identification as indigenous peoples', '[h]istorical continuity with precolonial and/or pre-settler societies', '[s]trong link to territories and surrounding natural resources', '[d]istinct social, economic or political systems', and '[d]istinct language, culture and beliefs'.[2]

Yet as Martin Hébert has argued, the meaning of 'indigeneity' has been contested, and groups decide differently whether and how it applies to them. He writes:

> Some groups have been associated with indigeneity for centuries by eurocentric discourses, but are reluctant to refer to themselves as being subsumed within a broader global set of 'Indigenous peoples'. Other groups, especially in Asia and Africa, have not historically been part of global Indigenous politics and rather were situated as ethnic minorities or tribal groups until they started to link their struggles for self-determination with the rights outlined in international documents.[3]

[1] Duncan Ivison, *Can Liberal States Accommodate Indigenous Peoples?* (Polity Press 2020) 13–14.

[2] United Nations Permanent Forum on Indigenous Issues, 'Fact Sheet: Who are indigenous peoples' (UN.org, 9 May 2006).

[3] Martin Hébert, 'Indigenous Spheres of Deliberation' in André Bachtinger and others (eds), *The Oxford Handbook of Deliberative Democracy* (OUP 2018) 100.

Deliberative Peace Referendums. Ron Levy, Ian O'Flynn, Hoi L Kong, Oxford University Press (2021). © Ron Levy, Ian O'Flynn, and Hoi L Kong. DOI: 10.1093/oso/9780198867036.003.0007

We understand that the use of 'indigeneity', as well as its cognates, is controversial and that some groups advocate avoiding their use altogether, preferring instead 'to be named or referred to by their specific nation or tribe names which themselves are sometimes contentious'.[4] According to the UN Permanent Forum on Indigenous Issues (which promulgated the definitions above), 'the most fruitful approach is to identify, rather than define, indigenous peoples. This is based on the fundamental criterion of self-identification as underlined in a number of human rights documents'.[5] While we acknowledge these definitional controversies, we adopt the term 'indigenous' in part because it has been used by authors with whom we engage. In addition, because we are concerned with constitutional and legal questions in this chapter, and international legal documents (eg, the UN Declaration of the Rights of Indigenous Peoples) use the term, it seems appropriate for us also to use it rather than alternatives. Finally, we use the term because it focuses our theoretical and institutional analysis by enabling us to identify general and shared characteristics of some groups engaged in conflicts in colonial societies.

Among these characteristics is the experience of a common set of harms that is the focus of the conflicts we address. Hébert identifies indigenous peoples' shared experiences of '[d]ispossession of land, incorporation and subalterneity within the institutional structure of a state, and cultural assimilationist policies'.[6] James Tully similarly writes of an experience that varies in its details across indigenous-settler contexts, but is constant in its broad outlines. He relates the colonial practices in Canada that imposed a constitution without consent, and sought to erase the institutions and societal context in which indigenous peoples could promote their own interests as members of distinct nations.[7]

Histories of this kind are also a source of violent intergroup conflict, and the objects of constitutional settlement in some indigenous-settler societies. In some of these societies, referendums have been held in attempts to achieve or restore a measure of formal independence for the indigenous population. The focus of this chapter will be on a specific kind of independence referendum—the *delayed independence referendum* (DIR)—because, as we shall see, its design features may be adapted to respond to challenges that indigenous-settler conflicts pose to DPRs. For our purposes, the DIR is a species of independence

[4] Michael A Peter and Carla T Mika, 'Aborigine, Indian, Indigenous or First Nations?' (2017) 49(13) Educational Philosophy and Theory 1229, 1229.
[5] United Nations (n 2).
[6] Hébert (n 3) 101.
[7] James Tully, *Strange Multiplicity: Constitutionalism in the Age of Diversity* (CUP 1995) 20.

referendum, and, when it incorporates key aspects of the DPR, it is *also* a form DPR that responds to a set of context-specific challenges.

Also for the purposes of this book, we distinguish independence from secession. Independence is an umbrella term that here refers to a range of cases in which a territory that had been colonized separates itself, legally and politically, from the colonial power, which may or may not be geographically distant. By contrast, secession refers to a specific situation in which one part of what had been a territorially unified state separates from that state. Both independence and secession may yield full state sovereignty at the international level, but independence, especially, may leave intact remaining formal associations with the original state (eg, under the British Commonwealth).[8]

Independence referendums have been held in many societies riven by conflict between colonial powers and indigenous liberation movements. The record of these referendums as part of peaceful settlements is at best mixed, and characterized by halting forward steps (and some backward ones). In some cases, referendums were part of ultimately successful movements towards stable constitutional settlements, but even such 'successes' were accompanied by eruptions of violence. For instance, we previously described the 1961 Algerian mandate referendum on independence. Given its success at ending French domination, in an important sense it helped to bring about a new constitutional settlement. But a referendum the following year, called to endorse a signed peace agreement between Algeria's National Liberation Front and France, was followed by intense violence.[9] Moreover, after a referendum in 1958 that led to Guinea's independence from France, significant economic hardship resulted from French policies (including withdrawal of capital),[10] and a new autocratic Guinean government imposed restrictions on civil liberties and other freedoms.[11] Yet despite an order from de Gaulle to bring down the newly established government, and despite multiple coup attempts,[12] at least one of which led the Guinean government to mete out reprisals,[13] there was no society-wide violence immediately following independence.

[8] Independence and secession are partly overlapping concepts. Some cases (eg, that of a colonized territory that separates from a territorially unified state) involve both secession and independence.

[9] JNC Hill, 'Remembering the War of Liberation: Legitimacy and Conflict in Contemporary Algeria' (2012) 23(1) Small Wars & Insurgencies 4, 12.

[10] Elizabeth Schmidt, *Cold War and Decolonization in Guinea, 1946–1958* (Ohio University Press 2007) 171–72.

[11] Lansiné Kaba, 'Guinean Politics: A Critical Historical Overview' (1977) 15(1) Journal of Modern African Studies 25, 32.

[12] Schmidt (n 10) 175.

[13] Kaba (n 11) 33–34.

In general, indigenous-settler conflicts raise at least two sets of challenges to the institutional design and theoretical arguments that we have advanced in this book. In Section II, we will address institutional challenges that focus on the *scope* and *duration* of DPRs. As we have argued in previous chapters, DPRs should be focused on generalized public values and involve time-limited processes (namely the referendum campaign and final vote). The critic might claim that this is not enough, given the scale of socioeconomic and political injustices suffered by indigenous peoples and their long histories of being dominated by colonial powers. A more adequate response may need to involve comprehensive and detailed changes to policies and laws, as well as a shift in cultural attitudes that would take years, if not decades. We will argue that DPRs can be designed to respond to these criticisms by adopting design principles from DIRs, which as we shall see, provide space for these kinds of long-term and systemic changes. The DIR model, albeit without key DPR features, has been followed, for instance, in New Caledonia.

In Section III, we will address problems of *incommensurability*. Some scholars suggest that discursive differences between indigenous and non-indigenous peoples are so great as to preclude deliberation of the kind that we argued for in earlier chapters. This incommensurability problem may particularly disrupt public-value deliberation. A related argument is that any constitutional regime that claims exclusive authority is inconsistent with indigenous concepts of sovereignty. We will respond to these challenges by specifying how the theory of democratic constitutionalism (which we initially explored in Chapter 5) can be applied to indigenous-settler conflicts, and how DPR design may adapt to settlements in those contexts.

Referendums may not be necessary in order to settle indigenous-settler conflicts. Indeed, democratic deliberation in other institutions designed to receive the claims of indigenous peoples (eg, indigenous representative bodies, treaty processes, and truth and reconciliation processes) may yield constitutional settlements that address indigenous peoples' experiences of 'political domination and dispossession of territory'.[14] However, for reasons that we identified in previous chapters and elaborate on below, a DPR may have unique potential to produce a constitutional settlement for indigenous-settler conflict societies.

[14] Ivison (n 1) 8–10, 13–14.

II. Challenges of Scope and Duration

A. Preconditions for Deliberation

We have focused throughout this book on the DPR as a moment that can help to catalyse a constitutional settlement. And we have called for a public-value approach, wherever possible, to framing referendum questions in this moment: the DPR should generally avoid including extensive institutional details or non-public values in referendum questions and in publicly promulgated information. A general objective is to avoid conceptual descent. Thus in Chapter 3, we distinguished our approach from those of Kanra and Addis. Unlike those authors, we generally do not require any gradual social movement towards wider trust, learning, social integration, or shared identities, because we expect that under conditions of violent conflict this approach may be unrealistic. Yet, given the pervasiveness of disadvantage and the extent of harms that we alluded to above in an indigenous-settler conflict, a referendum that focuses on public values and is time-limited might itself seem unrealistic.

Some critics of deliberative democracy have doubted the capacity of deliberative democratic processes to resolve indigenous-settler disputes. Writing in the Australian context, Katherine Smits argues that reconciliation should precede deliberation. By this she means that '[d]eliberation can only proceed when each party is recognised by all others as interlocutors. . . . As this suggests, deliberation is not, as is often assumed, a synchronic event, but is in fact a temporalized process, with stages through which it must proceed'.[15] Bashir Bashir similarly criticizes deliberative democrats (and Habermas in particular) when he writes that 'whereas the principles of equality and reciprocity ask unequal parties to treat each other as if they were equals in public reasoning, the principle of acknowledgment demands the explicit recognition of asymmetries and unbalanced power relations'.[16]

We understand Smits and Bashir to be arguing that, in indigenous-settler conflicts, indigenous groups assert claims under conditions of profound disadvantage that the colonial state has created. During an independence referendum campaign, the colonial state may exploit these conditions to intimidate indigenous populations and to underscore their dependence on colonial economic support. The general conditions of disadvantage may also mean that

[15] Katherine Smits, 'Deliberation and Past Injustice: Recognition and the Reasonableness of Apology in the Australian Case' (2008) 15(2) Constellations 236, 237.

[16] Bashir Bashir, 'Reconciling Historical Injustices: Deliberative Democracy and the Politics of Reconciliation' (2012) 18(2) Res Publica 127, 138.

indigenous communities themselves will not view certain referendum outcomes to be plausible. For instance, indigenous groups may doubt that independence from a colonial state is a realistic possibility, in part because the state has systematically undermined their institutional and socioeconomic capacity to govern. Mark Bennett extends these arguments about the effects of inequality on indigenous-settler deliberation, claiming that in order to deliberate on equal terms with the settler colonial state, credible claims for separation 'may be conceptually necessary in order to secure equal negotiation between Indigenous peoples and the state'.[17]

These authors' concerns about deliberative democracy's relevance in indigenous-settler conflicts are well-founded, particularly in the context of independence referendums. In several examples, the colonial power attempted to influence outcomes by physically intimidating voters and exerting economic pressure. For example, according to John Braithwaite and his co-authors, in the lead-up to the 1999 independence referendum in East Timor, Indonesia adopted 'a conscious military strategy to intimidate people, using Timorese militias armed by the military as proxies, against voting for independence. Quite a lot of terror was executed and directed by the military as well'.[18]

In 1958, when France presented many places still under its colonial control with referendums, the referendums offered the colonized populations a stark choice: they could continue their colonial relationship with a promise of greater autonomy, or they could select immediate independence from the French Union, with a consequent severing of all economic aid. As Klaas van Walraven notes, this economic threat meant that 'the referendum was tinged by blackmail'.[19] In Guinea—the only territory to vote for independence in the 1958 referendums—France exerted direct pressure during the referendum campaign and did so, according to the governor, 'to demonstrate the consequences of a negative vote'.[20] These measures included preventing teachers who had been vacationing overseas from returning just before the beginning of the school year—at a time when it would have been impossible to replace them. Elizabeth Schmidt argues that this measure aimed to have 'a profound psychological and moral effect. It would prove that France would carry through on its threats to terminate all aid to the rebel state'.[21] And days before the referendum,

[17] Mark Bennett, '"Indigeneity" as Self-Determination' (2005) 4 Indigenous Law Journal 71, 76.

[18] John Braithwaite, Hilary Charlesworth, and Adérito Soares, *Networked Governance of Freedom and Tyranny: Peace in Timor-Leste* (ANU Press 2012) 95.

[19] Klaas van Walraven, 'Decolonization by Referendum: The Anomaly of Niger and the Fall of Sawaba 1958–1959' (2009) 50(2) Journal of African History 269, 273.

[20] Schmidt (n 10) 166.

[21] ibid 166–67.

the French Overseas Minister issued a warning about the consequences of a vote for independence in *Le Monde*, saying: 'General de Gaulle said unequivocally that a territory that wanted to separate itself from the Community would be free to do so, but, it is well understood, with risks and perils'.[22]

These examples show that in indigenous-settler conflicts, imbalances of power may sometimes render remote the prospects for meaningful deliberation on relatively equal terms during a referendum campaign. Yet inequality in this context does not only manifest itself when colonial powers use their superior economic position and military force directly to intimidate indigenous populations. In some cases, those populations may themselves conclude that the cumulative effects of inequitable social, political, and economic policies have ruled out certain means of removing colonial influence—including a vote on independence. For example, in 1991, the pro-independence party in French-administered New Caledonia agreed to delay a referendum because it 'was not confident in its capacity to win a majority vote in favour of the self-determination process, given the minority position of the Kanaks among the overall population'[23]—a result of immigration policies.[24] Advocates for independence further hoped that a delay would enable the Kanak population to 'develop the expertise needed to manage an independent New Caledonia . . . and build more support for it among non-Kanak'.[25] The New Caledonian example suggests that power imbalances per se may preclude meaningful debate about independence. And in situations where these kinds of referendums appear to be promising routes to resolving a conflict, a lasting peace may be precluded as a result.

It would seem, then, that to make deliberation meaningful in the indigenous-settler context, where deliberation on unequal terms can render an outcome illegitimate, a polity may first need to address the widespread disadvantage suffered by indigenous peoples. This may be so especially in the specific circumstances of a referendum campaign on independence. Of course, imbalances of power are features of some other kinds of intergroup conflict, where relationships of imposed dependency may also arise. Unequal relationships arguably are deeper and more consistent features of indigenous-settler societies, and

[22] Quoted (and translated) in ibid 167.

[23] Guillaume P Blanc, 'The Elevation and Isolation of the Constitutional Status of New Caledonia: A Case Study of the French Interim Constitutional Reform' (2015) 2 Journal of South Pacific Law A39, A43.

[24] Nic Maclellan, 'From Eloi to Europe: Interactions with the Ballot Box in New Caledonia' (2005) 43(3) Commonwealth and Comparative Politics 394, 403.

[25] Denise Fisher, 'New Caledonia's Independence Referendum: Redefining the Future' (2019) 54(2) Journal of Pacific History 202, 206.

such relationships tend to be entrenched by the specific barriers to indigenous-settler deliberation and peacemaking that we will discuss later on. But some of what we say in this chapter may indeed have purchase for other kinds of conflict.

Thus change in (at least) the indigenous-settler context may need to involve certain sweeping and detailed modifications to government programmes and institutions that would need to be undertaken over years and decades. In the extent of conceptual descent and the length of time required, these changes would seem to require more than a DPR can deliver. Bashir and others who are sceptical of applying deliberative democratic principles to indigenous-settler contexts might suggest that we broaden our focus beyond the design of a DPR. These critics could argue that we should examine the background conditions under which DPRs are to be held, as these conditions may limit the scope and quality of deliberation. A DPR may need to be embedded in a widespread and long-term process of social change, of the kind for which Kanra and Addis advocate. We will respond to this challenge next.

B. The Delayed Independence Referendum

In previous chapters we discussed what we called 'exposure of agreement'. We said that a DPR may reveal existing but latent intergroup agreements, either about the desirability of signing a constitutional settlement generally, or of doing so on certain broad terms. The DPR may do this particularly by reframing peacemaking deliberations: from technical or non-public terms that generally defy agreement, to public values that are generalized such that most people reasonably can be expected to endorse them. We also pointed out that such pre-existing agreement is not so rare as one may expect. Even amid some of the most apparently intractable conflicts, when the parties shift perspective from non-public to public values, or from the desires of certain prominent classes of elites to those of non-elites, agreement was sometimes already widespread.[26] Yet there still may be worries that the conditions are not yet in place to enable the deliberation needed to expose (and much less to create) agreement. In particular, as we have just said, indigenous peoples' experiences of deep and pervasive disadvantage may not allow for deliberation on equal terms about possible constitutional settlements to indigenous-settler conflicts.

[26] Chapter 4.

In this light, it is notable that Katherine Collin has categorized a model of 'delayed' peace referendum comprising three essential elements: 'some form of regional autonomy, staged implementation and [a] territorial referendum at the plan's conclusion'.[27] A delayed peace referendum essentially has two decision points: (i) the initial decision to provide for regional autonomy and to delay the running of a territorial referendum until a later point; and (ii) the delayed territorial referendum vote itself. (Collin uses 'territorial referendum' here to refer to a vote about group sovereignty, such as a vote about secession or independence.)

Drawing on Collin's work, we apply the notion of a delayed peace referendum process to the independence context: hence a 'delayed independence referendum', or 'DIR'. On this model, the first key decision would set in motion processes that aim to reduce the inequalities between indigenous and settler communities—including by providing institutions for regional autonomy—and, in our view, this decision provides time for any needed economic, social, political, and cultural changes to take hold before a vote on independence is called.[28] This first decision typically results from negotiations among elites, although the results of those negotiations may be ratified by a referendum. The second decision addresses, via a referendum, the possibility of independence. It is that second decision that may address the harm of denial of prior sovereignty of an indigenous people by putting an option for a final, rather than transitional, constitutional settlement in front of voters.

Variations of this model have been attempted in a range of colonial conflicts, including Algeria (1962), South Sudan (2011), and Bougainville (2019), and also proposed for East Timor and Western Sahara.[29] We will discuss uses of this model in New Caledonia. Using this example, we will begin by identifying the interests that independence referendums in indigenous-settler contexts may aim to vindicate. We will then demonstrate how the two-stage decision-making process of the DIR can be adapted to satisfy DPR design principles and to respond to the challenges of scope and duration that we have described. And we will argue that the innovations we propose may provide for more equal deliberation during a referendum aimed at a final constitutional settlement in an indigenous-settler conflict.

[27] Katherine Collin, 'Peacemaking Referendums in Oceania: Making or Delaying Peace in New Caledonia and Bougainville' (2019) 18(2) Ethnopolitics 139, 139–40.

[28] Collin notes that the Nouméa Accord in New Caledonia aimed at both establishing autonomy for the Kanak and 'economic rebalancing between settlers and Kanak communities': ibid 145. She also notes, however, that according to a variety of socioeconomic indicators, '[d]espite gains in human development in Kanak-majority areas, parity among New Caledonians is distant': ibid 146.

[29] ibid 140.

(1) The nature of the interest: self-determination and prior sovereignty

Recall that the core principle of the democratic constitutionalist framework is that no individuals should be excluded arbitrarily from participating on an equal footing in decision-making processes that bind them. It follows from this principle that, given their fundamental nature and wide-ranging effects, constitutional reforms should rest on consent that is extensive within the populations affected. In Chapter 5, we argued that the principle could be extended to groups in the context of constitutional reform. In what Margalit and Raz call 'encompassing groups', individuals find 'a culture which shapes to a large degree their tastes and opportunities, and which provides an anchor for their self-identification and the safety of effortless secure belonging'.[30] The achievement of self-government, or what we referred to in the previous chapter as *constitutive* self-determination, is valuable insofar as it enables groups of this kind to make the political decisions necessary to protect the relevant individual interest.

The right to national self-determination is perhaps the classic instance of a group right. The right is grounded in the interests of its individual members,[31] but it is a right held by the group *qua* group rather than by its members severally: the interests grounding the right are interests that are shared. As Raz and Margalit argue, in belonging to an encompassing group, individual members gain a significant part of their self-identity from belonging to, and having been socialized in, the group.[32] A right to *ongoing* self-determination protects the ability of groups, or group members, to determine 'the character of their social and economic environment, their fortunes, the course of their development and the fortunes of their members by their own actions'.[33] And so, in acts of constitutional reform it would seem that the consent of encompassing groups is necessary for the reform to be legitimate. By participating in the reform of a constitution, these groups aim to guarantee their ability to make political decisions that safeguard the cultural context that is essential to their members' identities.

It is uncontroversial that indigenous peoples have the characteristics of encompassing groups. It follows that they should benefit from a right to ongoing self-determination, that is, a right to control their internal affairs in order

[30] Avishai Margalit and Joseph Raz, 'National Self-Determination' in Wil Kymicka (ed), *The Rights of Minority Cultures* (OUP 1995) 448.

[31] Chapter 5.

[32] Margalit and Raz (n 30) 456–57; see also Joseph Raz, *The Morality of Freedom* (Clarendon Press 1986) 208.

[33] Margalit and Raz (n 30) 440.

to safeguard the relevant interests of their members.[34] In some circumstances, the right to self-determination may also be constitutive in nature: it may include a claim to constitute an independent polity. In any case, a general right to make political decisions about the affairs of 'encompassing groups'[35] should be protected in all exercises of constitutional reform affecting indigenous peoples. The protection of such a right satisfies the democratic-constitutionalist requirement of consent. That right flows in part from the fact that, as Tully notes, 'they have the status of independent, self-governing nations, in virtue of prior sovereignty, grounded in the practice of governing themselves by their own laws'.[36] Duncan Ivison makes a similar point when he claims that if 'Indigenous peoples were sovereign and self-determining at the time of settlement', then the sovereignty of the colonial state can only be 'reconciled with their sovereignty through some mechanism of consent, or at least through means consistent with their freedom and equality'.[37]

Let us illustrate these claims by examining the situation of the Kanak in New Caledonia. We focus on this single example, in part, to avoid making unwarranted generalizations about pan-indigenous identity. As Sarah Maddison has argued, such generalizations can 'risk obscuring the diversity of Indigenous nations and communities'.[38] Before colonial contact, the Kanak society on the territory of New Caledonia was clan-based, and each clan consisted of 'individuals from different families who shared common ancestry and had a specific attachment to a territorial area'.[39] European settlement of the archipelago began in the 1840s and, in 1853, the area became a French possession.[40] In the decades that followed, waves of European immigration impacted the agrarian practices, the health, and the culture of the Kanak population.[41] As a result of a decision by the colonial Governor of New Caledonia, and a series of French government decrees, the Kanak were dispossessed of their land, confined to 'government-created reserves' and subjected to the 1887 *Indigenat*, 'an

[34] Robert N Clinton, 'The Rights of Indigenous Peoples as Collective Group Rights' (1990) 32(4) Arizona Law Review 739; Patrick Macklem, 'Normative Dimensions of an Aboriginal Right to Self Government' (1995) 21(1) Queen's Law Journal 173.

[35] Margalit and Raz (n 30) 447.

[36] James Tully, 'A Just Relationship between Aboriginal and Non-Aboriginal Peoples of Canada' in Curtis Cook and Juan D Lindau (eds), *Aboriginal Rights and Self-Government* (McGill-Queen's University Press 2000) 47.

[37] Ivison (n 1) 36.

[38] Sarah Maddison, 'Indigenous Peoples and Colonial Borders: Sovereignty, Nationhood, Identity and Activism' in Nancy A Naples and Jennifer Bickham Mendez (eds), *Border Politics* (New York University Press 2014) 165.

[39] Jacqui Zalcberg, 'The Kanak Indigenous Peoples of New Caledonia: Decolonization and Self-Determination in Practice' in Duncan French (ed), *Statehood and Self Determination* (CUP 2013) 380.

[40] ibid.

[41] ibid 380–81.

oppressive code of conduct promulgated by the French Government'.[42] In 1887 and 1917, there were two 'Kanak revolts'[43] that were used as justifications for the 'official violence that followed—deporting a certain number of survivors and turning the others into slaves'.[44] These acts of domination and violence helped seed later violent conflict between the Kanak and the settler society of New Caledonia in the 1970s and 1980s.[45]

(2) DIRs as DPRs

In New Caledonia, a DIR was introduced against this backdrop of colonial domination and indigenous-settler conflict. The parties to the conflict were the 'central state' (ie, France) and 'pro-integration and pro-independence groups'.[46] There were two DIR processes, set in motion by agreements that elites negotiated after a period of violence: the first by the Matignon Accords (1988) and the second by the Nouméa Accord (1998). The latter was negotiated at the end of the Matignon Accords' timetable for a constitutional referendum, because the parties believed that a referendum held at that time would exacerbate conflict. We focus here on the Nouméa Accord, which required that a referendum on New Caledonia's independence from France be held by November 2018.[47] In the event of a 'no' vote (which indeed has now occurred), the Accord provided for two more referendums on the same question in 2020 and 2022 if one-third of the Congress 'so request'.[48] In the event that all referendums return a negative verdict, the Accord provided that the 'political partners' would 'meet to consider the situation'.[49]

These delays created time for power imbalances to be addressed and for a measure of reconciliation to be achieved—before the independence referendums were to be held. The Nouméa agreement is complex, and we only

[42] ibid 381.

[43] Régis Lafargue, 'The Unity of the Republic vs Living Together on the Same Land: New Caledonia from Colonization to Indigenousness: Law at the Centre of a Major Cultural Issue' (2014) 46(2) Journal of Legal Pluralism & Unofficial Law 172, 174.

[44] ibid. Those who were enslaved were 'awarded' to clans that Lafargue refers to as 'allied' with the colonial authority.

[45] The history of Bougainville is similar, although the history of effective colonial control was shorter and the violence—both intra-group and against colonial authorities—was more intense: Anthony Regan, *The Bougainville Referendum Arrangements: Origins, Shaping and Implementation Part One: Origins and Shaping* (Department of Pacific Affairs 2018).

[46] Collin (n 27) 142.

[47] Fisher (n 25) 206.

[48] *Nouméa Accord*, France-Rally for Caledonia in the Republic-Kanak and Socialist National Liberation Front, signed 5 May 1998 (approved by referendum 8 November 1998) s 5 (English translation).

[49] ibid (English translation). Comparably, the Bougainville Peace Agreement emerged from a decade-long civil war and provided for a delayed referendum on independence that would not be binding on the Papua New Guinea parliament, but would be the basis for consultations: Regan (n 45) 11.

highlight some key features that aim to achieve these ends. The agreement provided the Kanak with greater governance autonomy. The Nouméa Accord established a Kanak Customary Senate that was given legislative power over laws touching on 'customary civil status and customary lands'.[50] The Accord also created 'consociational institutions, including a power-sharing executive and territorial Congress, drawn from the provincial assemblies on a proportional basis'.[51] In addition to governance instruments and statements recognizing the Kanak as the indigenous population and culture (eg, a statement in the preamble recognizing that the 1853 annexation 'did not constitute a legal agreement with the Indigenous peoples'),[52] the Nouméa Accord committed France to investments, including in infrastructure, that sought to address 'structural inequities' between Kanak and non-Kanak regions.[53]

The Accord thus provided for what Smits might call the conditions for reconciliation that precede meaningful deliberation. It created institutions and set social and political conditions that aimed to redress imbalances in power and recognize historical wrongs. One effect of these measures was to make independence a more credible option, which, as we saw above, can be a precondition for greater equality in engagements between indigenous and settler communities. A statement by a spokesperson for the pro-independence side reflected this intention after the release of referendum results in November 2018:

> We lost on the numbers, but for us it's a victory. For the Kanak people, the first people, this is a great victory, as we have loudly and clearly expressed our perspective without ambiguity and without recourse. Who now will contest the justice of our struggle, who now will challenge our very existence?[54]

Moreover, in a move arguably further instituting political equality among indigenous and settler populations, all French nationals living in New Caledonia, including New Caledonian citizens, were made eligible by the Nouméa Accord to vote in French National Assembly and presidential elections, as well as in

[50] Rowena Dickson Morrison, 'The Charter of the Kanak People: in Pursuit of "Cooperative and Balanced Legal Pluralism" in New Caledonia' (2016) 48(3) Journal of Legal Pluralism and Unofficial Law 476, 484.

[51] Collin (n 27) 145. Similar governance mechanisms, and instruments of reconciliation were provided for by the Bougainville Peace Agreement: Regan (n 45).

[52] David A Chappell, 'The Noumea Accord: Decolonization without Independence in New Caledonia?' (1999) 72(3) Pacific Affairs 373, 385.

[53] Collin (n 27) 146.

[54] Quoted in Nic Maclellan 'We Lost on the Numbers, But for Us It's a Victory: New Caledonia's 2018 Referendum for Self-Determination' (2019) 54(2) Journal of Pacific History 224, 225.

national referendums, elections for the European Parliament, and local town councils.[55]

These deliberative ends are salutary, but we suggest that incorporation of DPR design principles can render DIRs more reliably deliberative and more inclusive and, as a consequence, more legitimate on the terms that we set out in earlier chapters. DPR design may also render the DIR model more consistent with the values of democratic constitutionalism, and specifically those that bear on indigenous peoples as holders of rights to self-determination. We divide our discussion between institutional proposals for the first decision point (ie, the decision to defer the final referendum and introduce structural changes) and second decision point (ie, the deferred referendum itself).

(i) The first decision point: The decision to defer could, on the one hand, simply be an elite choice. Empowered elites may feel compelled to reach an accord after an outbreak of violence, and that accord may contain terms calling for referendum deferral (eg, as in the Nouméa Accord and the Bougainville Peace Agreement).

On the other hand, recall from previous chapters our preference that DPRs should be *mandate* referendums. One way of compelling elite negotiations towards a final settlement is to solicit input from a broad societal cross-section.[56] And the most robust form of such input is the mandate referendum, which reaches over the heads of certain recalcitrant elites to try to lend momentum to the process—giving to elite representatives an authoritative direction to negotiate a constitutional settlement in good faith.[57] The mandate referendum is typically, then, run early in a process of peacemaking (eg, in South Africa and France/Algeria). This perhaps suggests that a mandate referendum should run at the first decision point. On this approach, at the first decision point a mandate DPR would ask voters to endorse the running of another DPR to be held later on at the second decision point—with work on equalization and other structural reforms to occur in the interim. It may seem a contradiction to suggest deferring a peace referendum until a later point, and nevertheless to hold a referendum at the first stage as well. Yet the creative use of two, and even three, referendums in a carefully timed sequence is not unusual, as we saw above (and indeed we proposed something similar in the previous chapter).

[55] *Nouméa Accord* (n 48) s 5 (English translation); Mathias Chauchat and Vincent P Cogliati-Bantz, 'Nationality and Citizenship in a Devolution Context: Australian and New Caledonian Experiences' (2008) 27(2) University of Queensland Law Journal 193, 213.

[56] For examples of civil society inclusion in negotiations during peace referendum negotiations, see Joana Amaral, *Making Peace with Referendums: Cyprus and Northern Ireland* (Syracuse University Press 2019) 24–26.

[57] Chapter 3.

As ever, these and other design options must be weighed case-by-case. The main problem that an early mandate referendum would raise is precisely that which we identified above: that structural inequalities leading to indigenous-settler conflict may reduce the robustness of referendum deliberation. Thus one option, about which one of us has previously written, is to limit initial mandate voting to just the settler population; for instance, in the 1992 mandate referendum held in South Africa, voting was limited to the White population.[58] President de Klerk believed that only that population was divided on the question of whether constitutional reform should go forward. One could argue that the limitation of the vote in that case was therefore justified. Limiting an initial mandate referendum, in the context of DIR-DPRs, in a similar way may avoid problems associated with deliberations among groups with unequal status.

Though the constellation of circumstances for the 1992 referendum was of course particular to South Africa, a similar kind of mandate referendum could be held in other situations of indigenous-settler conflict—where, for instance, support for negotiations is widespread in the indigenous population, and there is elite opposition but broad popular support in the settler population. The notion that only one community—and a dominant, racially-defined community no less—should vote sits uncomfortably with principles of equal democratic citizenship. Yet arguably it is a 'second-best' option, which holds at least some appeal where peacemaking otherwise would founder.[59] The circumstances of widespread conflict may be such that any expedient that can move conflict settlement forward may be worth attempting.

But another option may lack the same effect of exclusion. The initial mandate referendum could gauge consent concurrently. Even though we said earlier that inequality affects whether indigenous people will believe that they can self-govern, it may be feasible to run a certain kind of concurrent mandate DPR at the first decision point. This DPR would include indigenous people but would not ask them about independence directly; instead it would ask only whether a referendum about independence ought to be held at a later date (with the promise that measures reducing inequality will be implemented in the meantime). And so even if, due to inequalities, at the first decision point indigenous people doubt whether they can self-govern, they may still say at that point that they would be willing to consider independence at a later date.

[58] Hoi L Kong, 'The Deliberative Mandate Referendum' (2020) 53 University of British Columbia Law Review 179.

[59] Chapter 6.

Again, each case will raise its own balance of concerns. For instance, in South Africa it may not have hurt the chances for an affirmative mandate vote had Black voters been counted in parallel. The time was already perhaps ripe for a concurrent mandate referendum in South Africa, as most Whites had come to recognize apartheid as normatively untenable.[60] Yet referendum designers might fear that including indigenous voters at the height of a conflict may be counterproductive. For instance, South Africa's reformist leadership may have assumed that involvement of Blacks in the referendum would have drawn down the affirmative vote among Whites (ie, Whites may have reacted negatively to being pressured into accepting reforms). It is also possible that, among many White voters, adopting a concurrent consent approach could have been seen as prejudging the very question that was (to them) still in doubt: whether the indigenous population should be accorded equal toleration and full democratic rights. Although a majority of Whites did accept this proposition, that fact was not apparent and widely recognized until after the Whites-only mandate referendum.

Hence at the first decision point, a mandate referendum is a possibility but not a necessity. As we said, it may be that running no referendum at all during the first decision-stage is the best choice. In either case, the deferral period of a DIR potentially allows time for improved deliberation on all sides, including time to mitigate political and other inequalities.

(ii) The second decision point: Regardless of whether a mandate referendum has run at the first decision point, a referendum should run at the second decision point. The latter referendum should in our view be a(nother) mandate referendum that, if passed, requires elites to negotiate a final settlement. Recall from Chapter 3 that a mandate ballot designed using DPR design principles should have either two or three segments: first, public-value questions at the top of the ballot; second, the mandate (or post-settlement endorsement) question itself; and (optionally) third, a set of very broad substantive reform options.

We previously said that *public values* at the top of the ballot could direct voters in a conflict society to look beyond their non-public (or comprehensive) views, rule out preferences that cannot be reasonably justified to differently

[60] The appeal of rights to equality—which, in South Africa for example, had come to be widely accepted as being at stake in the conflict—is hard to deny. Such rights may provide a clear and intuitive organising frame for deliberation: see, eg, Stuart J Kaufman, 'The End of Apartheid: Rethinking South Africa's "Peaceful" Transition' (Conference Paper, African Studies Association Conference, 29 November 2012). See also Ron Levy and Graeme Orr, *The Law of Deliberative Democracy* (Routledge 2016) 124.

situated others, and, as a consequence, uncover any common ground already available (but latent) in a conflict. A public-value ballot potentially confers on constitutional settlements a kind of legitimacy that is in line with both our democratic constitutionalist commitment to popular consent and our Rawlsian commitment to public reason.[61]

We also previously noted that values formulated as *rights* may be useful in the group-sovereignty context. Rights can stand for equal regard towards, and for the legitimacy of, multiple distinct groups and individuals. We suggested that including human rights on a ballot concretizes relatively vague notions of mutual toleration, dignity, respect, and the like. We suggest now that rights framing may similarly assist voters in understanding the interests at stake in indigenous-settler independence referendums. One such frame can be a variant of what Steven Curry, writing on the indigenous-settler context, has called 'the sovereign right': does 'every individual [have] the right to seek to fashion a society which will best promote their interests, provided they recognize the same right on the part of others and do not do any unnecessary harm to the interests of others'?[62] This is a right that is overtly generalized and reciprocal in nature. It is a right of the individual to decide how best to aggregate into stable groups with others, and of any groups so formed to direct at least some of their own affairs. Inclusion of the sovereign right on the ballot connects to democratic constitutionalist assumptions. One key assumption, as we previously saw, is that any self-defined group of people—not least a group that can plausibly claim preexisting sovereignty—enjoys democratic rights to decide foundational questions about whether and how to live in concert with others.[63]

As the sovereign right identifies much of what is essentially at stake in indigenous-settler conflicts, some version of it should appear as a proposition on the ballot. So, too, should rights addressing what tends to be at issue in many indigenous-settler conflicts: the contradictory demands of each community for use of lands and waters and their resources (eg, 'Groups *X* and *Y* should each enjoy fair use of lands and waters, and to the resources therein'). While including rights on these matters will be contentious especially among the dominant community, as we said in Chapter 2 it is often not possible to settle a conflict if we ignore the principal value disagreements that underlie it.

The benefits of a public-values ballot may include those that we previously laid out. The ballot can encourage a reframing of conflicts in public-value

[61] Chapter 5.

[62] Steven Curry, *Indigenous Sovereignty and the Democratic Project* (Routledge, 2004) 132. For reasons mentioned in Chapter 5, 'sovereignty' itself should not appear in the ballot's values segment.

[63] Chapters 5 and 6.

terms. The ballot may broaden voters' perspectives and lead them to reason in terms that can be reasonably justified to differently situated others. Given the normative and epistemic divides that can separate indigenous and settler communities, and the complex nature of indigenous rights to self-determination,[64] we suggest it is particularly important here to use a DPR to underline common ground (a point to which we will later return).

The second segment of the ballot should be the *mandate question*. The mandate should not be understood as a decision to sue for independence. Instead, a mandate expresses a popular view that negotiations should begin and be conducted (and ideally concluded) in good faith and on a broad substantive basis. The mandate question should provide certainty that, whatever the precise outcome of the referendum, the parties will negotiate. Hence a vote rejecting outright independence should not automatically amount to an endorsement of the colonial status quo.[65]

In the optional third segment of the ballot, *substantive constitutional reform options* would lay out, again in broad terms, the constitutional changes that each community wishes to see go forward if a constitutional settlement is achieved. In the case of an indigenous-settler conflict, the set of options put to voters could each aim to yield a measure of indigenous sovereignty and might include: outright independence (ie, international statehood), (greater) regional autonomy, or a non-territorial form of sovereignty that, according to Tully, 'does not refer to state sovereignty, but rather, to a stateless, self-governing and autonomous people, equal in status, but not in form' to the state.[66] Again, there should be no option to endorse the constitutional status quo; assuming that a referendum has endorsed a negotiating mandate, then some kind of constitutional reform should be taken as a given.

We note here, as we did in Chapter 6, the risk that due to the *concurrent consent* structure of a referendum, each community counted may favour settlement on different terms (or not at all). Running a concurrent consent DPR may reveal differences that could undermine our expectation that a DPR can yield common ground. For example, though an indigenous community may favour their own full independence, other communities may oppose this and instead

[64] Curry (n 62) 144.

[65] The *Nouméa Accord* envisaged potential elite involvement after a referendum vote: a final 'no' vote to independence gives rise to a duty on 'political partners' to meet to consider options: *Nouméa Accord* (n 48) s 5. Similarly, according to the Bougainville Peace Agreement, whatever the outcome of a referendum, consultation between the parties was mandated and the Papua New Guinea Parliament held final decision-making authority: *Bougainville Peace Agreement*, Papua New Guinea-Bougainville Revolutionary Army, signed 30 August 2001 ss 323, 325.

[66] James Tully, *Public Philosophy in a New Key, Volume I: Democracy and Civic Freedom* (CUP 2008) 280.

vote for options closer to the status quo. In Chapter 6, we said that giving a referendum vote to the larger existing state in a secession case would amount to a veto that can frustrate rights of self-determination. This may be so, too, in indigenous-settler cases in which independence is one of the options on the table. One solution may be again to depart from concurrent consent, and to give only the indigenous community a vote on substantive reform options (eg, the 2019 Bougainville independence referendum did not allow people in other parts of Papua New Guinea to vote).

On the other hand, in some cases it may still be useful to retain the concurrent consent model, especially if outright independence is only one of the plausible reform options. A peace referendum that includes substantive guidance from more than one community—even if that guidance differs in each community—may at the end point, when negotiations begin, usefully indicate where the starting positions of each of the groups lie.

Interestingly, New Caledonia did not opt for the concurrent consent model, and the New Caledonian experience provides us with another possibility for defining eligibility criteria. Here the ability to vote was predicated not on ethnic identity but on length of residency. This kind of proxy measure might be attractive in the context of indigenous-settler conflicts, because boundary debates about the scope of indigenous identity and membership can be fraught.[67] The New Caledonian case's eligibility criterion had the advantage of expressing a value that is in some sense neutral with respect to identity, and thus sidestepping difficult questions about how to define indigenous identity. Length of residency could be taken to be a proxy for the degree of a voter's investment in New Caledonian constitutional matters.

At the same time, the criterion addresses a specific, identity-related concern, namely that the Kanak population's voting power in a referendum could be diluted as a result of past immigration policies that sought to tip the scales in debates about independence in favour of the anti-independence or pro-integrationist side. The New Caledonian case can be distinguished from other settings of indigenous-settler conflict, where processes of immigration, among other state policies, have over generations and centuries, rather than decades, reduced the indigenous population to a minority. Whether the kind of proxy measure used in New Caledonia is available in a given context, then, is a contingent matter. But where the measure is available, boundary issues can

[67] See, eg, Sébastien Grammond, 'Disentangling Race and Indigenous Status: The Role of Ethnicity' (2008) 33 Queen's Law Journal 487.

be addressed without directly engaging intractable debates about the scope of group identity.

In other indigenous-settler settings, other kinds of proxy measures could be chosen. For example, in jurisdictions where indigenous populations are the majority in some geographical regions, but the minority in others, a referendum may require the consent of all regions. Here again, place of residence would be a proxy measure that does not require defining indigenous identity.

In sum, we have considered the claim that the DPR's focus on general values and time-limited decision-making may make it incapable of addressing the vast inequalities that separate indigenous and settler populations in many conflict settings. That inequality would seem to make implausible the prospect of deliberation on equal terms about a final constitutional settlement. We have responded to this criticism by introducing and adapting features of DIRs. With specific reference to experiences in New Caledonia, we suggested how incorporating design elements of DPRs into this form of referendum might allow the DIR to be made more deliberative, inclusive, and democratic. However, apart from the challenges of social and political inequality, or the problems of drawing boundaries around groups, the indigenous-settler context also presents other, arguably even more fundamental hurdles to referendum deliberation.

III. Challenges of Incommensurability

A number of authors express the concern that there may be no common measures, or no agreed standards of comparison, to which indigenous and settler deliberators can appeal.[68] This poses challenges to our uses of constitutional and deliberative democratic theory in the indigenous-settler context. First, Jorge Valadez argues that *empirical, normative, and epistemic incommensurabilities* can render a common democratic framework, shared between indigenous and settler communities, impossible. Second, Taiake Alfred argues that indigenous conceptions of *sovereignty* are incompatible with a theory and practice of constitutionalism that focuses on the exclusive authority of constitutions. Third, Monique Deveaux argues that it may be that modes of engagement prescribed by deliberative democratic theory have no place for *cultural difference*. These criticisms imply that constitutions and deliberative democratic processes risk

[68] For a general discussion of the problem of incommensurability see, eg, Richard Bernstein, *The New Constellation: The Ethical-Political Horizons of Modernity/Postmodernity* (MIT Press 1992).

perpetuating injustices suffered by indigenous peoples. We consider these three related commensurability challenges in turn.

A. Empirical, Normative, and Epistemic Incommensurabilities

Valadez provides examples of incommensurable 'empirical beliefs, normative principles and epistemic procedures'[69] that pose barriers to deliberations between indigenous and settler communities. Consider first an instance of incommensurable empirical beliefs that touch on the relationship between humans and the non-human world. Many indigenous people may believe that 'non-human animals have souls or that spirits inhere in mountains and rivers while members of the majority society do not share those beliefs and regard them as patently false'.[70] This kind of incompatibility with respect to empirical beliefs may give rise to normative incommensurability when indigenous groups extend obligations of 'moral reciprocity' to animals, whereas many people in non-indigenous communities do not.[71] And epistemic incommensurability arises when different groups rely on different 'sources of knowledge' that give rise to conflicts over 'what counts as reliable evidence for establishing the truth or justifiability of particular claims'.[72]

As a first note, recall that on a 'wide view' of public reason, comprehensive doctrines are not excluded from debates over public values, so long as they are (and are eventually shown to be) compatible with those values.[73] This is important because, as we said, it can demonstrate the sincerity of people's commitments and build mutual trust and confidence. We suggest that if DPRs reflect the distance between the comprehensive views of indigenous and settler populations, but nonetheless describe the common ground upon which a constitutional settlement can be fashioned, then problems of incommensurability need not block the achievement of an enduring settlement.

[69] Jorge M Valadez, 'Deliberation, Cultural Difference, and Indigenous Self-Governance' (2010) 19(2) Good Society 60, 60.

[70] ibid 63.

[71] ibid.

[72] ibid.

[73] Chapter 2. We recognize that public values themselves may give rise to problems of incommensurability. For instance, freedom and equality may conflict and there may be no way of adjudicating a conflict between them. We do not, therefore, deny the reality of deep conflict—empirical, normative and epistemic; sometimes people see the world in different ways. However, the measures we propose aim to manage these kinds of conflicts.

How might a DPR do this? As we have in previous chapters, we note here that a deliberative mini-public is often an effective forum for airing even foundational differences. It may be better to air them in a DPR than in negotiations between elites. Elites of many kinds, for reasons that we have described, may exploit what conceptual fault lines do inevitably persist to spoil a settlement, or to advance their own special preferences strategically.[74] However, we previously said that, among their other benefits, mini-publics may prompt participants to engage in open-minded ways with others who have identities and views different from their own.[75] And we have also said that a mini-public should, in particular, have equal representation from each of the main groups to be granted rights of concurrent consent in the subsequent referendum vote.[76] This kind of intergroup equality may go some way towards ensuring that indigenous perspectives are robustly heard and considered. What we often find in practice when deliberative mini-publics run is the accommodation, or at least the respectful airing and mutual acceptance, of two groups' sets of beliefs.[77]

As for indigenous views specifically, from other institutional contexts we know that there is—at least in some cases—nothing inherent in the nature of indigenous and non-indigenous knowledge to make them irreconcilable. For instance, and notably, some settler states have managed to mainstream indigenous and conservationists' conceptualizations of the natural environment.[78] Granted, there may be genuine obstacles to such epistemic reconciliation. For instance, rules of standing in traditionally adversarial legal systems may be such that no group of human beings seems to represent environmental and non-human animal interests adequately. But in practice such obstacles have not always been insurmountable.

With broadly similar objectives of epistemic reconciliation, DPR methods may go beyond mini-public deliberation to target referendum voters themselves. Because voters cannot be presumed to know about the history and conditions of indigenous peoples on their territories, nor to have knowledge of colonization or alternative forms of political organization (such as those in pre-contact indigenous societies), publicly-promulgated information sources

[74] ibid.
[75] Chapter 3.
[76] Chapter 5.
[77] Chapter 3. For an example see David M Farrell and others, 'When Mini-Publics and Maxi-Publics Coincide: Ireland's National Debate on Abortion' (2020) Representation 1.
[78] See, eg, in New Zealand, Andrew Geddis and Jacinta Ruru, 'Places as Persons: Creating a New Framework for Māori-Crown Relations' in Jason Varuhas and Shona Stark (eds), *The Frontiers of Public Law* (Hart Publishing 2019) 255.

of the kinds discussed in Chapter 3 can be imperative. A mini-public run at an earlier stage should have drafted information for tutorials or for more traditional materials such as information booklets; these methods should extensively circulate among voters before the referendum.[79] Information and deliberative engagement may assist voters in understanding, for instance, the various reform options for sovereignty set out in a referendum. The included information should also include a clear account of the distinctive empirical beliefs, normative principles, and epistemic procedures of the indigenous peoples involved.

B. Sovereignty

Alfred criticizes the concept of sovereignty and its uses by states. Specifically, he rejects the idea that indigenous peoples should work within the terms set by the colonial concept of sovereignty or aim to achieve a status analogous to that of colonial sovereign states.[80] Alfred notes that assertions of state sovereignty by European powers reflected an 'exclusively European discourse' and 'in both a legal and political sense were made strictly vis-à-vis other European powers'.[81] This European concept of sovereignty evinces an 'imperial demand for conformity to a single language and way of knowing'.[82] Thus he insists that a strategy of working within the terms set by European conceptions of state sovereignty, with its presumption of 'the superior posture of the state',[83] is self-defeating for indigenous peoples.[84] Such a strategy compromises their autonomy as they 'enter the state's legal and political framework'[85] and abandon indigenous values, including those that support 'noncoercive forms of authority'.[86]

Alfred argues for an alternative to forms of governance that are premised on norms of state sovereignty. He advocates for an indigenous nationalism that aims at 'reinstituting systems that promote the goals and reinforce the values

[79] For discussion see, eg, Katherine Knobloch, John Gastil, and Robert Richards, 'Vicarious Deliberation: How the Oregon Citizens' Initiative Review Influenced Deliberation in Mass Elections' (2014) 8 International Journal of Communication 62.

[80] Taiaiake Alfred, 'Sovereignty' in Joanne Barker (ed), *Sovereignty Matters: Locations of Contestation and Possibility in Indigenous Struggles for Self-Determination* (University of Nebraska Press 2006) 42.

[81] ibid 34.

[82] ibid 47.

[83] ibid 46.

[84] ibid 44.

[85] ibid 39.

[86] ibid 45.

of indigenous cultures'.[87] If adopted, Alfred claims, these values could restructure the relationship between the state and indigenous peoples into a 'regime of respect' that seeks to 'build frameworks of respectful coexistence by acknowledging the integrity and autonomy of the various constituent elements of the relationship'.[88]

Alfred's criticisms of state sovereignty seem to represent a direct challenge to our concept of constitutionalism. Recall that according to our view—derived in fact from sources in Western legal theory—constitutional norms must be capable of clearing the ground around them of alternative kinds of legal or social action. Once established, the norms must be able to guide action almost exclusively along those cleared paths.[89] Our arguments about this exclusivity function of constitutions would appear to bring us close to making Alfred's 'imperial demand for conformity'.

But we should distinguish between a constitution's status as an exclusive norm on the one hand, and certain objectionable instances of exclusion on the other. Consider Alfred's claim that European assertions of state sovereignty did not impinge upon the 'law or politics, the rights and status of Indigenous nations'. One might interpret this claim to be a description of the exclusive authority of indigenous constitutionalism. That is, one might take Alfred to be arguing that European claims of sovereignty did not apply to indigenous nations because they were excluded by indigenous constitutions. Hence, the attempt by European states to impose themselves upon the constitutional orders of indigenous peoples, and to thus claim exclusive authority in the relevant territories, was objectionable. But that does not mean that the exclusivity function of a constitution is objectionable in all cases. Indeed, in this instance, this function of indigenous constitutions is to be defended against the unwarranted claims of European states.

The foregoing suggests why our understandings of DPRs and democratic constitutionalism are compatible with the view of indigenous constitutionalism that Alfred describes. Recall that, according to Rawls, public reason consists of reasons that members of a plural society can share. When a constitution purports to offer reasons for excluding individuals or groups from its ambit, but does so on terms that those subject to the constitution cannot reasonably be expected to accept, the constitution and the resulting exclusions are objectionable.

[87] ibid 40.
[88] ibid 46.
[89] Chapter 4.

We suggest, however, that when a constitution is made according to the prescriptions of a DPR, it can reduce the risk of a constitution's including these kinds of exclusions. Throughout this book we have argued that, even in conflict societies, an enduring constitutional settlement can be achieved if constitutional essentials build upon normative common ground that all parties to a conflict can endorse. And in this chapter we have argued that a DIR, designed in accordance with DPR principles, can achieve this end, even in the specific circumstances of indigenous-settler conflict. Ultimately, group consent—if it is met under conditions of relative deliberative equality—may yield settlements of indigenous-settler conflicts that will not subject indigenous peoples to alien systems of law or authority. In the ideal case, such a settlement will yield instead a constitutional order characterized by respectful and peaceful coexistence and in which indigenous systems of value may thrive. And it is important to note that the resulting constitutional order would make claims of exclusive authority with respect to all other constitutional norms and systems. Thus, although the constitutional order resulting from the settlement would be inclusive in relation to the relevant settler and indigenous communities, it would serve the exclusivity function that we understand to be essential to all constitutions.

C. Responding to Difference

Finally, Deveaux identifies two concerns centring on the accommodation of cultural difference (variants of which first arose in Chapter 2). Both could perhaps be levelled against DPRs. First, according to Deveaux, deliberative democrats require 'one party to set aside its culturally specific ways, while the other party has the luxury not only of having its style of conflict prevail but also of believing that its style is culturally unmarked and universally applicable'.[90] Second, she may charge us with failing to adequately value the role of 'identity-based differences' and of treating 'difference itself [as] something to be transcended because it is partial and divisive'.[91] We offer two responses to these criticisms.

[90] Monique Deveaux, 'Deliberative Democracy and Multiculturalism' in Andre Bachtiger and others (eds), *The Oxford Handbook of Deliberative Democracy* (OUP 2018) 158, quoting David Kahane, 'What is Culture? Generalizing about Aboriginal and Newcomer Perspectives' in David Kahane and Catherine Bell (eds), *Intercultural Resolution in Aboriginal Contexts* (UBC Press 2004) 42.

[91] Deveaux (n 90) 160, quoting Iris Marion Young, *Inclusion and Democracy* (OUP 2000) 42.

(i) Indigenous practices of deliberation: We suggest that DPRs will typically include debates within indigenous groups that will unfold in the style most convincing to their own members. If the objection about style is primarily that our proposals impose on indigenous peoples a deliberative mode of argument, we would respond that deliberation is, in a variety of contexts, understood to be a primary source of indigenous law and an essential means by which indigenous people engage with non-indigenous institutions. Although writing in a Canadian context, indigenous scholar John Borrows makes broad claims about indigenous law when he argues that deliberation is 'an especially broad source of Indigenous legal tradition' that underwrites or 'is the proximate source of most Indigenous law'.[92]

Borrows does not refer to Rawls when he writes of deliberation in indigenous legal systems, but there are points where he expresses ideas similar to Rawls's wide view of public reason. Recall that Rawls says that groups may introduce comprehensive doctrines into public political discussions, provided that 'in due course, proper political reasons—and not reasons given solely by comprehensive doctrines—are presented that are sufficient to support whatever the comprehensive doctrines are said to support'.[93] Borrows argues that indigenous legal traditions are 'attentive to foundational principles of civil, political, social and economic rights and responsibilities upon which legal systems rest'.[94] We understand Borrows to be claiming that such foundational principles—which indigenous and non-indigenous legal systems share—shape indigenous legal systems. Indeed, he goes further, arguing that these principles frame and provide the substance for indigenous criticisms of colonial systems of law.[95] The commitment to human dignity entailed by these principles would seem, therefore, to bring them within the ambit of Rawls's 'proper political reasons' or what we have called in this book, public values.

According to Borrows, decisions about whether to harmonize indigenous laws with external legal influences or to remain distinct from them will be 'based on what counts as persuasive to the group involved in the debate'.[96] Hébert notes, moreover, that 'regional, national and international Indigenous organizations' engage deliberatively with non-indigenous bodies. Some, including 'the Customary Senate of New Caledonia have a formalised status as the State's interlocutors', while 'other organizations are set up to function as

[92] John Borrows, *Canada's Indigenous Constitution* (University of Toronto Press 2010) 35.
[93] John Rawls, *Political Liberalism* (Columbia University Press 2005) 462.
[94] Borrows (n 92) 37.
[95] ibid.
[96] ibid 36.

governments'.[97] He gives as an example of the latter Bolivia's 'first officially recognized autonomous Indigenous government'.[98]

To Borrows and Hébert, then, deliberation is essential in indigenous law, forms part of the process for deciding whether to incorporate external norms, and sets the terms by which non-indigenous entities, including states, are engaged. Far from requiring indigenous peoples to set aside their cultural modes of expression, deliberation in the context of a DPR would seem to be consistent with an essential way in which indigenous peoples make decisions about law, including law external to indigenous communities. Indigenous peoples participating in a constitutional settlement, by means of a DPR, may engage in a deliberative law-making process that would be familiar to many. In our view, then, neither the deliberative processes of the DPR in general, nor its public values approach in particular, could be seen as being imposed on or foreign to participating indigenous peoples.

(ii) Cooperative institutions: Where a DPR mandates negotiations, particular perspectives and divergent views (epistemic, empirical, and normative) should be explicitly considered, where relevant, before the negotiating parties arrive at a settlement. And at least in some circumstances, if incommensurable views were raised in negotiations they would not need to be directly engaged. For instance, if divergent views of the political standing of the natural world were to be presented in negotiations about specific constitutional norms, the truth of those claims may not need to be addressed directly. Instead, the debate may concern the shape of institutions that can accommodate that diversity through, for instance, an independent state, the conferral of jurisdiction over the relevant matter to regional governments, or regulation of the matter through a legal regime that applies differently to indigenous and non-indigenous individuals. The negotiations would be over what Rawls calls 'fair terms of cooperation', rather than the contents of the parties' comprehensive worldviews.

Similarly, Ivison argues for 'institutional innovation' that will create 'the conditions in which . . . complex and sometimes conflicting claims can be discussed and mediated'.[99] In settler colonial states these innovations would involve developing: 'ways of deliberating about the past democratically;'[100] the capacity 'to see the world from the perspective of another'; and 'a shared set of practices and reasons for going on together'.[101] We suggest that the DPR is one

[97] Hébert (n 3) 105.
[98] ibid.
[99] Ivison (n 1).
[100] ibid.
[101] ibid 58.

such institutional innovation. Although we initially justified it in the terms of Western political theory, we believe that the DPR can respond to the plurality of normative orders that exist on the territories of modern states, and especially, colonial states. We expect that if designed and deployed with care, the DPR can be responsive to what indigenous and settler groups and their members view to be distinctive about the institutions and theories of their respective normative orders, even in circumstances of conflict. Our hope is therefore that if deployed widely, the DPR can provide Ivison's 'shared set of practices and reasons for going on together' in the sense that the parties approach the achievement of a final settlement together.

To be sure, the scope of the challenge of indigenous cultural difference may depend on whether the dominant worldview is (or is seen to be) fundamentally at odds with indigenous constitutionalism. Ivison, for one, identifies one version of this challenge when he notes that even expansive conceptions of rights that acknowledge the prior sovereignty of indigenous peoples are 'grounded in liberal conceptions of the person and political institutions' that cannot be easily reconciled with distinctively indigenous 'political theories and institutions'.[102] Aaron Mills sets out a stronger version of the challenge. He writes: '[b]ecause of liberalism's view of persons as autonomous and because of its anthropocentric view that only humans are persons, from my perspective it's irredeemably committed to violence'.[103]

A critic who held this latter view of liberal constitutionalism, in particular, might argue that using a DPR to resolve indigenous-settler conflicts will necessarily yield a constitutional settlement that is irredeemable. We cannot meet this challenge by appealing to Ivison's view of institutional dialogue; this kind of dialogue will amount to a colonial imposition if it is conducted within, and according to the norms of, a liberal democratic institution such as the DPR, rather than in an indigenous institution and in accordance with indigenous constitutional values.

Yet we suggest that even if the DPR and its attendant theory of constitutionalism were incompatible with indigenous legal orders in this fundamental way, a DPR may yield a constitutional settlement that can be authorized by those orders. It may be that a conflict resolution mechanism, designed by indigenous peoples and according to indigenous political principles, would be a first-best

[102] Ivison (n 1) 42.

[103] Aaron Mills, 'The Lifeworlds of Law: On Revitalizing Indigenous Legal Orders Today' (2016) 61(4) McGill Law Journal 847, 865.

solution to indigenous-settler conflicts. But a DPR may nonetheless be a serviceable second-best solution.

In a similar vein, Tully argues that the best way for members of a dominant settler society to set the groundwork for a non-colonial future would be to engage directly with indigenous political theories. But a 'next-best approach is to draw on the resources of critical self-reflection available within the dominant Western language of political thought to . . . present a non-colonial alternative'.[104] Similarly, a DPR—despite being a political instrument that we have defended in the language of Western political theory—can lead to a constitutional alternative to a colonial status quo. Ultimately, in order to be legitimate, that alternative would need to be authorized by the relevant indigenous legal system, on terms that are acceptable to it. In our view, such authorization could flow, at least in part, from the consent of the affected indigenous peoples, as expressed in a DPR. Therefore, even if the DPR itself may be incompatible with a given indigenous legal system and its principles, a constitutional settlement that results from a DPR need not be.

IV. Conclusion

In this chapter, we have sought to extend the arguments from past chapters on group sovereignty and secession to indigenous-settler conflicts. We selected this context because we believe it represents a particularly demanding test-case for our theoretical and institutional design arguments. Our model of public-value deliberation within the confines of the DPR is tested by the sharp divides between indigenous and settler populations. Moreover, our assumptions about institutional design are challenged by long histories of domination and violence that make the prospects for deliberation from a position of relative parity seemingly remote. Indeed, in some cases, such as South Sudan and Western Sahara, conflicts only intensified during a period of delay or led to an indefinite delay of the independence vote.[105] Nonetheless, in this chapter we proposed variations on DPR institutional design features and made normative arguments that attempted to show how the DPR may help to meet such challenges. We hope to have demonstrated, in the process, the flexibility of the DPR as a model and theory of conflict settlement in societies riven by conflict.

104 Tully, *Public Philosophy in a New Key* (n 66) 277.
105 Collin (n 27) 140.

We conclude by noting that we intend to make our arguments with humility and with an awareness of the limits of our ability to fully understand the indigenous contexts that we have analysed. We have, where possible, tried to focus our attention on specific conflicts in order to avoid making unwarranted generalizations. We centred our attention on New Caledonia because it is the case that most closely approximates our model for a DIR that can be adapted to the design requirements of a DPR. We do not intend to deny the very real differences that separate cases. Yet we do hope that the insights and prescriptions that we have offered will assist in finding ways out of seemingly intractable conflicts.

PART IV

CONCLUSION

8
Conclusion

Much like most peace referendums of the past, a deliberative peace referendum (DPR) is a referendum intended to aid the process of peacemaking in conflict societies. The difference is the level of attention to design in the DPR—design with the objective of improving deliberation in the run up to the vote and, as we have explained, during the vote itself. Deliberation is often precisely what is lacking between groups in conflict. And when deliberation is wholly or largely lacking in the attempted solutions to conflict, the attempt may not be worth the effort. Standard peace referendums, though increasingly prevalent, risk only setting off a backslide into conflict. When we look at cases from the past, we see that this is at least as likely an outcome as is progress towards a lasting peace settlement.

We have therefore attempted in this book to outline an alternative approach to peacemaking by referendum that connects to the wealth of prior contributions on the theory and the design of deliberative democracy. And we have gathered these efforts into a generic model that we call the DPR. As we described it, the DPR can include a set of four key features of institutional design: the public-values ballot; limits (especially deferral) on elite involvement in the early and middle stages of the referendum; the deliberative mini-public; and several, interconnected ways of managing campaign information with deliberative objectives in mind. While we think that the DPR should ideally include all of these features, in some cases not all of them will be feasible or appropriate.

Thus while the DPR is a distinct model, it is also a flexible model. Of course, there are limits. For instance, a DPR that did not reserve a central place for public-value deliberation or that did not seek to empower ordinary people relative to elites would not be a DPR as we have defined it. We also see merit in always including a mini-public of some description. But within these broad parameters, there is plenty of room for institutional variation.

However, the notion of a DPR is ultimately broader than just the sum of the parts that we recommend. The DPR label can attach to any concerted attempt to make a peace referendum more deliberative using purposive institutional

Deliberative Peace Referendums. Ron Levy, Ian O'Flynn, Hoi L Kong, Oxford University Press (2021). © Ron Levy, Ian O'Flynn, and Hoi L Kong. DOI: 10.1093/oso/9780198867036.003.0008

design. The ideas that we have put forward doubtless do not exhaust all of the possibilities in the field. Equally, the approaches in our generic model may need to be modified for particular genres of conflict—a point that we often made in Part III of this book, where we explored some variations on the theme of the DPR. Many more variations are conceivable—a point to which we will return shortly.

Whatever the precise institutional contours of the DPR, we also repeatedly made an argument that provided the conceptual spine of this book: that even though it is almost always exceedingly difficult, a DPR may prompt the *achievement* of a constitutional settlement, and may thereafter help the constitutional settlement to *endure*. Initially, the DPR may prompt a settlement to be reached by switching attention from elites to non-elites, and by focusing popular discussion on public values that any person committed to democratic ideals could reasonably be expected to endorse. This may expose, or even prompt, a brief meeting of minds about the need for a constitutional settlement. We do not think that widespread cultural change is liable to happen at this early stage. But neither do we think it is necessary. The act of exposing an agreement leading to settlement is, in the first instance, just a temporary scaffolding exercise: a way to ensure that groups in conflict come together long enough to reach a settlement. Yet we also showed how the DPR may also help to constitutionalize the settlement, once achieved, and may even help the settlement to remain stable and to induce people to adhere to its dictates.

In short, a DPR should aim to institutionalize a kind of deliberation centred around public values in order to reframe the issues germane to a conflict and to expose and encourage agreement among ordinary people. The DPR may also help to secure a lasting constitutional settlement by relying on what we coined 'deliberative popular legitimation'.

Some readers may wonder how and whether our work will fit the wealth of parallel contributions on the value of grass-roots, or ground-up, peacemaking. In one sense, we sought to build on such efforts. Our approach draws on the democratic voice of the people in a conflict society as whole. However, as others have,[1] we argue that ground-up processes are not enough, and that a complementary process from above is also needed. The DPR is at once a ground-up and a top-down model of peacemaking. It draws on the democratic voice of the people in a conflict society as whole, but it connects this voice to a formal and consequential vote—a choice on the actual complexion of constitutional

[1] John Braithwaite and others, *Reconciliation and Architectures of Commitment: Sequencing Peace in Bougainville* (ANU Press 2010) 133.

norms that will govern the society and be implemented and applied by state institutions.

Clearly, in practice none of this is easy. Indeed, we said much to downplay any suggestion that we have identified a magic bullet that can be universally applicable and universally successful. If readers had doubts throughout the book about particular points, or worries about certain destabilizing factors, in general we shared them. At many points we therefore took care to explain why our book, though aimed at broad innovation, avoided making unrealistic claims. The reasons were in the many provisos along the way, offered in order to hem in our claims and ensure they never got away from a realistic grounding in the practically achievable:

- Our claims, empirical or normative, were always claims of *degree*. When referring to deliberation, we had in mind improved or enhanced deliberation, not deliberation as an ideal readily achieved, much less perfected. The best we can hope for (though to hope for this is itself noteworthy) is incremental improvement. For instance, it is possible that a DPR may be unable to resist spoilers (drawn, for example, from the ranks of motivated online warriors or empowered elites). Ultimately, however, we believe that all forms of peacemaking are susceptible to this kind of influence; therefore the question is whether the DPR has advantages that allow it to improve, by increments, on the alternatives.
- The example above also underscores a further feature of this book: that nearly all of our claims have been *comparative* in nature. Whenever we referred to 'improving' deliberation, we had in mind improvements over either the status quo or as against some other concrete alternative. Often we made the point, for example, that non-elite deliberation is frequently flawed—and sometimes profoundly so. The nub of our empirical claims was that the public-value deliberation of non-elites was likely to be more robust than that of certain types of elites.
- The comparisons we made were also *institutionally grounded*, reflecting the institutionalist deliberative democrat's expectation that deliberative capacities will probably not be realized in any meaningful way until the tools for their realization exist.[2] We think this is, or at least should be, uncontroversial. Just as the voter cannot express any choice absent the

[2] John Parkinson, 'Legitimacy Problems in Deliberative Democracy' (2003) 51 Political Studies 180, 186–87.

institutional forms required to do so (eg, polling station, ballot, and ballot box), the deliberator cannot arrive at a reasoned view or judgement absent certain institutional conditions (eg, balanced information, and time and opportunities to discuss the issues with people from different walks of life).

- Our claims about the potential to improve deliberation were also bounded by the *time-limited* nature of the deliberation that we have in mind. That is, our aim, as noted, is to bring disparate groups to the point of being able to agree at least fleetingly, but with lasting effects. That is never likely to be easy, but it is at least far more likely in the confined time and space of a referendum than in other decision-making contexts. The referendum (as we saw Dicey observing in an earlier chapter) lacks the substantive chaos of a legislative election; it is usually just a choice on a single subject and its underlying values. More important, the referendum campaign itself lasts a short time—typically several weeks—during which widespread deliberation about constitutional essentials is more feasible than at other times. Some deliberation about the implications of constitutional change is, in both the normative and sociological senses, required before any constitutional settlement can be achieved and endure. This is not likely to occur in ordinary times, when ordinary people must focus on their daily work and concerns. Yet in the brief moment of the referendum—an event with a high profile due to the time, expense, and opportunity for concrete engagement and decision-making—deliberation becomes more plausible. That time will fade. But before it does, deliberative design of the referendum can build on what may already be a public ready for deliberation.
- As noted, we have specifically advocated for tools to enable and improve *public-value deliberation*. This kind of deliberation is itself far more limited in scope than other kinds of deliberation: it focuses on those few, essential constitutional values that, in principle, can be reasonably agreed to by everyone. As we said above, anything bigger and broader than this—such as deep and immediate cultural change—is unrealistic. But what perhaps *is* realistic is change grounded in considerations that all sides already share.
- Moreover, with an eye to making public-value deliberation itself more feasible, we sought to make clear that only those public values germane to a conflict ought to be deliberated in the DPR. We called this the condition of *minimalism*.
- While our approach was indebted to Rawls, we generally (but with a few exceptions) limited our use of his ideas to the proposition that what a DPR, or any exercise in public-value deliberation, can achieve is an *exposure of*

agreement—not its creation from whole cloth. Exposing agreement means shifting the way we look at values, from using non-public (self-focused) to public (generalizing) language and concepts. There may be some movement by deliberators to bracket some of their comprehensive doctrines, or to bend (in Rawls's description) those doctrines towards public values. But we mainly expect that a DPR—given, again, its short duration—is far more likely to reveal what public-value agreement already exists, rather than to stretch that capacity itself. This was a key plank of our arguments in the foundational part of the book.

- The final proviso was that everything we said in the book regarding institutional innovation was *of necessity partly speculative*. The simple reason was that no *bona fide* DPR has yet run. We found some features of the DPR in past cases—for example, the attention to public values in the lead up to the Belfast Agreement referendum. But never has even a majority of the suite of DPR features that we put forward been adopted in one place. For this reason, much of the book's orientation has been towards what ought to happen in future cases. In essence, we have sought to create a new conceptual category of peace referendum by describing its main contours, and showing why past incomplete cases, certain empirical clues (eg, about what motivates sociological legitimacy), and arguments in a normative and theoretical mode point to the usefulness of this new model. In this way we have sought to fill a wide gap in peace referendum design.

Those were the main provisos that attached to our conception of the DPR, which we presented in order to ensure that our project was not cast in an overly (that is, unrealistically) optimistic light. Equally, however, we have tried not to downplay what we have meant to achieve by writing this book:

- As we said at the start of Chapter 4, the DPR and the theory and explanation around it contribute to what we think, hopefully without undue immodesty, is a new *theory of the peace referendum*. In Chapter 2 we pointed to how public values had figured in a number of past works on peacemaking in general. But the literature on peace referendums had scarcely taken notice. And neither had that literature appreciably connected with the recent parallel literature on deliberative referendums. A 'deliberative peace referendum' is where these main conceptual tributaries join up to form something that is, we think, unique—and especially distinctive in its explanatory power.

- The very constraints listed above—our many provisos—we believe strengthen the claims made around the prospects for DPRs. That is because recognizing the downsides of the DPR, and especially its potentials to misfire, is part of a process of testing the concept and defining the boundaries of the DPR's effective use in practice. Whether a settlement achieved via a DPR will in practice endure, or whether the parties will reach a settlement in the first place, we obviously cannot say with any certainty. However, by tracing the likely limits of the DPR's usefulness, we hope that we have provided a *guide to its effective use* by governments (or others), and to its analysis by other scholars.
- A claim that we made the middle of this book particularly deserves to be drawn out and repeated. It was that the referendum, designed with care to exclude the undue influence of elites, uniquely may have the ability to *rival the persuasive political force of elites*—including elites who are bent on spoiling or soft-pedalling peacemaking. A referendum's instrumentalization of popular sovereignty in the service of peacemaking works, when it does, in part because it is the most direct democratic expression available. Particularly when coupled with deliberation, as we saw, the referendum and its capacity for deliberative popular legitimation may eclipse the sociological legitimacy of elites. What we called the 'realization thesis' was the notion that, when referendums include extensive institutional supports for deliberation, the referendums may at last come to avoid certain common criticisms of referendum deliberation. In this way they may live up to their potential as potent tools of constitutional legitimation.
- Another key possibility to recall is that the DPR may provide what is lacking in most conflict societies, but what is needed if peacemaking is to move forward, namely a context within which deliberation seems plausible to participants. In the normal situation, conflict draws down intercommunal trust. Hence even if members of a given group are willing to deliberate (including in the ways that we have noted may be helpful for peacemaking), they may find it hard to credit the other side with any similar willingness. In a situation so far-gone that widespread intergroup violence has become common, or is heading in that direction, often there will be a prevailing assumption by members in each camp of the abjectness of the other side—including that the other side's members are lost causes: morally craven and irresponsible, and thus hardly capable of engaging in genuine discussions about common purposes. One of the principal aims of the DPR is to provide a time-limited *institutional reset of the*

conditions for deliberation. In and around the DPR, deliberation may be seen, at last, as a possibility. Experience with deliberative mini-publics seems to make clear that something like this is possible under certain circumstances. But the project of this book has been aimed at reproducing this possibility on a larger—though still not unbounded—scale.

- Finally, our focus on *deliberative and constitutional theory in combination* is another aspect that makes this book largely unique in the peace and conflict field. The settlement achievement-endurance paradigm that we developed relies critically on the constitutional nature of settlement. It is only because a constitutional norm—once formed through a credible, socially-recognized process—has a certain amount of promise for cementing an intergroup agreement that even an initially fleeting agreement may come to endure. Deliberative popular legitimation, as well as the norm exclusivity that public-value deliberation entails, may be part of this process of constructing a settlement as something constitutional and lasting.

These, we trust, are not overly sanguine views. Rather, by outlining the DPR's areas of promise, as well as the provisos that attend them, we have sought to provide a balanced view of where peacemakers may take DPRs. In Part III of this book, we began to speculate about certain DPR variations suited to particular contexts: to group-sovereignty conflicts in general (Chapter 5), and more particularly secession conflicts (Chapter 6) and conflicts between putatively sovereign indigenous and settler groups (Chapter 7). Yet there remain many DPR applications left to articulate or explore further. For instance:

- Our chapter on secession alluded to a category of referendum that one could call the 'rogue referendum'—that is, a referendum held without the formal legal sanction of the ultimate authority in a jurisdiction. In some cases, the referendum may have been authorized by a state, devolved, or local government, but not by the central or federal authority (eg, in Catalonia, Kirkuk). This will mean that the referendum cannot translate voters' choices directly into legal reforms, and sometimes (more contentiously) that the higher authority may disallow or criminalize the running of the referendum. In still another set of cases, the rogue referendum is not authorized by any government at all, but neither it is disallowed: it may simply be a private exercise of the rights of expression or association required to organize a collective exercise in 'do-it-yourself democracy'[3]

[3] Caroline W Lee, *Do-It-Yourself Democracy: The Rise of the Public Engagement Industry* (OUP 2014).

(eg, Hong Kong's 2015 'Referendum' associated with the Umbrella-Revolution). We can read the effects of the vote, in all of these cases, through the legitimacy lenses discussed in Chapters 4 and 6, and particularly according to the distinction between formal legitimacy as pedigree or as expression. A rogue referendum by definition lacks the former to any appreciable degree, but may yet vindicate the latter, expressive kind of legitimacy. This is important because, as we have said, in many cases elites are reluctant peacemakers. If a rogue referendum that altogether bypasses empowered elites presents a viable way forward, then this may be a way around the problem of elite recalcitrance.

- Can a DPR usefully run in a situation short of 'hot' conflict and violence? In many societies what widescale violence exists is (to many) not obvious, but is rather internalized into a society's repressive legal and other norms. For instance, key human rights (eg, equality, self-determination, cultural association) may be denied to a defined sub-group. Commentators do not necessarily define such cases, which we can call 'cold' cases, as conflicts. Indeed they fall short of conflict as we defined it in Chapter 1 for this book's purposes. But would a DPR nevertheless be appropriate for this type of case? The question is an open one especially in light of observations that we offered at the conclusion of Chapter 3. There we noted how the DPR's methods may be mildly coercive. To the extent that is so, the DPR's use is perhaps not justified in cases short of conflict. It is the imperative of peacemaking—of managing the coercive social reality of conflict—that, we said, still warrants running a DPR, even if the DPR is modestly coercive too. Though an exploration of this point will have to wait for future work by ourselves or others, it seems to us that the DPR's methods may also sometimes be justified in cold conflicts, which—as we have just defined them—are coercive enough that they involve the denial of the foundational rights of a weaker party.
- In some cases, peacemaking has been tried in the past and failed, leading to a situation where intergroup trust has sunk to lower levels and the prospects for any future peacemaking efforts to succeed are widely discounted (eg, in Israel/Palestine). The question this raises is whether a DPR may have little hope of reaching its primary aims, or whether on the other hand the DPR is one of the few options still open to impose a 'reset' to prevailing cycles of distrust and violence. In the latter case, can the DPR represent a last-ditch attempt to sustain—or revive—a peace process?

There is a great deal more to consider in the future, both in terms of the range of applications of the DPR and in terms of the range of its designs.

To conclude, it is worth saying a few words about what it was that led us to write this book in first place: our sense that, while peace settlements are almost always required to bring a conflict to an end, and while such settlements require popular support, peace referendums have a mixed record. When they go wrong, conflict can resume, and with increased intensity. Human suffering continues and hope gets replaced with despair. But we have shown that peace referendums can be more skilfully designed. And while referendums are just one part of a larger, complex picture, they can be a decisive part. Referendums are never just about the act of voting. They are also about contests of ideas and norms in the broader society. In that sense, the DPR is a distinct approach not just to peace referendums, but to peacemaking more broadly.

Index

For the benefit of digital users, indexed terms that span two pages (e.g., 52–53) may, on occasion, appear on only one of those pages.